State, Labor, and the Transition to a Market Economy

# State, Labor, and the
# Transition to a Market Economy

*Egypt, Poland, Mexico, and the Czech Republic*

AGNIESZKA PACZYŃSKA

The Pennsylvania State University Press
University Park, Pennsylvania

LIBRARY OF CONGRESS CATALOGING-IN-PUBLICATION DATA

Paczynska, Agnieszka, 1967–
    State, labor, and the transition to a market economy : Egypt, Poland, Mexico, and the Czech
    Republic / Agnieszka Paczyńska.
        p.       cm.
Includes bibliographical references and index.
Summary: "Explores what facilitates or hinders social group attempts to influence the process of
economic restructuring and reconstruction of state-society relations by focusing on organized
labor's response to privatization of the public sector during the first decade of reforms. Compares
Poland, Egypt, Mexico and the Czech Republic"—Provided by publisher.
ISBN 978-0-271-03436-2 (cloth : alk. paper)
ISBN 978-0-271-03437-9 (pbk. with epilogue 2012 : alk. paper)
1. Capitalism—Cross-cultural studies.
2. Privatization—Cross-cultural studies.
3. Labor unions—Political activity—Cross-cultural studies.
4. Political culture—Cross-cultural studies.
5. Industrial relations—Cross-cultural studies.
I. Title.

HB501.P128 2009
338.9'25—dc22
2008030465

The Pennsylvania State University Press is a member of
the Association of American University Presses.

It is the policy of The Pennsylvania State University
Press to use acid-free paper. This book is printed on
Natures Natural, containing 50% post-consumer waste,
and meets the minimum requirements of American
National Standard for Information Sciences—
Permanence of Paper for Printed Library Material,
ANSI Z39.48–1992.

*To my mother and to the memory of my father*

# Contents

# Tables

...............................................

## Acknowledgments

The idea for what eventually became this book first came about in the early 1990s in Cairo during a lecture by a World Bank official. He compared Egypt's economic reform program to the one that Poland was implementing at the time, and in particular the debt-forgiveness deal both countries made with their international creditors. This unlikely comparison intrigued me and would become the core of this study. Along the way the support of numerous people and institutions made the completion of this project possible.

I would first like to thank William Quandt, Arista Cirtautas, and Krishan Kumar for all their advice during the research and writing process. I want to thank William Quandt, whom I met while working as his research assistant at the Brookings Institution, for convincing me to come to the University of Virginia for my doctoral studies. He has been a wonderful friend and mentor since those Washington days. My greatest intellectual debt goes to David Waldner. David pushed me relentlessly, drove me crazy, and frustrated me to no end when I was his student. I will be forever grateful to him for all the amazing insights he provided (even if I didn't always appreciate them at the time). His unrelenting constructive criticism resulted in my producing a much better study than I would have otherwise. David has become a great friend, a wonderful sounding board for ideas, and an invaluable supporter of this project.

I would also like to thank the many people in both Poland and Egypt who agreed to talk to me, answered my endless questions (and only occasionally giggled at my horrid Arabic pronunciation), and helped me better understand the process of privatization and labor's role in public sector reform. This study would have been impossible to write without their generosity.

Many friends and colleagues in the United States, Egypt, and Poland made the completion of this project possible. I want to thank my dear friends Ranjit Singh, Beata Czajkowska, David Skully, Jillian Schwedler, Nicola Pratt, Paul Amar, Khalid Medani, Neda Zawahri, and Suzanne Simon for reading and discussing this project with me. I also want to thank Marsha Pripstein Posusney, Diane Singerman, Hilary Appel, Bob Vitalis, Bassam Haddad, Samer Shehata, Agnieszka Rybczyńska, and members of the DC Workshop on Contentious Politics, especially Christian Davenport and Virginia Haufler, for commenting on parts of this manuscript. I would also like to thank the two anonymous reviewers. Their collective insights were invaluable and their comments significantly strengthened this book.

I also want to thank Anthony Shadid, Hossam Barakat, Gasser Abdel Razek, Abdel Monem Said Aly, Mustafa Kamel al-Said, Carrie Johnson, and Wilson Jacob for all their help during my research in Egypt; and Leszek Gilejko, Juliusz Gardawski, Iza Ksiażkiewicz, Rafał Towalski, David Ost, and my Polish friends and family, especially Marta Adamska, Baśka Adamska, Guśka, Piotrek, Jaś and Antek Popławscy, Iza Stypuła, Atka Tynel, and Monika Kalinowska, for all their help during my research in Poland.

Finally, I want to extend my thanks to friends in the United States who kept me sane during this long process. I especially want to thank Andrea Akel, Liz Pelcyger, Margrete Strand Rangnes, Stevens Tucker, Aileen St. George, Peter Mandaville, Katerina Vogeli, Susan Finlay, Karen Semkow, Eva Busza, Mona Russell, Molly O'Brien, Lynn Khadiagala, Lora Lumpe, and Jim Cason. I also want to thank the Barracks Row Babysitting Co-op for allowing me to have those wonderful nights out every now and then during the revisions process.

I would also like to thank the institutions whose financial assistance made this research possible: the Woodrow Wilson International Center for Scholars, the International Research and Exchange Board, the Social Science Research Council, the American Council of Learned Societies, the University of Virginia, and the Global Studies Center at George Mason University. I also want to thank Foreign Language Area Studies and the Center for Arabic Studies Abroad for making it possible for me to acquire enough Arabic to conduct research in Egypt. Additionally, I would like to thank the School of Humanities and Social Sciences at the American University in Cairo and the Sociology Department at the Warsaw School of Economics for welcoming me when I was conducting my field work. Finally, I would like to thank the School for Conflict Analysis and Resolution at George Mason University and all my wonderful colleagues, and especially Andrea Bartoli, Susan Hirsch, Sandy Cheldelin, and Sara Cobb, for supporting me during the final revisions on this manuscript.

My family has been a constant source of support and love over the years. I cannot thank them enough. My brother, Martin, has been my constant and always wonderfully reliable traveling companion ever since our American adventure began in 1981. My parents, Hanna Paczyńska and Bohdan Paczyński, passed on to me their love of books, learning, and exploration. They also were a two-person grant-making institution for much of my educational career.

My deepest thanks go to my husband, Terrence Lyons, who has lived with this project for more than a decade. He never tired (or if he did, he never let me know) of listening to me talk about it and of reading the various drafts countless times. I want to thank him for all his amazing insights and for putting up with all my sometimes bizarre work habits. Most important, I want to thank him for being in my life, for being my best friend, and for his love.

I don't think my daughter Nell really liked the process of my writing this book especially once she discovered that it would not have any colorful illustrations. But her exasperated sighs whenever I had to stay at work late did wonders to motivate me to do the final revisions. Her exuberance, her wit, and her excitement at discovering the world have been a source of constant inspiration. She truly is a wonder. Nell has also been a source of joy and hope during a time when life took many difficult turns in the final years of writing. Shortly after Nell was born, my father was diagnosed with brain cancer. In midst of grim news she made all of us smile and that was a tremendous gift. When my father passed away in April 2007, Nell's hugs, cartwheels, and never-ending chatter injected a bit of much-needed and wonderful chaos into his funeral and memorial service. Her laughter and the special bond between her and her little cousin Asher also helped the Lyons clan as it struggled with the tragic death of my brother-in-law Brian in September 2007.

My greatest regret is that my father did not live long enough see this book published. But I am grateful that he could celebrate with me when I signed the contract for this manuscript. I will forever miss his presence in my life. I dedicate this book to my mother and to my father's memory.

# Acronyms

| | |
|---|---|
| AFL-CIO | American Federation of Labor—Congress of Industrial Organizations |
| ASU | Arab Socialist Union |
| AWS | Solidarity Electoral Action |
| ČMKOS | Czech-Moravian Confederation of Trade Unions |
| CROC | Revolutionary Confederation of Workers and Peasants |
| CROM | Regional Confederation of Mexican Workers |
| CRZZ | Central Council of Trade Unions |
| ČSKOS | Czechoslovak Confederation of Trade Unions |
| CT | Labor Congress |
| CTM | Mexican Labor Federation |
| ETUC | Egyptian Trade Union Confederation |
| IMF | International Monetary Fund |
| KOR | Workers Defense Committee |
| KSČ | Czechoslovak Communist Party |
| LR | Liberation Rally |
| NDP | National Democratic Party |
| NU | National Union |
| OPZZ | National Confederation of Trade Unions |
| PAN | National Action Party |
| PNR | National Revolutionary Party |
| PPR | Polish Workers Party |
| PPS | Polish Socialist Party |
| PRI | Institutional Revolutionary Party |
| PRM | Party of the Mexican Revolution |
| PRON | Patriotic Movement of National Rebirth |
| PSL | Polish Peasant Party |
| PZPR | Polish United Workers Party |
| RCC | Revolutionary Command Council |
| RUH | Revolutionary Trade Union Movement |
| SD | Democratic Alliance |
| SL | Peasant Alliance |
| SLD | Social Democratic Left |
| TD | Democratic Tendency |
| USAID | United States Agency for International Development |

# Introduction

..............................................................

In the 1980s, sharp increases in foreign debt and severe macroeconomic instability combined to produce urgent economic crises throughout the developing world. Drawing on newly influential economic analyses that identified state intervention as the primary culprit, reform programs sought to confine the state to a minimal regulatory role while permitting unrestrained market forces to set relative prices and thus govern resource allocation. The emerging dominance of the neoliberal paradigm was further reinforced by the changes in the structure of production, finance, and communications technologies associated with economic globalization.

The recalibration of state-economy relations was as profound as the construction of welfare systems among industrialized capitalist economies during the 1930s. In that decade, the state took on an important role in economic management. Now the state was seen as the problem rather than the solution and the politicians who ran it as corrupt, rent seeking, and ineffective. The policies that flowed from this new neoliberal analysis meant that governments facing profound crises would have to fundamentally restructure their economies. As a result, social contracts that had been in place between the state and society would have to be renegotiated. Employment guarantees would be scrapped, consumer goods subsidies would no longer be provided, and employment possibilities and prices would now be determined by market forces.

Not surprisingly, groups that had benefited from previous arrangements were often deeply concerned about the impact of these changes. How did they respond to the restructuring of the economy? And more important, were social actors able to influence and shape these structural adjustment policies? The empirical record is mixed. In some cases, social actors played a significant role, while in others reforming governments had the ability to push through restructuring policies with little input from social actors, be they business associations or labor unions. What explains these differing patterns of social groups' influence?

This book explores what facilitates and what hinders social group attempts to influence the process of economic restructuring and hence the reconstruction of state-society relations. It examines the reasons for the very different responses of social actors to economic restructuring programs and their vastly different abilities to shape and influence the content and pace of implementing these reforms. It explores these dynamics by focusing on one social group, organized labor, and one feature of structural adjustment policy programs, the privatization of the public sector during the first decade of reforms. Specifically, it analyzes how organized labor in Egypt, Poland, Mexico, and the Czech Republic responded to and attempted to shape the processes whereby privatization programs were designed and implemented.

All four states, Mexico in the 1980s and Egypt, Poland, and the Czech Republic in the 1990s, faced deepening economic crises and embarked on ambitious economic restructuring programs. Among other reforms, all four programs contained plans for selling most public sector enterprises to private investors. Organized labor in the state-owned firms targeted for divestiture was keenly interested in how these privatization programs would be designed and implemented. Yet its ability to shape the design and implementation of public sector reform in the four cases differed. In Egypt and Poland organized labor was able to significantly influence both phases of the reform program. In Mexico and the Czech Republic, by contrast, organized labor had difficulty in effectively inserting itself into these policy debates or shaping the content of restructuring plans. This variation is not well explained by the extant studies of the political economy of reforms.

This book advances a two-stage argument to account for the observed variation in labor's ability to shape privatization policies. The first stage of the argument explains the variation in organized labor's influence on privatization policies by pointing to the resources available to labor organizations at the time when structural adjustment programs began. Among the most important resources are legal prerogatives and the financial autonomy of labor from the state as well as experiences of past confrontations with the state. Labor organizations that have acquired these resources before reforms begin have a greater ability to ensure that their voices become part of the debate about the shape of the reforms themselves. Their ability to draw on legal prerogatives, financial resources, and historical experience means that the political costs of silencing labor organizations are much higher than in cases where labor organizations do not have such resources.

This explanation, however, raises another question, namely, how and through what processes organized labor acquires these resources in the first place. The second stage of the argument addresses this question, through a theoretical framework that links labor resources to the historical legacies of labor's prior relationship with the state. Specifically, this book traces how the inability of ruling parties in Poland and Egypt to construct corporatist labor institutions meant that over time these parties were forced to grant more concessions to labor in order to retain workers within their political coalition. It locates the reasons behind the unsuccessful corporatist experience in the continuing internal struggles within the ruling parties and, in particular, in the lack of adequate incentive structures to enforce the loyalty of party members and punish their disloyalty. By contrast, the ability of the ruling parties in Mexico and Czechoslovakia to manage elite conflicts facilitated maintaining effective corporatist institutions.

## Privatization and Organized Labor

Having identified excessive state intervention in economic matters as the main cause of the crisis, the neoliberal prescription for restoring growth focused on reducing the state's control over and involvement in the economy. Dubbed the Washington Consensus, the policy recommendations had a number of common features. Structural adjustment programs emphasized restoring fiscal discipline, reducing public expenditures, allowing the market to set interest rates, making the exchange rate competitive, liberalizing the trade regime, encouraging foreign direct investment, and privatizing the parastatal sector.[1]

Privatization became a central component of restructuring programs and one of the most important mechanisms for curtailing state involvement in the economy. Neoliberalism viewed public sector enterprises as inherently inefficient.[2] In many developing countries state elites had historically turned to public sector enterprises to fulfill production quotas as well as to ensure high employment levels. Public sector firms also provided the means for the distribution of political patronage. In the long term, these varied economic, social, and political goals resulted in overstaffing, inefficiencies, stifled initiative and innovation, and mounting debts that were a drain on the state budget.

1. See, for example, John Williamson, "What Washington Means by Policy Reform," in *Latin American Adjustment: How Much Has Happened?* ed. John Williamson (Washington, D.C.: Institute for International Economics, 1990), 7–20.

2. World Bank, *Bureaucrats in Business: The Economics and Politics of Government Ownership; A World Bank Policy Research Report* (New York: Oxford University Press for the World Bank, 1995), 33–50; John Waterbury, *Exposed to Innumerable Delusions: Public Enterprise and State Power in Egypt, India, Mexico, and Turkey* (New York: Cambridge University Press, 1993), 107–34.

Selling state-owned enterprises, according to reform proponents, would therefore have a multitude of benefits. Not only would these enterprises no longer have to be financed by the state, thereby reducing the persistent budget deficits, but the taxation of newly privatized companies would provide new sources of revenue for the state. Furthermore, once in private hands, these enterprises, relieved of their social and political roles, would be able to produce more efficiently. Through a process of letting the market perform its magic, rather than one of allowing inefficient and overstaffed industrial mammoths to remain on life support, those entities that could not survive in a free-market environment would simply go bankrupt. By making the whole economy function more dynamically, these bankruptcies would in the long run result in higher economic growth rates, higher employment levels, and improved standards of living. Although later experience with implementation of reforms in general and privatization in particular exposed deep flaws in this neoliberal logic, during the first decade of economic restructuring, shedding of the public sector was firmly at the very center of the reform agenda. At the same time, precisely because of the central role that state-owned enterprises played in economic, social, and political life, privatization became one of the most contentious components of economic restructuring programs.

Although all social groups were affected by economic restructuring, the costs and benefits of reform were not distributed evenly. While some benefited from the changes, others quickly found themselves struggling to cope in the new economic environment. Similarly, the costs and benefits of discrete reform measures varied for different social groups. Consequently, we can anticipate that different groups will attempt to mobilize and influence different components of the structural reform package. Farmers are likely to watch carefully debates revolving around agricultural subsidies. Trade unions, by contrast, can be expected to pay particularly close attention to restructuring and privatization proposals, since such measures have an immediate and direct impact on workers within the public sector. While many other reforms associated with structural adjustment will affect workers' standard of living and job prospects, the effects of measures such as trade liberalization are likely to be more diffuse and not as readily apparent. They are therefore less likely to trigger labor mobilization. Privatization that threatens job security as well as benefits and wage levels is likely to be immediately felt by workers and hence more likely to elicit labor response.

Labor's ability to respond to these threats, at least theoretically, is much greater than that of many other interest groups within society. Not only do unions have established institutions that can be used in organizing collective

action, but such flexing of the political muscle is not easily ignored by governments. Strikes can have profound impact beyond the factory gates and affect
broader macroeconomic conditions within a country.[3] Even in countries with
low union density in which much of the population is involved in either
agricultural production or is employed within the informal sector, unions
are usually present within the public sector. Industrial enterprises also tend
to be clustered together in urban areas, thereby facilitating interaction and
communication between workers. Furthermore, as Zolberg has noted, in
many developing countries even when trade unions appear weak and not well
organized, "it is relatively easy for them to make trouble for their employer, and
since their employer often happens to be the state their behavior is politically
threatening."[4] Privatization, therefore, directly affects what is frequently one
of the few organized groups within society.

Despite organized labor's anticipated interest in state sector reforms and
potential ability to translate that interest into policy influence, the actual experience with public sector reform design and implementation has proven to be
more complex. Many early observers of economic reforms anticipated that
organized labor was likely to present a major challenge to the implementation
of structural adjustment. In their view, overcoming labor resistance was crucial
to consolidating the reforms.[5] When reforms were not abandoned, the analytic
pendulum swung in the opposite direction and initial concerns about the
power of organized labor were brushed aside. Geddes summed up this emerging
consensus on labor's powerlessness well when she pointed out that the lack of
political upheavals such as "regime breakdown" or "defeat of incumbents at
the polls" or "wholesale abandonment of market reforms" made evident that
organized labor was unable to affect reform dynamics.[6] Empirical evidence
suggests, however, that neither view is fully persuasive. In some cases, organized
labor was able to significantly shape both stages of the reform agenda. In other
cases, it was not.

3. J. Samuel Valenzuela, "Labor Movements in Transition to Democracy: A Framework for
Analysis," *Comparative Politics* 21, no. 4 (1989): 447.

4. Aristide R. Zolberg, *Creating Political Order: The Party-States of West Africa* (Chicago:
Rand McNally, 1966), 72.

5. Stephan Haggard and Steven B. Webb, introduction to *Voting for Reform: Democracy,
Political Liberalization, and Economic Adjustment,* ed. Stephan Haggard and Steven B. Webb (New
York: Oxford University Press for the World Bank), 1994, 16–18; Adam Przeworski, *Democracy and
the Market: Political and Economic Reforms in Eastern Europe and Latin America* (New York: Cambridge University Press, 1991), 180–87.

6. Barbara Geddes, "Challenging the Conventional Wisdom," *Journal of Democracy* 5, no. 4
(1994): 111.

## The Reform Experience

### Poland

In Poland organized labor emerged as an influential player during the first decade of public sector reform design and implementation. Polish organized labor that emerged following the 1989 political transition was highly fragmented. However, most workers belonged to one of two large union federations, the National Confederation of Trade Unions (OPZZ) or Solidarity. These groups, because of their divergent affiliation with two different political currents, were frequently in conflict at least at the national level. Both federations fielded candidates in parliamentary elections. However, Solidarity chose to play a much more direct role in politics and it both offered political backing to governing coalitions and formed its own political organization, becoming directly involved in governing. Alongside trade unions, each state-owned enterprise had a workers' council. In spring 1990 the government submitted its privatization program to the parliament, setting the stage for the first significant confrontation between the state and organized labor. The government proposal emphasized the need for a quick sale of state assets and gave state agencies the power to initiate and oversee the sales process. The reaction of organized labor was both swift and negative. One of the main points of contention between the government and organized labor was the issue of actual ownership of public sector firms. Union-backed deputies quickly presented the parliament with an alternative privatization plan which proposed greater social control over the process.

The final version of the privatization program represented a major victory for labor. Workers' councils were granted the right to initiate restructuring and privatization procedures and to decide on the privatization path for their enterprise. Most important, without the approval of the workers' council, sale of the company could not move forward.[7] Labor organizations thus managed to significantly modify the privatization program during the design phase and played an equally significant role during implementation. In the first years of reform both trade unions and workers' councils did little to block the restructuring of enterprises and in many cases were active promoters of these changes. At the national level, Solidarity extended a "protective umbrella" over the reforms, containing strike activities and promoting enterprise restructuring.

---

7. As a former deputy minister of privatization put it, "Privatization did not so much entail getting the state out of enterprises, but rather getting worker self-management out of them." Author interview, Warsaw, April 27, 1999.

When organized labor's support for reforms became more tenuous and workers' councils became reluctant to approve restructuring measures, the pace of sales of state firms slowed noticeably.

The change in organized labor's stance forced the government to rethink its public sector restructuring strategies. The resulting Commercialization and Privatization Act of 1996 gave organized labor additional incentives to back privatization programs through allocation of free shares in enterprise and increase in workers' representation on company supervisory boards. The new law, however, did little to accelerate the pace of sales or to make the first decade of reforms less contentious. Polish labor organizations thus managed to significantly influence the process of privatization implementation by affecting the privatization methods employed as well as the pace of sales.


*Egypt*

In Egypt organized labor also became an influential player in the process of reform design and implementation. The way it pursued its goals differed, however, because of the lack of political opening that accompanied market reforms in Poland. In fact, as the Egyptian regime sought to liberalize its economy, it began retreating from the political liberalization experiment of the 1980s. Despite growing political repression, organized labor succeeded in modifying the privatization program during the design phase, shaped other pieces of legislation directly affecting the pace of divestitures, and significantly slowed the implementation of the public sector restructuring program.

The first confrontation between the Egyptian Trade Union Confederation (ETUC) and the government erupted during the parliamentary debate in the summer of 1991 over the adoption of the Public Enterprise Law (Law 203), which was to guide the privatization process. The ETUC opposed the original government proposal. Because the government wanted the ETUC's endorsement before adopting the plan, however, it agreed to a number of concessions, including guarantees against mass layoffs of workers and that only the adoption of a new labor code could override these provisions. In addition, the ETUC was guaranteed participation in all future decisions affecting the public sector.

As the privatization program moved into the implementation phase, the ETUC continued to have substantial influence over the process. Two government proposals directly related to the implementation of the privatization program encountered especially strong objections from organized labor. One involved changes in the labor code and the other concerned the adoption of an early retirement scheme for public sector workers. The most contentious were negotiations over new labor market regulations. Both government and business groups wanted more flexible employment contracts that would allow employers to dismiss unneeded workers. Labor opposed this change but wanted the right to strike, which business and the government rejected. The negotiations lasted almost a decade and the lack of progress contributed to the slowdown in the pace of sales. Negotiations over the early retirement scheme were also contentious. In the end the ETUC succeeded in ensuring a higher compensation package and the voluntary nature of the program. The latter provision in particular affected the pace of enterprise restructuring and sales. At the same time and without ETUC approval or support, many restructuring measures also came up against enterprise-level labor opposition. Because the regime feared social unrest, the intensification of labor protests made the implementation of public sector restructuring policies politically difficult.

### The Czech Republic

In the Czech Republic organized labor had little input into the design and implementation of public sector restructuring. In March 1990, following the fall of the Communist regime, a congress of trade unionists officially dismantled the seventeen industrial unions of the Revolutionary Trade Union Movement and established the Czechoslovak Confederation of Trade Unions (ČSKOS), which grouped labor organizations of both the Czech and Slovak republics. As in Poland, trade unions were initially supportive of the economic reform program, though not of all proposed restructuring measures. Unlike in Poland, however, the unions had difficulty in formulating counterproposals and ensuring that they would be considered by the parliament and the government as the reform program was being designed in the second half of 1990. The privatization plan adopted by the parliament in January 1991 did not reflect trade union demands.

Once the privatization program was approved by the parliament, unions proved equally powerless to influence the process of implementation. Large-scale privatization, which included most state-owned assets in industry, agriculture, and trade, was implemented in two stages in 1993 and 1994. Although unions were concerned about the decline in real-wage levels, they did not manage to affect the pace of divestitures or to shape other reforms, in particular, the new labor code. The Tripartite Council, which was to facilitate government-business-labor negotiations, proved a source of frustration to unions. They felt that the government treated the council, not as a forum where agreements could be hammered out, but as a rubber stamp for decisions already taken. Yet during the first decade of reforms, even čskos's threats of strikes and demonstrations did little to influence the process of reform implementation.

## Mexico

As in the Czech Republic, in Mexico organized labor was unable to shape the process of privatization design and implementation. However, the interaction between organized labor and successive Mexican administrations was more complex. The labor movement was composed of official unions affiliated with the ruling Institutional Revolutionary Party (PRI) as well as independent unions. All the major official trade union confederations, the Mexican Labor Federation (CTM), Revolutionary Confederation of Workers and Peasants (CROC), and Regional Confederation of Mexican Workers (CROM), were organized under the umbrella of the Labor Congress (CT). Also belonging to the CT were a number of smaller federations and a few large industrial unions. There were also independent unions not affiliated with the PRI.

When the economic reform program began during the administration of Miguel de la Madrid (1982–88), the official unions were willing to back the government if it guaranteed adequate minimum wages. The willingness of the government to disregard that pledge was the first sign that the PRI was prepared to abandon its long alliance with organized labor as the former shifted economic policies.

Here too privatization of the public sector was at the center of the restructuring program. Despite the long and close relationship between the official labor unions and the ruling PRI, the administration of de la Madrid and that of Salinas (1988–94) did not consult the unions during the process of privatization design and, despite intense lobbying, the CTM was unable to ensure that provisions offering protection to employees of privatized companies would be included in the program.

Initially the CTM responded with caution and was unwilling to mount outright opposition to the program's implementation. Some independent union organizations as well as official union locals did on occasion resist restructuring plans. However, the government was prepared to ignore such opposition and, if necessary, crush it. When the worsening economic situation led to increasing criticism from the lower levels of the official union hierarchy and from the rank and file, the CTM and CT took a more confrontational stance and demanded a rethinking of restructuring policies. This shift in official union position, however, did little to change government policies. Nevertheless, despite its inability to shape public sector reform policies, the CTM and CT were never prepared to completely break their traditional alliance with the party and join forces with the independent unions.

## Framing the Question

The ability of organized labor to influence and shape the process of privatization design and implementation thus varied across the four cases. However, the four cases differ significantly in their cultural, historical, regional, and political background. Additionally, during the first decade of economic restructuring programs, two cases remained under authoritarian rule, while two made a dramatic transition from authoritarianism to democracy.[8] In particular, studies of both Central and Eastern Europe and of the Middle East have tended to present these regions as unique or even exceptional as a result of their particular sociocultural, religious, and political dynamics. In light of these differences, can we draw any broader conclusions about what factors shape organized labor's ability to influence reform process?

Despite these differences, the struggles over the form of the new economic order playing out in Central and Eastern Europe, Latin America, the Middle East, and elsewhere stem from similar sources and are a response to similar pressures. In all these regions, deep economic crises and high levels of foreign debt forced these state-dominated economies to initiate market reforms. These structural adjustment policies had many similar features and posed a challenge to groups that had benefited from previous socioeconomic arrangements. By comparing the experiences of state-labor encounters we can thus gain a better understanding of the complex dynamics of social response to economic restructuring that are relevant across a wide range of cases. The choice of these four cases, which despite many differences shared a number of crucial similarities in the pre-reform period, allows for a systematic investigation of the factors that shape organized labor's influence on economic change.

What are these crucial similarities? Prior to reform initiation, all four states were authoritarian ones in which the ruling party explicitly appealed to the working class for political support and promised revolutionary socioeconomic

---

8. This study examines the interaction between the state and organized labor in Mexico in the period prior to the 2000 elections when the ruling PRI was voted out of office. Hence, Mexico is classified here as an authoritarian state.

Table 1   Public sector restructuring

|  | Number of SOEs at the start of reforms | Number of SOEs privatized ten years after the start of reforms |
|---|---|---|
| Poland | 6,864 | 4,511 |
| Egypt | 314 | 130 |
| Mexico | 1,155 | 916 |
| Czech Republic | 2,700 | 2,500 |

SOURCE: Data from the World Bank, OECD, Polish Central Statistic Office, and the Egyptian Ministry of Economy. The number of companies privatized can vary in different data sets. It is often a matter of dispute when a given firm is considered privatized, given the variety of sales methods employed by countries. In this table, for example, the figures for Egypt do not include companies that sold only minority shares. Figures for Poland, by contrast, include companies that have been "commercialized," or have become joint-stock firms owned by the Treasury. If "commercialized" companies are excluded, the number of enterprises privatized drops to 2,984.

restructuring of the society. In all four cases, the ruling party sought to construct corporatist labor organizations with the dual goal of politically mobilizing labor in support of the ruling party while at the same time establishing firm control over unions and workers. While labor was expected not to challenge the state, in return for its political quiescence workers gained access to a whole host of subsidies and other privileges that resulted, at least for a time, in improved standards of living.

In the decades prior to the initiation of market reforms, all four countries pursued import-substitution policies, relying heavily on the public sector both as the driving force behind economic development and as a means of achieving other sociopolitical goals. All four faced a deepening economic crisis and began implementing structural adjustment programs. In all four, privatization of public sector enterprises was a central component of the reform agenda.

At the same time, while Egypt and Mexico initiated economic restructuring without transforming their political systems, Poland and the Czech Republic simultaneously embarked on market reforms and democratization. This case selection thus allows me to investigate whether and in what ways the legacies of the dynamics of state-labor relations persist over time and survive dramatic breaks with the past such as those that took place in Eastern Europe.[9] It also permits a careful exploration of the extent to which historical legacies affect the patterns of labor influence during economic restructuring.

9. The importance of exploring the role of historical legacies in shaping posttransition political life in Eastern and Central Europe has become increasingly clear in recent years. See, for example, Grzegorz Ekiert and Stephen E. Hanson, eds., *Capitalism and Democracy in Central and Eastern Europe: Assessing the Legacy of Communist Rule* (New York: Cambridge University Press, 2003).

In other words, as the following section will further elaborate, our case selection allows for controlling for various explanatory variables that have often been central to explaining reform dynamics in the extant literature. For instance, there is no correlation between how labor is organized institutionally and its ability to shape and affect policies. Neither centralized nor fragmented trade unions are a good predictor of labor's influence on public sector reform policies. The existence of technocratic teams also proves to be a poor predictor of organized labor's ability to shape reform processes. Similarly, contrary to arguments in numerous studies of economic reform, political regime type is not a good explanatory variable for the observed variation. Among the cases analyzed here, there is no correlation between the nature of the political regime and the influence of labor organizations on privatization policies. In one democracy, the Czech Republic, organized labor's demands were largely ignored during the design and implementation of the privatization program, while unions in the other democratic example, Poland, came to play a prominent role during both phases of the reform project. Similarly, in one authoritarian state, Mexico, organized labor was unable to influence the public sector reform program, whereas in the other, Egypt, organized labor was able to significantly shape both phases of the restructuring program. The age of the regime, also sometimes noted as an important variable explaining the level of interest group influence, does not correlate with the empirical evidence that emerges from these cases.

In other words, the nature of the regime does not significantly affect the ability of organized labor to influence reforms. This at first glance seems surprising. As will be discussed below, many analysts have argued that authoritarian regimes are more readily able to push through painful reforms because they can silence opposing voices more easily than is the case in democracies. Authoritarian regimes can resort to coercion and break up a strike; place union activists in jail; or even, in extreme cases, shoot and kill protesters without fear that they will have to pay for using repression and violence at the ballot box. Yet authoritarian regimes are sometimes very reluctant to resort to outright violence to quell the protests and ignore the demands of workers. Democratic governments, by contrast, sometime ignore popular protests and demonstrations and push through highly unpopular policies.

This does not mean that regime type is irrelevant. However, as these four cases will demonstrate, regime type matters in shaping strategies used by organized labor as it seeks to shape privatization program design and implementation. Strategies that are useful in a democratic context—for instance, lobbying parliamentarians—are less practical in an authoritarian system. How effective these different strategies are in influencing policy, however, seems to depend more on variables other than regime type. Specifically, the legal, financial, and experiential resources that organized labor acquired prior to reform initiation shape its ability to translate these different strategies into policy influence. By comparing states where authoritarianism has persisted with states that experienced a transition to democracy, I am better able to show how historically acquired resources can persist across even dramatic breaks with the past and shape policy dynamics.


## Theoretical Approaches

One of the most important variables in the extant studies explaining interest group influence on economic policy making has been the regime type. The role political institutions play in shaping interest group influence has long been a matter of controversy. Many of the arguments marshaled during the debates between modernization theorists and those working within the bureaucratic authoritarianism tradition that took place in the 1960s and 1970s are reflected in contemporary studies. Modernization theorists posited that democracy and economic development were compatible with each other.[10] Critics pointed out that democracy in fact posed numerous challenges to launching successful economic development because special interest groups and popular participation generated increasing demands on the state. The state, lacking adequate resources, could not satisfy these demands without sacrificing economic efficiency. These studies, drawing in particular on Latin American experiences, argued that authoritarian systems are more capable of undertaking ambitious development projects, thanks to their greater insulation from popular pressures. Democratic governments, however, are constrained by their need to win elections. They are therefore more likely to yield to political pressures from special interest groups and more hesitant to push through policies that may facilitate long-term economic growth, but undermine short-term electoral support.[11]

10. Seymour Martin Lipset, "Some Social Requisites of Democracy: Economic Development and Political Legitimacy," *American Political Science Review* 53, no. 1 (1959): 69–105; Karl W. Deutsch, "Social Mobilization and Political Development," *American Political Science Review* 55, no. 3 (1961): 493–514.
11. Samuel P. Huntington, *Political Order in Changing Societies* (New Haven: Yale University Press, 1968), 32–92; Philippe Schmitter, *Interest Conflict and Political Change in Brazil* (Stanford: Stanford University Press, 1971), 3–19; Samuel P. Huntington and Joan M. Nelson, *No Easy Choice: Political Participation in Developing Countries* (Cambridge: Harvard University Press, 1976), 1–16; Guillermo A. O'Donnell, *Modernization and Bureaucratic-Authoritarianism: Studies in South American Politics* (Berkeley and Los Angeles: University of California Press, 1973), 51–111.

In other words, according to this approach, the ability of interest groups to influence policy making is directly linked to the regime type: in democracies interest groups will have a greater capacity to shape reform policies, whereas in authoritarian systems such influence is less likely to occur. These debates gained new currency as more countries began to initiate structural adjustment policies in the 1980s. The cases analyzed in this study, however, suggest that regime type provides at best an incomplete explanation.

As more democratic governments began to undertake economic restructuring, it became apparent that in fact democratically elected governments can impose heavy costs on their populations and still remain in power and, more important, continue policies that often hurt politically important social groups.[12] This resilience of some democratic governments suggested that regime type may not be a fully satisfactory explanation of interest group influence on economic policy making. An alternative set of explanations looked to not just the regime type but also regime age. Some argue that consolidated democracies and authoritarian states have the ability to repress social demands and hence may have advantages in initiating economic reform programs. Newly established democracies, by contrast, face particular challenges, since they must simultaneously attempt to consolidate the new political system and initiate economic restructuring.[13] Alternatively, others predict that newly established representative governments are likely to benefit from a honeymoon period, when large reservoirs of popular trust, support, and willingness on the part of the public to incur even substantial hardships means that few social groups will attempt to block the reforms being implemented.[14]

These explanations of interest group influence, however, do not fully account for the patterns observed in the four cases examined here. Although

12. Glen Biglaiser and Michelle A. Danis, "Privatization and Democracy: The Effects of Regime Type in the Developing World," *Comparative Political Studies* 35, no. 1 (2002): 83–102.

13. Robert Kaufman and Barbara Stallings, "Debt and Democracy in the 1980s: The Latin American Experience," in *Debt and Development in Latin America,* ed. Robert Kaufman and Barbara Stallings (Boulder, Colo.: Westview Press, 1989), 201–24; Stephan Haggard and Robert Kaufman, "Economic Adjustment in New Democracies," in *Fragile Coalitions: The Politics of Economic Adjustment,* ed. Joan M. Nelson (Washington, D.C.: Overseas Development Council, 1989), 57–59; Joan M. Nelson, "How Market Reforms and Democratic Consolidation Affect Each Other," in *Intricate Links: Democratization and Market Reform in Latin America and Eastern Europe,* ed. Joan M. Nelson (New Brunswick, N.J.: Transaction Books, 1994), 1–36.

14. Stephan Haggard and Robert Kaufman, introduction to *The Politics of Economic Adjustment: International Constraints, Distributive Conflicts, and the State,* ed. Stephan Haggard and Robert Kaufman (Princeton: Princeton University Press, 1992), 6–8; Przeworski, *Democracy and the Market,* 161–71; Bela Greskovits, *The Political Economy of Protest and Patience: East European and Latin American Transformations Compared* (Budapest: Central European University Press, 1998), 69–92.

the type of political regime in existence when reform began shaped the types of strategies labor organizations employed to press their claims, their ability to make their voice heard was influenced by variables other than regime type and age. While none of the four cases examined in this book qualified as consolidated democracies when reforms were initiated, the other anticipated variation between states does not hold. In one old authoritarian system (Mexico), labor found it extremely difficult to have much input into policy making, while in the other (Egypt), labor had substantial influence. Similarly, in one new democracy (the Czech Republic), trade unions were unable to influence the privatization program, while in the other (Poland), their input was considerable.

Other studies suggest that it is the internal characteristics of a state rather than political regime type that accounts for the differences in the ability of governments to push through reforms without interest group influence. In this view, the cohesion and autonomy of the state are crucial variables affecting restructuring processes and the role that social actors come to play.[15] Especially significant, and signaling autonomous state decision making, is the existence of change teams, insulated from popular pressures and with the bureaucratic capacity to push through the measures that shape the process of economic reform implementation.[16] Such change teams are seen as indispensable to reform promotion, since they are composed of people who possess technical knowledge about the restructuring process and are not beholden to or dependent on old political patronage networks.[17] Advocates of the so-called shock therapy approach to economic restructuring, in particular, have emphasized the importance of technocratic teams, fully committed to reforms. As Sachs has pointedly noted, "In times of crisis there simply is no consensus to build upon, only confusion, anxiety, and a cacophony of conflicting opinions. . . . The reform team must make

15. Stephan Haggard, *Pathways from the Periphery: The Politics of Growth in the Newly Industrializing Countries* (Ithaca: Cornell University Press, 1990), 42–46; Stephan Haggard and Robert Kaufman, "The Politics of Stabilization and Structural Adjustment," in *Developing Country Debt and Economic Performance: Selected Issues,* ed. Jeffrey Sachs (Chicago: University of Chicago Press, 1991), 209–54; Peter Evans, *Embedded Autonomy: States and Industrial Transformation* (Princeton: Princeton University Press, 1995), 43–73.

16. Joan M. Nelson, "Introduction: The Politics of Economic Adjustment in Developing Countries," in *Economic Crisis and Policy Choice: The Politics of Adjustment in the Third World,* ed. Joan M. Nelson (Princeton: Princeton University Press, 1990), 3–32; Miguel Angel Centeno, *Democracy Within Reason: Technocratic Revolution in Mexico* (University Park: Pennsylvania State University Press, 1994), 21–41.

17. John Waterbury, "The Heart of the Matter? Public Enterprise and the Adjustment Process," in *The Politics of Economic Adjustment: International Constraints, Distributive Conflicts, and the State,* ed. Stephan Haggard and Robert Kaufman (Princeton: Princeton University Press, 1992), 182–220.

its reforms an accomplished fact."[18] Similarly, Balcerowicz, both a theoretician and a practitioner of this approach, has argued that change teams, working far away from the political limelight, must make use of the period of extraordinary politics that frequently exists at the beginning of the reform process and, swiftly, without engaging in much political debate, initiate reforms.[19] Moments of political transition when a new political elite comes to power may thus be a particularly auspicious time for pushing through reforms without interest group interference.

From this perspective, the existence of change teams not only makes interest group influence on policy making less likely, but such lack of influence is unambiguously seen as essential to successful reform process. Although change teams may indeed facilitate state autonomy from interest group pressures in some instances, the cases examined in this book suggest that such teams are at best a necessary but not sufficient condition for blocking interest group influence on policy making. The Polish case in particular suggests that the existence of a technocratic change team in itself does not block interest groups from being able to shape the reform process.

Analyses of structural adjustment and economic globalization have also explored how these processes have affected organized labor. A mixed picture emerges from these studies. In the view of some analysts, organized labor is no longer the powerful social, economic, and political force it once was and is unlikely to again reclaim its position. According to the pessimists, a nearly perfect storm has permanently weakened unions. On the one hand, structural adjustment policies have targeted the bastion of union strength, the public enterprise sector, and have shifted winning political coalitions toward the business sector and away from labor. On the other, changes associated with globalization appear to have further undermined the power of organized labor. Others, however, are less pessimistic both about how organized labor has fared in the changed economic environment and about what its future is likely to be.

For the pessimists, two distinct, albeit interrelated, changes associated with globalization have had a profoundly negative impact on this social group. First, the emergence of truly global multinational corporations, the segmentation of production, and the just-in-time production process have combined to create

18. Jeffrey Sachs, "Life in the Economic Emergency Room," in *The Political Economy of Policy Reform,* ed. John Williamson (Washington, D.C.: Institute for International Economics, 1994), 503–26.

19. Leszek Balcerowicz, "Understanding Post-Communist Transitions," *Journal of Democracy* 5, no. 4 (1994): 75–89.

an increasingly integrated global economy, thus heightening competition between workers in different locales. Corporations can now use the threat of moving production elsewhere, thereby undermining labor's bargaining power.[20] Workers across cases have been caught in a relentless "race to the bottom" of lower wages, lower social spending, and less worker-friendly market regulations.[21] Second, many analysts contend that globalization processes have been weakening state sovereignty, thus reducing the scope of economic decision making available to national governments. This has led to the convergence of macroeconomic policies that favor business over labor interests. The pressure toward policy convergence is especially acute in developing countries that have been saddled with foreign debt, which further reduces state decision making autonomy.[22] Many students of Eastern European transitions are among the most pessimistic about organized labor's ability to continue playing a significant role in the contemporary era.[23] Among the telling signs of labor's weakening in this view are dwindling union membership rolls, the decline in the number of labor disputes and strikes, the move away from manufacturing and the growth of the service sector, and the shrinking of enterprise size.[24] As posited by the pessimists, we should expect to see a uniform lack of organized labor's influence on policy making. Yet there is great variation in the four cases examined in this study.

Not all studies of how organized labor has responded to and been affected by the processes of globalization and marketization have been so pessimistic.

20. Bruce Western, "A Comparative Study of Working-Class Disorganization: Union Decline in Eighteen Advanced Capitalist Countries," *American Sociological Review* 60, no. 2 (1995): 179–201; Michel Chossudovsky, *The Globalization of Poverty: Impacts of IMF and World Bank Reforms* (Penang, Malaysia: Third World Network, 1997), 69–94; Jay Mazur, "Labor's New Internationalism," *Foreign Affairs*, January/February 2000, 79–84.

21. See, for example, Alan Tonelson, *Race to the Bottom* (Boulder, Colo.: Westview Press, 2000), 53–80.

22. Evelyne Huber, Dietrich Rueschemeyer, and John D. Stephens, "The Paradoxes of Contemporary Democracy: Formal, Participatory, and Social Dimensions," in *Transitions to Democracy,* ed. Lisa Anderson (New York: Columbia University Press, 1999), 195.

23. Paul Kubicek, "Organized Labor in Post-Communist States: Will the Western Sun Set on It Too?" *Comparative Politics* 32, no. 1 (1999): 83–102; Paul Kubicek, *Organized Labor in Postcommunist States: From Solidarity to Infirmity* (Pittsburgh: University of Pittsburgh Press, 2004); Stephen Crowley and David Ost, eds., *Workers After Workers' States: Labor and Politics in Post communist Eastern Europe* (New York: Rowman and Littlefield, 2001); Stephen Crowley, "Explaining Labor Weakness in Post-Communist Europe: Historical Legacies and Comparative Perspective," *East European Politics and Society* 18, no. 3 (2004): 394–429.

24. See, for example, Michael Shalev, "The Resurgence of Labor Quiescence," in *The Future of Labour Movements,* ed. Marino Regini (London: Sage, 1992), 102–32; Aristide Zolberg, "Response: Working-Class Dissolution," *International Labor and Working Class History* 47 (Spring 1995): 28–38; James A. Piazza, "Globalizing Quiescence: Globalization, Union Density, and Strikes in Fifteen Industrial Countries," *Economic and Industrial Democracy* 26, no. 2 (2005): 289–314.

A number of analyses suggest that social groups, including organized labor, have reacted to these changes in more complex ways. Such studies maintain that the structure of domestic-level institutions and political struggles at the local level continue to influence the shape of macroeconomic, regulatory, tax, and other policies.[25]

Various institutional factors emerge from these studies as playing a particularly significant role in shaping labor's response to economic restructuring. For instance, Murillo argues that the ability of labor organizations to affect policy reform varies both across countries and across sectors within countries, depending on "incentives created by partisan loyalties, partisan competition and union competition."[26] Levitsky and Way note that "the strength of the government party, level of union competition, organizational overlap and autonomy of union leaders from party-controlled resources and the rank and file" accounts for government-labor cooperation.[27] In a similar vein, Bellin argues that key to understanding labor response is its dependence, both political and financial, on the state as well as the degree of organized labor's aristocratic position within broader society.[28] Burgess sees the explanation for the variation in union support for government policy in the ability of affiliated party leaders to punish disloyal unionists and the degree to which there is a strategic contradiction between loyalty to the party and loyalty to workers among union leaders and locates the sources of variation in union responses in the costs imposed on them by political leadership. Depending on the distribution of these costs, union leaders may choose exit, voice, or loyalty strategies.[29] Alexander, by contrast, points to workplace institutions as the crucial explanatory variable of effective labor mobilization when confronted by privatization.[30] Finally, Pripstein Posusney

25. Christopher Candland and Rudra Sil, eds., *The Politics of Labor in a Global Age: Continuity and Change in Late-Industrializing and Post-Socialist Economies* (New York: Oxford University Press, 2001); Beverly J. Silver, *Workers' Movements and Globalization Since 1870* (New York: Cambridge University Press, 2002).

26. Maria Victoria Murillo, "From Populism to Neoliberalism: Labor Unions and Market Reforms in Latin America," *World Politics* 52, no. 1 (2000): 137. See also Maria Victoria Murillo, *Labor Unions, Partisan Coalitions, and Market Reform* (New York: Cambridge University Press, 2001), 11–26.

27. Stephen Levitsky and Lucan Way, "Between a Shock and a Hard Place: The Dynamics of Labor-Backed Adjustment in Poland and Argentina," *Comparative Politics* 30, no. 2 (1998): 172.

28. Eva R. Bellin, "Contingent Democrats: Industrialists, Labor, and Democratization in Late Developing Countries," *World Politics* 52, no. 2 (2000): 175–205.

29. Katrina Burgess, *Parties and Unions in the New Global Economy* (Pittsburgh: University of Pittsburgh Press, 2004), 8–16.

30. Christopher Alexander, "The Architecture of Militancy: Workers and the State in Algeria, 1970–1990," *Comparative Politics* 34, no. 3 (2002): 315–19.

argues that workers will oppose government policies when they perceive them as breaking the social contract.[31]

The present study builds on the insights of these recent works on organized labor responses to economic restructuring, which point us in the direction of domestic-level institutions as key variables to understanding how and with what consequences for state-society relationships international economic pressures are translated into the local context. Pripstein Posusney's analysis alerts us to the central fact that the existence of corporatist labor institutions should not be equated with organized labor's inability to shape policies. Studies by Murillo and Burgess provide valuable explanations of particular strategies that organized labor chooses when confronted with market reforms. Murillo goes further and also explores under what conditions these strategies are effective in extracting concessions from the state. However, she sees historical legacies primarily in terms of organized labor's dependence on the ruling parties and how that dependence shapes union and partisan competition.[32] By downplaying other resources that organized labor can draw upon as it seeks to influence policies, this model overestimates the extent to which both kinds of competition weaken labor and lead to "resistance" or "unsuccessful militancy."[33] Polish coal mining unions, for instance, despite high levels of partisan and union competition, retained their ability to affect sectoral restructuring policies. As we shall see, this capacity was a result of resources that organized labor acquired in the pre-reform period.

Furthermore, both Murillo and Burgess limit their analysis to cases where market reforms are initiated by parties with institutional links to organized labor and where the initiation of neoliberal reforms puts strains on these relationships. But in many countries changes in either the regime type or governing party preceded the initiation of market reforms. In this study I explore two questions left unanswered by Burgess and Murillo: First, how does organized labor that used to benefit from a close relationship with a ruling party react to structural adjustment in cases in which the regime has changed? Are these responses different from those of organized labor in which labor-based parties have retained power, and if so how? Second, and more important, are there significant differences in whether organized labor can influence economic reform measures between cases where labor-based parties retained power and where political transitions occurred?

31. Marsha Pripstein Posusney, *Labor and the State in Egypt: Workers, Unions, and Economic Restructuring* (New York: Columbia University Press, 1999).

32. Murillo, *Labor Unions, Partisan Coalitions,* 50–51.

33. Murillo, "From Populism to Neoliberalism," 153.

To answer these questions, I emphasize the importance of resources that organized labor can draw upon as it confronts a state undertaking structural reforms. Levitsky, Way, and Bellin note the importance of fiscal autonomy in explaining organized labor's ability to influence policy reform. In addition to fiscal autonomy from the state I highlight the importance of two other resources in shaping labor's ability to affect reform policies—legal prerogatives that organized labor had won prior to reform initiation and experiential resources gained from past contentious encounters with the state.

The book is organized as follows: In the following chapter I develop the theoretical framework of the study and explore the linkage between the conflicts over economic restructuring between states and organized labor with the historical patterns of state-labor interaction. Chapter 2 traces the internal dynamics within the Communist parties in Czechoslovakia and Poland from their creation following World War II and the transition to democracy and explores how the differences in these dynamics affected the ruling parties' relationship with organized labor and shaped the types of resources that labor was able to acquire in the decades prior to reform initiation. Chapter 3 explores these dynamics within the ruling parties in Egypt and Mexico and examines how they affected the parties' relationship with organized labor. Chapters 4, 5, and 6 examine how organized labor in the four cases sought to influence the process of privatization design and implementation during the first decade of reforms. Here I focus both on the strategies that organized labor used in attempting to shape the two phases of the reform process as well as on the degree of success of these strategies. In these chapters I explore how the resources that organized labor had at its disposal when governments in the four cases initiated market reforms influenced their ability to shape privatization policies. I also link the financial, legal, and experiential resources available to organized labor when economic restructuring commenced to the pre-reform dynamics of state-labor relationship analyzed in Chapters 2 and 3. Finally, the Conclusion revisits the main themes discussed in the previous chapters. Here I also briefly explore the continuing institutional changes of the following decade of reforms. Finally, I discuss the implications of this study for understanding patterns of state-society interaction as well as institutional change.

# 1 PARTIES, UNIONS, AND ECONOMIC REFORMS

As we saw in the Introduction, the ways in which organized labor reacted to changes associated with structural adjustment—and, more important, whether it succeeded in influencing the shape of privatization policies—differed markedly in Poland, Egypt, Mexico, and the Czech Republic. As we have also seen, the extant literature, while providing many important insights into the dynamics of reform experience, does not satisfactorily account for this observed variation. In this chapter, I lay out the theoretical framework that links the historical patterns of interaction between ruling parties and organized labor, the resources that organized labor extracts from the ruling parties over time, and the ability of unions to insert themselves successfully into policy debates once economic restructuring programs are adopted.

## Labor Strategies

To tease out how union interest in public sector reform is translated into policy influence, I distinguish between two phases of divestiture programs: design and implementation. Labor organizations can seek to influence one or both phases. During the design phase, labor organizations may attempt to influence the scope and speed of the envisioned program, the privatization methods that will be employed, and the prerogatives that workers will be granted within the program. Although regime type does not explain well whether organized labor succeeds or fails in shaping policy, what strategies labor chooses as it seeks to influence the process of privatization design does depend on the broader political context in which it exists. Hence, these strategies are likely to differ in democracies and authoritarian systems, since strategies that prove most effective in pluralistic context may well be of little value in an authoritarian environment. In democracies, unions are more likely to concentrate their efforts on lobbying government officials and parliamentary deputies, making alliances with political parties that are sympathetic to labor demands and interested in unions' electoral support, presenting alternative restructuring proposals, and appealing to the broader voting public through the media and protest actions.

Similar tactics are likely to be of less utility in a context of limited political pluralism. Even if parliament and multiple political parties are present, it is unlikely that the incumbents can be voted out of office during the next electoral cycle. Therefore, lobbying parliamentarians and threatening to shift alliances to another political party prior to electoral contests are unlikely to have much influence on how government privatization proposals are formulated. More efficacious strategies entail direct lobbying, often behind the scenes, of regime officials and relying on established clientelistic networks.

Once the program is designed and approved, labor organizations can seek to alter the process of implementation. While the early literature on economic reforms generally assumed that influence at the implementation stage would be manifested primarily in terms of labor organizations attempting to block restructuring and sales of enterprises, labor's reactions to privatization tend to be more complex. During this phase, labor organizations may seek to modify the privatization methods employed as well as to influence the pace at which sales are realized. At this point, labor is also likely to turn its attention to modifying and shaping other reform measures that generally accompany privatization and are of immediate interest to workers, for example, changes in the labor code.

At both stages of the process, labor organizations can also attempt to influence policies by staging strikes, protests, and demonstrations. Through such actions they can signal to political leaders their preferences. They can also make it more difficult for politicians to ignore their demands by making their dissatisfaction public and making appeals to broader sections of the society. These strategies at both phases of the reform process may or may not be successful.

I evaluate whether organized labor was able to shape the design phase of privatization programs by examining the extent to which initial government proposals were modified to reflect worker demands. I assess the extent of organized labor's ability to shape the implementation phase by examining the original timetables offered by the government in terms of the pace of divestitures, the methods of privatization the government was interested in pursuing, and the extent to which the pace and methods were modified to reflect labor demands.

Table 2    Unions and privatization

|  | Design phase | Implementation phase |
| --- | --- | --- |
| Objectives | Scope of privatization | Pace of divestitures |
|  | Speed of privatization | Methods of privatization |
|  | Workers' prerogatives within privatization | Related legislation |
|  | Methods of privatization |  |
| Strategies | Lobbying | Promoting sales |
|  | Alliance making | Opposing sales |
|  | Presenting alternative proposals | Modifying sale methods |
|  |  | Lobbying |
|  | Appealing to broader public |  |
|  |  | Strikes/demonstrations |
|  | Strikes/demonstrations |  |

Additionally, I assess whether organized labor was able to shape pieces of legislation that were directly related to the privatization program, such various labor market regulations.

Clearly, a variety of factors affect the ability of governments to implement privatization programs. The process of company valuation often proves technically difficult and politically challenging; private investors prove less willing to purchase companies offered for sale; and the politically thorny issue of foreign ownership of previously state-owned firms can affect the pace and methods of privatization, as can the global economic climate, to name just a few factors. Nonetheless, drawing on official documents; media accounts; and interviews with policy makers, union leaders, international observers, and local analysts, it is possible to assess the degree to which organized labor's actions influenced and shaped the dynamics of public sector reform implementation.

While unions in all four cases examined here wanted to see public sector restructuring programs modified, they did not always seek to block reform measures. In fact, initially unions were fairly supportive of aspects of the economic reform programs. In Mexico, for example, unions were concerned about the high rate of inflation and believed that addressing this problem would benefit their rank-and-file members. Polish unions, disillusioned with the centrally planned economy and the inefficiencies of state firms, were initially eager to see them reformed. Among Egyptian labor leaders, despite concerns about threats to job security that public sector restructuring posed, there was a willingness to accept market mechanisms provided that their introduction was accompanied by other changes, for example, the creation of unemployment insurance and job-retraining programs similar to those in existence in Western Europe.

Polish unions pursued a wide variety of strategies in their efforts to modify government privatization design proposals. They made alliances with parliamentarians and presented an alternative privatization program for consideration at the same time as the government sent its proposal to the parliament. They also appealed to the public for support. The Czech unions, by contrast, concentrated on lobbying parliamentarians and presenting alternative proposals, while largely eschewing strategies aimed at attracting broader popular support for their cause. Mexican and Egyptian unions, functioning within an authoritarian environment, pursued very different strategies, concentrated primarily on the direct lobbying of government officials as the design of the privatization program was being considered.

During the implementation phase, Polish unions again pursued a variety of strategies. In the first years of reform, most unions and workers' councils supported sales of their companies, although they substantially modified the types of privatization methods employed. Later, as economic conditions deteriorated, unions moved more firmly to oppose the implementation of sales and fought for additional concessions. Czech unions looked to strikes and demonstrations as a means of putting their demands on the government agenda. Mexican unions, taking another approach, engaged in strategies to modify the program. While the official labor confederation concentrated primarily on lobbying government officials and occasionally staging demonstrations, the independent unions turned to strikes and protest actions. In Egypt, factory-level unions also sought to influence the implementation of the privatization program at particular companies through staging protests and strikes, while the confederation leadership concentrated on lobbying government officials and negotiating legislation whose passage was directly tied to progress in the implementation of the divestiture plan.

Organized labor is, however, not a unitary actor. Union leadership and the rank and file often have different preferences during times of economic transition. This can create profound tensions within labor organizations. Such differences exist both in democratic and authoritarian contexts and can have various consequences. In Poland, for instance, the differences between the leadership of Solidarity and the rank and file resulted in the union's varying and sometimes contradictory responses to economic restructuring and over time contributed to the decline in its membership.[1] Likewise in Egypt the policies pursued by the leadership of the ETUC created much opposition among the rank and file. The lack of internal accountability within the confederation and the inability of the rank and file to elect different representatives pushed them to engage in protest actions that confederation leaders did not sanction and often opposed. These actions, while not supported by the ETUC, nonetheless gave the organization a useful chip in bargaining and negotiating with the regime. Similar tensions between the rank and file and the official unions' leadership were also evident in Mexico, where the lower levels of the union hierarchy were prepared to be more vocal and active in their opposition to the proposed reform measures than were those in the CTM leadership. Chapters 4, 5, and 6 will explore in greater detail how these internal union dynamics shaped labor response to the privatization program.

It is this initial complexity of labor response to market reforms that was underestimated by early students of restructuring efforts. This divergence of expected and actual response stems from a number of sources. First, as Kingstone points out in his analysis of the role of Brazilian business in the country's economic restructuring program, "Economic crisis that usually precedes major reform programs can radically alter how business and other interest groups view their stakes in reform. Economic crisis leaves business much more open to policy innovation because they perceive the status quo as untenable."[2] Second, deep crisis can also make people more willing to take risks in anticipation of potential, if not guaranteed, payoffs.[3] Third, periods of reform are characterized by deep uncertainty. It is often difficult to anticipate who the winners of the reforms will be.[4] The difficulty of identifying winners of reforms means that those who are likely to benefit from the changes cannot mobilize in support of

1. A recent study argues that the anger caused by the hardships associated with economic reforms and the rank-and-file workers' perception of abandonment by both the political elites as well as their own union leadership has had a profound influence on the course of democratic consolidation in Poland. David Ost, *The Defeat of Solidarity: Anger and Politics in Postcommunist Europe* (Ithaca: Cornell University Press), 2005.

2. Peter Kingstone, *Crafting Coalitions for Reform: Business Preferences, Political Institutions, and Neoliberal Reform in Brazil* (University Park: Pennsylvania State University Press, 1999), 17.

3. See, for example, Kurt Wayland, *The Politics of Market Reform in Fragile Democracies: Argentina, Brazil, Peru, and Venezuela* (Princeton: Princeton University Press, 2002), 37–70.

4. See, for example, Robert H. Bates and Anne O. Krueger, "Generalizations Arising from the Country Studies," in *Political and Economic Interactions in Economic Policy Reform: Evidence from Eight Countries*, ed. Robert H. Bates and Anne O. Krueger (Cambridge, U.K.: Blackwell, 1993), 444–72; Joan M. Nelson, *Fragile Coalitions: The Politics of Economic Adjustment* (New Brunswick, N.J.: Transaction Books, 1994), 8–9.

these changes and provide valuable coalition partners to the reforming political elites. However, the identity of losers is less ambiguous, and they are therefore expected to mobilize in order to prevent those reform measures that are likely to cause deterioration in their economic position.[5] One of the reasons why labor was expected to block reform efforts was that organized labor was seen as one of the likely losers of the reforms.

Nevertheless, as Chapters 4, 5, and 6 will examine in detail, organized labor, although clearly concerned by many of the restructuring proposals, did not always see itself as just a loser of the reform effort during the first years of restructuring programs. Unions were often keen to address the deep economic crisis, since it negatively affected its rank and file. For example, reform measures aimed at bringing high inflation rates under control met with a positive response from labor. Additionally, unions in state-dominated economies often were well aware that public sector firms were inefficient, corrupt, dysfunctional, and in need of restructuring. A popular Polish saying from the pre-reform period, "We pretend to work, they pretend to pay us," indicated worker dissatisfaction with the condition of public sector enterprises. They were therefore sometimes willing to consider modifying rather than outright rejecting proposals to reform the public sector.[6]

The fourth reason that the expected and actual behavior of unions differed is that in cases where unions are engaged in a political struggle to displace an authoritarian state, they may well support privatization of the public sector as part of their oppositional political program. In other words, if an authoritarian state supports retaining control over enterprises, opposition unions may well support selling state firms as a way to undercut the power of the authoritarian political elite.[7] The fact that over the long term many of the policies initially supported by organized labor resulted in a deterioration of workers' standards

5. Hellman, however, argues that it is partial winners of reforms rather than losers who are the main groups blocking implementation of full reform packages. Joel S. Hellman, "Winners Take All: The Politics of Partial Reform in Post-Communist Transitions," *World Politics* 50, no. 2 (1998): 204–5.

6. A number of studies of Western European unions have shown that given credible assurances of future wage prospects and, more important, a role in investment decisions, unions have often been willing to set aside demands for short-term benefits. Thus, under certain conditions, rather than being adversaries during periods of reform, unions can become important government allies and policy supporters. See, for example, Peter Lange, "Unions, Workers, and Wage Regulation: The Rational Basis for Consent," in *Order and Conflict in Contemporary Capitalism*, ed. John H. Goldthorpe (Oxford: Clarendon Press, 1984), 56–73; R. Michael Alvarez, Geoffrey Garrett, and Peter Lange, "Government Partisanship, Labor Organization, and Macroeconomic Performance," *American Political Science Review* 85, no. 2 (1991): 539–56.

7. This was clearly the case in Poland but is has also been evident in, for example, Zimbabwe.

of living and employment prospects should not lead us to conclude that organized labor was unable to shape reform strategies.

## Evolution of Corporatist Labor Organizations

Unions employ different strategies to translate their interest in public sector reforms into policy influence. Sometimes these strategies prove successful; sometimes they are ineffective. How can we account for this variation in patterns of labor influence? As discussed in the preceding chapter, many accounts of interest groups' ability to influence policy making in periods of reform and of labor's reaction to economic restructuring provide useful insights into these complex transition processes. However, a fuller picture of the variation in labor influence on policy making during the design and implementation of economic restructuring programs is possible if the resources available to labor organizations when the reforms are commenced are more centrally incorporated into the analysis. Particularly important are legal prerogatives won by organized labor prior to reform initiation, financial autonomy from the state, and experience of successful past confrontations with the state. Whether these resources are available to organized labor depends on its relationship with the state during the pre-reform period.

Despite numerous differences between the four cases, they share a number of characteristics that makes comparative analysis fruitful. Most important, in the decades preceding the initiation of economic restructuring, all four were states in which the ruling parties looked to labor groups as one of their main pillars of political support. To harness that support and to ensure regime control over politically mobilized labor, these states created corporatist labor institutions.

In this study, I define ruling-party states as authoritarian political systems in which one political party serves as a tool of governance. While other political parties may be present, they tend to be small, repressed, and not allowed to challenge the ruling party's hegemony. Corporatist labor organizations are defined here as labor associations organized by the state, functioning under state supervision, and financed by the state. Their primary function, unlike that of other types of trade unions, is not the representation and promotion of workers' interests but rather the political mobilization and control of labor and support of state policies. In exchange for this political submission to the party-state and loss of autonomy and independence, labor received access to material benefits that ensured its privileged position within the domestic economy.

Many studies of corporatism suggest that such arrangements generally result in the subordination of the working class to the state. The centralization and hierarchical structure of labor federations and the tight control that the state exercises over nominations to union leadership positions and trade union finances make organized labor unable to mount effective action in opposition to the party-state.[8] The dependence of union leadership on the party-state for finances and career advancement, furthermore, isolates them from the rank and file, thereby redirecting their loyalties away from the workers they nominally represent and toward the party-state.

However, as Stepan points out, maintaining a corporatist system can be difficult.[9] Corporatist labor institutions do not always function as originally designed by the ruling elite. In some cases, during the pre-reform period the ruling parties succeeded in constructing and maintaining corporatist labor institutions in a subordinate position to the state. In these circumstances, corporatist institutions continued to perform their original functions and organized labor lacked the ability and resources to act as an autonomous interest group. In other cases, state control over corporatist labor organizations gradually weakened. Over time, organized labor extracted concessions from the state, concessions that gave unions the ability to act independently from the state. Thus, the balance of power between the state and labor groups may shift, thereby fundamentally changing the relationship between the two.

## Substantive and Procedural Concessions

In the four cases examined in this study, corporatist labor institutions continued to perform their original functions in Mexico and Czechoslovakia.[10] However,

8. See, for example, Kenneth S. Mericle, "Corporatist Control of the Working Class: Authoritarian Brazil Since 1964," in *Authoritarianism and Corporatism in Latin America,* ed. James M. Malloy (Pittsburgh: University of Pittsburgh Press, 1977), 303–38; Youssef Cohen, "The Benevolent Leviathan: Political Consciousness Among Urban Workers Under State Corporatism," *American Political Science Review* 76, no. 1 (1982): 46–47; David Collier and Ruth Berins Collier, *Shaping the Political Arena: Critical Junctures, the Labor Movement, and Regime Dynamics in Latin America* (Princeton: Princeton University Press, 1991), 51–55; David Collier, "Trajectory of a Concept: 'Corporatism' in the Study of Latin American Politics," in *Latin America in Comparative Perspective: New Approaches to Methods and Analysis,* ed. Peter H. Smith (Boulder, Colo.: Westview Press, 1995), 139–42.

9. Alfred Stepan, *The State and Society: Peru in Comparative Perspective* (Princeton: Princeton University Press, 1978), 301–16.

10. In this book I am focusing only on the Czech Republic and not including the Slovak Republic, since during the first decade following the political transition in Czechoslovakia very few economic reforms were attempted in the Slovak Republic.

in Poland and Egypt, ruling party control over these institutions gradually weakened, and organized labor succeeded in carving out ever greater autonomy from the state. More important, the types of concessions that the ruling parties were forced to make changed over time in the latter two cases. The types of concessions that organized labor extracted from the state can be divided into two categories. The state may offer organized labor substantive concessions, which include assorted material resources. Especially common are wage increases; expanded benefits packages, including health, pension, recreation and education benefits; housing and child care support; and subsidies on consumer goods. The other type of concessions is procedural, granting organized labor rights and privileges that allow it to have a voice in the management of state firms and in national policy debates on decisions affecting labor. Although both types of concessions are extended by the state in response to labor mobilization and protest, the long-term consequences of these concessions are different.

In cases such as Egypt and Poland, where corporatist labor institutions weakened over time, we can discern a particular pattern in the interactions between organized labor and the state. The state first responded to labor demands by extending substantive concessions. Although these had budgetary implications, they did not affect the overall balance of power between organized labor and the state. The higher wages, more attractive benefits packages, or additional consumer subsidies tended to defuse worker mobilization and protest, thus restoring social stability and maintaining labor within the ruling party's support coalition. However, over time recurring economic crises depleted the regime's resources. Consequently, the party had fewer material goods to offer organized labor as payment for the latter's continued political support. These financially strapped regimes had few alternatives but to offer organized labor procedural concessions, which were attractive when material resources were scarce, since they did not have an immediate economic price. Thus, by offering these procedural concessions the ruling party could silence labor opposition without incurring significant costs. In most cases, once the immediate crisis was over, the ruling party attempted to rescind the concessions by offering pay increases or other substantive benefits. This kind of an exchange, however, did not always succeed and many procedural concessions remained in place.

Although they were less costly in the short run, the procedural concessions won through confrontations with the state provided organized labor with important legal prerogatives that in the long term significantly augmented its power vis-à-vis the state. In Poland, for instance, concessions granted to labor during the 1980s gave workers' councils extensive powers in controlling the management of public sector enterprises. Once economic reforms began following the 1989 transition, the councils were able to make a compelling case that they had ownership rights within state firms, thus significantly altering the government's privatization plans. In Egypt, during the 1970s the ETUC extracted important concessions from the regime that gave them the legal right to participate in policy making affecting its membership base. The ETUC made use of this legal prerogative during debates about public sector restructuring and divestiture during the 1990s.

## Resources

As a consequence of contentious encounters between organized labor and the state, corporatist institutions can weaken over time and labor begins to acquire important resources. Crucially, such encounters often go beyond demands for improving workers' standard of living that can be satisfied, at least in good economic times, through substantive concessions. Frequently these contentious encounters revolve around issues of control over decision making within the labor organizations themselves as well as at the national level. The procedural concessions that the party is forced to grant both because it lacks material resources to extend substantive concessions and because of the nature of the demands go to the very heart of the corporatist arrangements designed to ensure labor's subordination to the regime. The price of maintaining labor's political support during periods of crisis is often the long-term reduction of the regime's ability to control labor organizations. By gradually expanding the autonomous space that labor institutions enjoy, labor's political loyalty to the ruling party becomes that much more difficult to enforce. This in turn increases the likelihood that during the next moment of crisis the unions will be that much more willing and able to demand and extract further concessions. In other words, changes in laws and regulations governing labor relations are valuable resources that organized labor acquires during contentious encounters with the state. Over time these legal prerogatives significantly reshape organized labor's ability to influence policy decisions it cares about.

These legal prerogatives are often accompanied by the acquisition of other resources. When the prerogatives are acquired through a bargaining process with an often reluctant state, labor organizations also gain a more intangible resource of experience. Thus labor organizations that had successfully extracted concessions from the state are more confident in their ability to challenge the state in the future and know how to do so. They had confronted the state previously and had witnessed the state backing down. Consequently, what once may have been perceived as a regime with large reservoirs of repressive tactics and a willingness to use them now comes to be seen more as an opponent that can be brought to the negotiating table. By the same token, during subsequent encounters the ruling party is aware that the once submissive labor organization has gained additional experiential resources that it can draw upon and knows how politically threatening labor unrest can be.[11]

Finally, the acquisition of legal prerogatives by labor organizations is also often accompanied by the expansion of fiscal autonomy from the state, through, for instance, greater control over the collection and expenditure of union dues and through the control of profit-generating ventures and economic initiatives that bypass the state, such as vacation resorts; housing; or, as was the case in Egypt, a bank. In other cases, as in Poland, organized labor can tap into foreign sources of funding that are outside state control. With greater financial autonomy, the ability of organized labor to effectively confront the state grows, since unions are now less concerned that in retaliation for insubordination the ruling party will be able to cut off all its financing. Furthermore, once acquired, these resources proved difficult to rescind and highly resilient even in the face of profound and far-reaching sociopolitical and economic transformation. Because the resources were acquired through contentious encounters with the state, workers were willing to defend them and resist attempts by the state to take them away. Chapters 2 and 3 will examine the evolution of corporatist labor institutions in the four cases. They will focus on how in two of them, Poland and Egypt, in the decades prior to reform initiation in 1989 in the former and 1991 in the latter, the contentious encounters between the state and organized labor resulted in unions' acquiring legal prerogatives, significant financial autonomy, and experience of successfully confronting the regime. These resources allowed them to insert themselves into policy making and shape privatization strategies that were adopted when governments initiated structural adjustment reforms. These chapters will also examine how organized labor in Czechoslovakia and Mexico traveled along a very different trajectory. Here, corporatist labor institutions remained effective and unions did not acquire the resources that would allow them to influence privatization policies during the first decade of reforms.

---

11. For example, the specter of the January 1977 riots that erupted in Egypt following President Anwar al-Sadat's removal of consumer subsidies continues to haunt Egyptian policy makers. Author interview with World Bank official, Cairo, August 25, 1998.

## Dynamics Within Ruling Parties

Why are corporatist labor institutions able to extract these recourses in some cases but not in others? After all, economic crises that triggered labor mobilization in Poland and Egypt also occurred in the other two cases, but with very different consequences for party-labor relationships. Why were ruling parties in two cases able to either prevent labor mobilization from happening in the first place even during periods of economic downturn or, when they did occur, to withstand the pressure to grant additional procedural concessions or accede to changes that resulted in greater union financial autonomy? Or put differently, why was the creation of effective mechanisms for elite conflict resolution so central to the Mexican and Czechoslovak regimes' ability to maintain control of corporatist labor institutions?

The single or ruling party, which Duverger has called one of the great inventions of the twentieth century, shares some features with other types of political parties.[12] It does, however, exhibit a number of unique characteristics that place it in a distinct category. The single or ruling party has historically emerged primarily either in states that have undergone revolutions or in those that were engaged in nationalist, anticolonial struggles. This particular context has influenced how the party defined its functions and goals and how it related to the bureaucratic apparatus of the state. Single parties that emerged from either revolutionary or nationalist struggles came into power with promises of a complete reorganization of both the political and socioeconomic order. In cases of nationalist struggle, the single party achieved a dominant position by virtue of being the most viable political organization in the new nation. In the revolutionary context, the single party engaged in displacing any other political actors who may have posed a challenge to its authority and to its program of fundamental restructuring of socioeconomic relations.[13]

The single party's tasks were enormous, both because of ambitious socio-economic-transformation projects and because of the need to politically consolidate what often were newly created nations. Given this environment, the party engaged in activities that in more consolidated states are performed by other institutions, such as the mass media, the courts, or social service delivery

---

12. Maurice Duverger, *Political Parties: Their Organization and Activity in the Modern State* (London: Methuen, 1969), 256.

13. For a discussion of the characteristics of dominant party states, see Samuel P. Huntington and Clement H. Moore, eds., *Authoritarian Politics in Modern Societies: The Dynamics of Established One-Party Systems* (New York: Basic Books, 1970).

organizations.[14] In addition, to promote and implement its goals of socio-economic transformation and working either in the absence of a well-developed bureaucracy or in a bureaucracy whose loyalty to the party's project was suspect, the party became engaged in mobilizing, controlling, and coordinating administrative tasks; served as the main conduit for the dissemination of information and development targets from the center to the peripheries; and became the main source of training and educating the population to prepare it for implementation of the sought-after changes. At the same time, the single party began extending direct control over such social organizations as labor unions and women's and youth leagues to make them unavailable to any other potential political entrepreneurs. This meant that while the ruling party and the government remained nominally independent of each other, in reality the two became fused.[15]

Ruling-party regimes, according to some studies, because of their extensive presence within societies and their dominance of the political space, may have a unique ability to initiate difficult policy decisions thanks to their control of the political arena and the means to mobilize public support.[16] However, if they are to have these capabilities, they must first build an effective party organization that allows them to mobilize and control the population, establish effective lines of communication between the leadership and the population, and ensure that the directives coming from the party leadership are implemented by the lower levels of the party machine. The primary goal of any party, however, is its self-preservation. Unless a party can marshal the necessary resources, create effective internal organization, and institutionalize mass support, it will not be able to perform any other functions and, in fact, may not survive at all.[17]

An effective party must therefore create mechanisms that allow internal party disputes to be resolved within the party itself and, once a consensus is reached within the party, to enforce that consensus.[18] Conflict within a political

14. See, for example, Zolberg, *Creating Political Order*; Leonard Binder, "Political Recruitment and Participation in Egypt," in *Political Parties and Political Development,* ed. Joseph LaPalombara and Myron Weiner (Princeton: Princeton University Press, 1966), 217–40.

15. See, for example, Henry Bienen, *Tanzania: Party Transformation and Economic Development* (Princeton: Princeton University Press, 1967); Gerald A. Heeger, "Bureaucracy, Political Parties, and Political Development," *World Politics* 25, no. 4 (1973): 600–607; Leonard B. Schapiro, *The Communist Party of the Soviet Union* (New York: Random House, 1960).

16. Stephan Haggard and Robert R. Kaufman, *The Political Economy of Democratic Transitions* (Princeton: Princeton University Press, 1995), 267–306.

17. See Samuel P. Huntington, *Political Order in Changing Societies* (New Haven: Yale University Press, 1968), especially 401–12.

18. As Haggard and Kaufman point out, "Divisions send mixed signals when policy decisions are taken and provide the opportunity for lower echelons to appeal or even challenge commands." *Political Economy of Democratic Transitions,* 271.

party is inevitable. What matters is how that conflict is managed by the party and, most significant, whether conflicts can be managed within the organization without spilling out into the public arena. A party can respond to internal disputes by moving toward greater internal centralization and authoritarianism; conversely, it can begin to fragment and become unable to effectively perpetuate itself as an organization or, if in control of the government, to govern effectively.[19]

A ruling party that fails to create an effective internal organization is prone to challenges in maintaining political control for a number of reasons. The jockeying for position within a party torn by internal disputes pushes the various factions to build up personal fiefdoms within the state bureaucracy. These factions are also likely to look for allies outside the regime as a means of bolstering their position: the dynamics of single ruling parties that have not created an effective internal organization come to resemble those in a fragmented or polarized multiparty system, with each faction seeking to acquire allies and build independent bases of power. Although conflicts may often appear as little more than personality clashes, those in the inner circle of the regime who preside over vast bureaucratic or military organizations have resources that can be drawn on to mount effective opposition to other factions.[20]

The existence of competition within the ruling elite creates a window of opportunity for interest groups to extract more concessions by allying themselves, whether formally or tacitly, with one of the competing regime factions. Conversely, when a party builds into the system incentives that promote loyalty and punish disloyalty among the elite, such a favorable opportunity structure does not exist.[21] In this context, it makes little sense for those within the party elite to look to social groups as a means of building alliances for promoting their careers. If anything, such attempts can undermine their ability to move up in the power hierarchy.

The internal management of the ruling party's disputes therefore is of key importance for the evolution of the corporatist labor institutions' relationship

19. See, for example, Robert Michels, *Political Parties: A Sociological Study of the Oligarchic Tendencies of Modern Democracy* (New York: Dover, 1959), 333–41.

20. See, for example, Robert Holt and Terry Roe, "The Political Economy of Reform: Egypt in the 1980s," in *Political and Economic Interactions in Economic Policy Reform: Evidence from Eight Countries*, ed. Robert H. Bates and Anne O. Krueger (Cambridge, U.K.: Blackwell, 1993), 179–224.

21. Doug McAdam, "Conceptual Origins, Current Problems, Future Directions," in *Comparative Perspectives on Social Movements: Political Opportunities, Mobilizing Structures, and Cultural Framings*, ed. Doug McAdam, John D. McCarthy, and Mayer N. Zald (New York: Cambridge University Press, 1996), 23–40.

to the party-state. In cases where party elite conflict is not contained within the party, labor organizations are able to more successfully make demands on the state, since factions within the party are interested in ensuring labor support. Over time, as labor gradually extracts more concessions, corporatist control over organized labor weakens and unions develop the means to act independently of the state. Conversely, when the elite manages to contain disputes, corporatist institutions continue to perform their original functions and labor lacks the ability and resources to act as an autonomous interest group.

The differences in the ability of unions to become influential players in the first years of reform in the four cases I examine can be traced back to the very different elite dynamics that existed in the four countries in the years prior to the initiation of reforms. These different dynamics affected the resources available to labor organizations as reforms were being considered. While the Czechoslovak and Mexican elites succeeded at constructing mechanisms for ensuring elite cohesion, neither the Polish nor the Egyptian elites were able to devise such mechanisms. In Mexico and Czechoslovakia, the elites constructed political parties that both served to ensure that elite conflicts could be managed constructively and established channels of communication with the public. In Poland and Egypt, by contrast, political parties did little to dampen elite conflict.

In Mexico and Czechoslovakia, while the mechanisms that were devised were quite different, what they did have in common was the incentive structure that rewarded loyalty and punished disloyalty among the elite. Given this incentive structure, those seeking to advance their political careers saw few benefits in making alliances with social groups, while the advantages of being faithful to the party line were unambiguous. In the Mexican case, the task of maintaining elite cohesion was facilitated by a number of factors. One of the most significant of these was the principle of no reelection to the presidency or to most other contested offices. This rule had two main consequences. In the first place, it gave assurance to the various factions within the Institutional Revolutionary Party (PRI) that they could reasonably anticipate having their turn at the helm, thereby encouraging them to work within the system. Second, the possibility of someday returning to an elective office made breaking with the party unattractive because promotion of one's political career did not depend on the control of a particular district or constituency but rather on the establishment of relationships with higher-ranked party members who controlled the promotion process. In most cases, these incentives were sufficient to ensure loyalty to the PRI. When, however, individuals attempted to break ranks, the reaction from the elite was swift and included expulsion from party ranks.[22]

In the Czechoslovak case, the costs of insubordination to the KSČ were even higher, entailing not just removal from the party but also the loss of professional opportunities. It made little sense for those within the ruling elite in Czechoslovakia to look to social groups as means of building alliances for promoting their careers. If anything, such attempts would undermine their ability to move up in the power hierarchy. The pressure to conform to the party line was reinforced by targeting family members as punishment for insubordination.[23]

In Poland and Egypt, such incentives remained underdeveloped and were not applied with any consistency. The punishments for disloyalty not only were less onerous but also were applied sporadically and selectively. In both cases, there were good reasons for politically ambitious individuals to believe that the path to promotion could lead through a variety of channels. In both countries, building up one's own power network and cultivating clients among various constituencies remained a viable path to political advancement. In Egypt, the very establishment of a political party proved problematic because of the deep distrust between various regime factions.[24] Here, rather than serving as a means for bringing about elite cohesion, the party and the state were frequently at loggerheads. Furthermore, unlike in the other three cases, the military was never fully subordinated to civilian control and became yet another player in elite power struggles. In fact, by the 1980s in Egypt it seemed that one of the best strategies for moving ahead was to openly break with the ruling National Democratic Party, since successful opposition candidates were regularly offered plum positions within the party and state administration as a way of enticing them back into the fold.[25]

22. See, for example, Bo Anderson and James D. Cockcroft, "Control and Cooptation in Mexican Politics," in *Latin American Radicalism: A Documentary Report on Left and Nationalist Movements,* ed. Irving Louis Horowitz, Josue de Castro, and John Gerassi (New York: Random House, 1969), 366–89; Rogelio Hernandez Rodriguez, "The Partido Revolucionario Institutional," in *Governing Mexico: Political Parties and Elections,* ed. Monica Serrano (London: Institute of Latin American Studies, 1998), 71–94; Jorge G. Castaneda, *Perpetuating Power: How Mexican Presidents Are Chosen* (New York: New Press, 2000), xix.

23. See Edward Taborsky, *Communism in Czechoslovakia, 1948–1960* (Princeton: Princeton University Press, 1961), 68–96; Vlad Sobell, "Czechoslovakia: The Legacy of Normalization," *East European Politics and Society* 2, no. 1 (1987): 35–68.

24. See two studies by Kirk J. Beattie: *Egypt During the Nasser Years: Ideology, Politics, and Civil Society* (Boulder, Colo.: Westview Press, 1994), 58–74; *Egypt During the Sadat Years* (New York: Palgrave, 2000), 189–98.

25. See Robert Springborg, *Mubarak's Egypt: Fragmentation of Political Order* (Boulder, Colo.: Westview Press, 1989), 89–105.

## Historical Legacies and Change

The relationship between the ruling parties and organized labor in the decades prior to reform initiation in Poland, Egypt, Mexico, and the Czech Republic influenced the ability of trade unions to shape debates about the restructuring measures that were of particular concern to these groups. The resources that organized labor acquired in Poland and Egypt before debates about privatization policies began allowed them to have an important voice during the phases of design and implementation. The lack of similar resources in the case of Mexican and Czech trade unions meant that they were unable to shape public sector policies. Therefore, even in cases where organized labor seems to be losing political power, for instance, where membership rolls have been dwindling, they may still retain important resources that allow them to continue playing a significant role in policy debates. In other words, once established, institutions often tend to persist even in the face of profound change.[26] Changing and restructuring institutions is, of course, possible. How easy a task that will be, however, will depend on how the existing institutional arrangements have distributed power among the relevant actors and on the willingness of promoters of change to incur the political costs of pushing reforms. That is, the most significant effect of historical legacies is not that they predetermine future choices but rather that they constrain them.[27] They do so through their effects on the distribution of resources among the state and social actors. They therefore affect the balance of power between them and influence the outcome of policy conflicts over the direction of economic reforms.

The evidence presented in this book thus suggests that the "punctured equilibrium" or "critical junctures" model of institutional change, which argues that change is most likely as a consequence of dramatic breaks with the past, overestimates the power of a political or economic crisis to precipitate a fundamental restructuring of the institutional environment.[28] Similarly, it suggests that the incremental and gradual process model, which argues that modifications

---

26. See, for example, Geoffrey Garrett and Peter Lange, "Internationalization, Institutions, and Political Change," *International Organization* 49, no. 4 (1995): 627–55.

27. David Stark and Laszlo Burszt, *Postsocialist Pathways: Transforming Politics and Property Rights in East Central Europe* (New York: Cambridge University Press, 1998), 80–105.

28. For a discussion of the "critical junctures" or "punctured equilibrium" model, see, for example, Stephen D. Krasner, "Approaches to the State: Alternative Conceptions and Historical Dynamics," *Comparative Politics* 16, no. 2 (1984): 240–46; Collier and Berins Collier, *Shaping the Political Arena*, 27–39.

to existing institutions take place slowly and primarily at the margins, under-estimates the potential influence of a crisis on processes of change.[29]

What crises do produce are windows of opportunity for change. However, while potential for change increases during these "critical junctures," whether this opportunity will be seized or not will depend on the existing institutional environment. Many of the potential transformations are likely to directly affect various groups that had a stake in the previously established institutions and hence will be seen by these groups as directly threatening their interests. But whether these groups can successfully resist change will depend on the resources they can bring to the negotiations over the form of new institutional arrange-ments. Those resources in turn will depend on how institutions developed in the past. In cases in which institutional evolution had redistributed resources away from a group threatened by change, it will have difficulty in challenging such transformations, and institutional restructuring can be rapid. Where historical developments have allowed these groups to amass resources, however, there will be no dramatic breaks with the past but rather a gradual change even in the face of a crisis.

29. For a discussion of the incremental change model, see, for example, Avner Grief, Paul Milgrom, and Barry Weinpast, "Coordination, Commitment, and Enforcement: The Case of the Merchant Guild," in *Explaining Social Institutions,* ed. Jack Knight and Itai Sened (Ann Arbor: University of Michigan Press, 1995), 27–56; Douglass C. North, *Institutions, Institutional Change, and Economic Performance* (New York: Cambridge University Press, 1990), 73–106. Kathleen Thelen argues that over the long term such incremental changes can profoundly reshape the institutional landscape. Kathleen Thelen, *How Institutions Evolve: The Political Economy of Skills in Germany, Britain, the United States, and Japan* (New York: Cambridge University Press, 2004), 31–36.

## 2  RULING PARTIES, ORGANIZED LABOR, AND TRANSITIONS TO DEMOCRACY

*Poland and Czechoslovakia*

When the Polish and Czechoslovak governments initiated economic reforms following the fall of Communism, they encountered very different labor organizations. Polish unions, as will be examined in Chapter 4, emerged as influential actors and significantly shaped the process of privatization design and implementation. Unions in Czechoslovakia, however, were unable to play such a central role during the reform processes. The source of this difference between the two cases can be located in the state-labor dynamics of the pre-reform period. The contentious encounters between the Polish ruling party and labor resulted in the acquisition by the latter of important resources, in particular, legal prerogatives, financial autonomy, and the long experience of successfully challenging the state. Thanks to these resources, Polish organized labor could not be brushed aside by the government as the latter sought to push through market reforms. Czechoslovak organized labor traveled along a very different trajectory that left it with few resources it could draw upon as it confronted structural adjustment reforms. This chapter will examine how despite similar initial conditions following the Communist takeover in both countries, organized labor entered the new democratic era with such differing resources.

### The Labor Movement in Communist Poland

In July 1944 on Polish territory controlled by the advancing Soviet army, the Polish Workers Party (PPR) announced the formation of a new government. A bloody and protracted civil war, with the Home Army supported by the Polish government in exile, based in London, followed as the PPR sought to consolidate power. Immediately following the end of World War II it appeared that an agreement hammered out in Yalta between the Soviet Union, the United States, and Great Britain that mandated free elections in Poland would hold. In June 1945 Stanisław Mikołajczyk, the prime minister of Poland's government in exile and leader of the Polish Peasant Party (PSL), returned and joined the PPR-dominated government. In January 1947 the PPR, which ran in coalition with the Polish Socialist Party (PPS) and two smaller parties, the Democratic Alliance (SD) and the Peasant Alliance (SL), won the parliamentary elections largely thanks to fraud and intimidation.[1]

Following the election the PPR quickly moved to consolidate power. In October 1947, facing imminent arrest, Mikołajczyk fled the country. In December 1948 the PPR merged with the PPS, forming the Polish United Workers Party (PZPR).[2] By 1949 the new regime had abolished all independent political parties and organizations and began the process of Stalinization, sending thousands of political foes to prison or into exile. The PZPR, led by first secretary Bolesław Bierut, also expanded the police apparatus extending surveillance over the population and the party itself. In March 1949 it created a special department within the Ministry of Security and charged it with the elimination of all opposition forces that may have penetrated the party. Within the next couple of years, in the name of the "battle for revolutionary vigilance," numerous high party dignitaries were expelled from the PZPR. Others were incarcerated. The PZPR also moved to transform the Polish economy, nationalizing industry and instituting central planning mechanisms. At the same time that the PZPR was busy eliminating its political rivals, it also sought to appeal to the rural and urban poor with promises to undertake revolutionary socioeconomic restructuring of the society.

Containing political opposition and mobilizing support also meant that the party had to extend control over organized labor, which had become increasingly militant in the 1930s. It entrusted Edward Ochab, a high-ranking party official, with formulating a plan to reshape union organization. In June 1949, a centralized trade union organization was formed, headed by Politburo member Aleksander Zawadzki, with branch unions subordinated to the Central Council of Trade Unions (CRZZ). Gradually, the number of branch unions was reduced from the prewar high of about three hundred to twenty-three. Forty-nine councils were established at the national level along with about thirty

---

1. For additional information about the rigging of the elections, see Teresa Torańska, *Oni* (Warsaw: Agencja Omnipress, 1989).
2. *Głos Ludu—Robotnik*, December 15, 1948.

thousand factory councils.[3] The party wanted to ensure that all workers joined the organization and the CRZZ membership quickly expanded. By 1949 it had 3.5 million members. In 1954 membership swelled to 4.5 million, leaving only 750,000 workers in state-owned enterprises outside union structures.[4]

In 1949 new labor legislation codified the hierarchical structure of labor organizations and defined the rights and responsibilities of the unions. At the lowest level, the factory unions were responsible for the administration of various social programs, such as those of health and recreation, that had been newly extended to workers. They were also responsible for ensuring cooperative relations between company management and employees and for fulfilling national economic plans. Additionally, they were expected to work closely with party cells that had been established in all firms to promote the ideological education of workers.[5] At the national level, the CRZZ was guaranteed consultative powers in designing national development plans and wage policies.[6]

The suppression of political dissent, the expansion of the party apparatus, and the centralization of labor organizations under the PZPR's control thus seemed to ensure that working-class activism would be channeled to support the new regime. The changes in economic policies provided further incentives for workers to remain within the new regime's coalition of support. These changes ushered in a period of unprecedented social mobility, opening previously inaccessible opportunities for educational and professional advancement. Peasants left the countryside in large number to find employment in the expanding industrial sector. Blue-collar workers moved into administrative and managerial posts and staffed party bureaucracy, local administration, and central government ministries.[7]

*The 1956 Confrontation*

Worker support for the regime proved to be more conditional than the PZPR had anticipated and was predicated on continued improvement in living standards.

3. George Kolankiewicz, "Poland, 1980: The Working Class Under 'Anomie Socialism,'" in *Blue-Collar Workers in Eastern Europe*, ed. Jan F. Triska and Charles Gati (London: George Allen and Unwin, 1981), 146.
4. Andrzej Paczkowski, *The Spring Will Be Ours: Poland and the Poles from Occupation to Freedom* (University Park: Pennsylvania State University Press, 2003), 227.
5. A. Witalec, "Organizacja partyjna pomocnikiem i inspiratorem związkowego działania," *Przegląd Związkowy*, no. 12 (1978).
6. For a further discussion of unions' role in the new political and economic system, see K. Ostrowski, *Rola związków zawodowych w polskim systemie politycznym* (Wrocław: PAN, 1970).
7. Alexander Matejko, *Social Change and Stratification in Eastern Europe: An Interpretative Analysis of Poland and Her Neighbors* (New York: Praeger, 1974), 50–56.

Within a few years of coming to power, however, the regime was facing a growing economic crisis, making it difficult to meet these worker expectations. Further, conflicts that had simmered within the PZPR from its inception presented challenges to devising a response to the crisis. The main disagreement pitted those within the party leadership who advocated a national development path and were skeptical about the wisdom of transplanting such Soviet ideas as farm collectivization, against those who argued that the Soviet model should be closely replicated in Poland and pushed for acceleration of the industrialization program. In the late 1940s, this second group, led by Bolesław Bierut and Hilary Minc, appeared to gain the upper hand when Stanisław Gomułka, leader of the "nationalists," was forced to resign from the party.

However, the push for agricultural reform proved futile. Peasants increasingly rebelled against forced collectivization and food production plummeted. As the economy began running into trouble by the mid-1950s, discontent among industrial workers grew as well. Workers' grievances concerned primarily wages, production norms, and working conditions but also dissatisfaction with the performance of trade unions in representing their interests within companies.[8] At the same time as discontent among workers grew, with the death of Stalin in 1953, political repression eased, press censorship weakened, and political discussions became increasingly open and often critical of the PZPR's policies. Critical discussions also took place within the party itself, with democratic reforms now openly mentioned. This political opening and the growing economic crisis for the first time since the establishment of the Communist regime presented workers with an opportunity to challenge the state and demonstrated that the labor institutions set up by the PZPR were hard pressed to contain and manage growing worker discontent.

Tensions boiled over in June 1956 when worker protests broke out in Poznań. The initial demands focused on working conditions at the Cegielski factory. When the PZPR responded with threats, workers marched to the city center, where they were joined by students and workers from other enterprises. The demands turned political and the demonstrators clashed with the security police, threw Molotov cocktails at police headquarters, and stormed party offices. Eventually, the PZPR called in an estimated ten thousand soldiers, who dealt brutally with the protesters. Official sources claimed that fifty-three were killed. However, foreign press put the number at two thousand to three hundred and

8. Jan B. De Weydenthal, "Poland: Workers and Politics," in *Blue-Collar Workers in Eastern Europe*, ed. Jan F. Triska and Charles Gati (London: George Allen and Unwin, 1981), 190.

two thousand arrested.[9] Although the protests were put down by force, concessions were immediately extended to workers to bring them back into the fold.

The 1956 workers' demonstrations proved to be a harbinger of future conflicts between the regime and labor, conflicts that would gradually tilt the balance of power between the two. This first eruption of discontent also signaled how the party elite would seek to control labor opposition. While repression was deployed in this instance and would be used in future encounters as well, those within the party leadership who viewed repressive measures as the preferred response never gained full control of the party apparatus. Rather, they were always forced to contend with the faction supporting an indigenous development path. This faction believed that social groups, whether peasants or workers, needed to be offered positive inducements to remain supportive of the PZPR and advocated offering substantive concessions in exchange for that support. When those were deemed insufficient, this faction was also prepared to consider procedural concessions as a way to diffuse labor opposition, with the understanding that once the immediate crisis was over, these procedural concessions would be withdrawn. At the same time, labor protests tended to exacerbate internal conflict within the party, thus providing a window of opportunity for labor to extract concessions.

During the first few decades when the PZPR had material resources at its disposal, it was still able to withdraw some procedural concessions by extending more material inducements. Over time, however, as economic crises became more frequent and those material resources increasingly scarce, procedural concessions became more difficult to abrogate. In other words, over time labor organizations gradually succeeded in acquiring more legal prerogatives and valuable experience in confronting the state, which gave them a say in the day-to-day management of state firms and, by the 1980s, a greater say in national economic decision making.

The bloody clashes in Poznań intensified tensions within the party. While the reformists within the Central Committee wanted to continue the democratic reforms begun earlier, the conservative faction that dominated the Politburo resisted these changes. Eventually, appealing to the disaffected public, the reformers gained the upper hand and voted for Gomułka to become the first party secretary. For a brief moment, it seemed that the concessions workers won in Poznań would stand.

9. Maryjane Osa, *Solidarity and Contention: Networks of Polish Opposition* (Minneapolis: University of Minnesota Press, 2003), 32–34.

Within a year the hope that changes that had been ushered in following Stalin's death would be permanent were dashed. At the Ninth Party Plenum in May 1957, as the PZPR embarked on internal reforms aimed at bringing an end to the divisiveness and factionalism of previous years, it sought to reestablish control over a restive organized labor. In particular, it moved to abrogate the procedural concessions granted after the Poznań protests. Especially targeted were workers' councils, established in response to workers' demands for more meaningful representation within enterprises, and which had oversight over management and controlled wage funds and premium distribution.[10] The party viewed this concession as potentially undermining the PZPR's control over organized labor. Indeed, when the party made similar procedural concessions in the 1980s, they significantly augmented labor's power.

During the plenum, the prerogatives of workers' councils were transferred to trade unions, and the December 1958 legislation that established the Conference of Workers' Self-Management effectively restored the PZPR's dominance within enterprises by giving the party a central position within the councils.[11] Thus, during the late 1950s the PZPR was still able to relatively easily withdraw procedural concessions once the immediate crisis was over. It could do so because it was still able to meet demands for wage increases and improved standards of living. In other words, the party could withdraw politically threatening procedural concessions by offering workers sufficiently attractive substantive concessions and therefore maintain its dominance over organized labor.

Despite the backtracking on these pledges, however, the events of 1956 were an important precedent in state-labor relations. Most significant, they made clear the tenuousness of workers' support for the regime, the inadequacy of political and union institutions in controlling labor, and the importance of worker self-management to labor groups. The substantive concessions, by contrast, proved for a time to be invaluable in ensuring labor quiescence, especially when the growth of a more organized opposition among the intelligentsia led in 1968 to a confrontation between this group and the regime. While students were demonstrating, workers were unwilling to join them in challenging the PZPR.

10. George Kolankiewicz, "Employee Self-Management and Socialist Trade Unionism," in *Policy and Politics in Contemporary Poland,* ed. Jean Woodall (New York: St. Martin's Press, 1982), 130.

11. Wojciech Roszkowski, *Historia Polski, 1914–1993* (Warsaw: Wydawnictwo Naukowe PWN, 1994), 231.

## The 1970 Confrontation

As the economy began running into trouble in the second half of the 1960s these substantive concessions became increasingly costly to maintain. The regime found itself in a predicament. Unless it undertook reforms to restore economic growth, social unrest sparked by declining standards of living could threaten political stability. Yet pushing through with restructuring was also fraught with danger, since it would inevitably entail belt-tightening measures. Intensifying factional struggles within the party elite made cobbling together a reform package difficult. Eventually, the PZPR agreed to measures aimed at spurring growth, improving industrial efficiency, and linking workers' remuneration to improvements in productivity. At the same time, in order to address the ballooning budget deficit, the party decided to raise the prices of some consumer goods.

Workers responded immediately to the December 1970 price hikes. On December 14 strikes broke out in the Gdańsk shipyard. Workers demanded withdrawal of price increases and granting of greater political freedoms. The police response was brutal and dozens of workers were killed, leading to massive demonstrations and the firebombing of the PZPR's headquarters. Within days protests spilled to other seaside cities. By the second part of the month similar protests erupted in Warsaw, Katowice, Poznań, Wrocław, Słupsk, Elbląg, Kraków, and Łòdź.[12]

The protests were a watershed in state-labor relations. Not only was the scale of protests unprecedented, but workers' demands were not just economic but also explicitly political. Furthermore, many local party and trade union activists, the very ones whom the regime relied on to maintain control over workers, joined the protests. In Gdańsk and Szczecin, workers elected strike committees that were responsible for maintaining channels of communication with other striking enterprises and for negotiating with regime representatives. For the first time, workers explicitly demanded the establishment of independent union organizations.[13]

---

12. Luba Fajfer, "December 1970: A Prelude to Solidarity," in *Poland's Permanent Revolution: People vs. Elites, 1956 to the Present*, ed. Jane Leftwich Curry and Luba Fajfer (Washington, D.C.: American University Press, 1996), 72–75. For a detailed account of the December 1970 events, see Lucjan Adamczuk et al., *Grudzień przed sierpniem: W XXV rocznicę wydarzeń grudniowych* (Gdańsk: Instytut Konserwatywny im. E. Burke'a, 1996).
13. Weydenthal, "Poland," 196.

Although force was used against workers in Gdańsk, the regime was immobilized by an intensifying struggle for control of the party being waged by three factions and appeared unable to decide how best to respond to the crisis. The strongest of these factions, led by Edward Gierek, party leader from the southern coal mining region, appealed to workers for support, promising substantive concessions. Criss-crossing the country, Gierek pleaded with workers not to abandon the party but to help resolve the economic crisis. To ensure that this help would be forthcoming, the Gierek faction pushed for measures that would guarantee improvements in workers' living standards.

By the end of January, the regime scrapped the new wage-determination system and in February rescinded price increases and extended additional subsidies and benefits.[14] Finally, as had happened following the 1956 riots, the PZPR sacked the top party leadership. Although the party ignored workers' political demands and only offered substantive concessions, the 1970 confrontation foreshadowed the more sustained mobilization of opposition forces that began in the second half of the 1970s and culminated in the formation of the independent trade union Solidarity in 1980. By then, the concessions that the party was forced to make by the increasingly militant labor opposition fundamentally reshaped the relationship between state and labor. The consequences of the PZPR's procedural concessions significantly constrained the policy-making options of posttransition governments.

### The 1976 Confrontation

The party elite was aware that the economic payoffs offered after the 1970 protests were only a stopgap measure and that it could not ignore the political demands articulated during the protests. The new party leadership thought the protests reflected unions' loss of worker support, trust, and respect. It therefore embarked on restructuring internal union organization. As one leader of the official unions pointed out, "Union institutions have been widely criticized for not adequately representing working people's interests and not fighting sufficiently for their rights. Consequently, in some enterprises labor organizations were bypassed when workers wanted to present and resolve their problems."[15]

---

14. David Ost, *Solidarity and the Politics of Anti-politics: Opposition and Reform in Poland Since 1968* (Philadelphia: Temple University Press, 1990), 51–52.

15. Ryszard Pospieszyński (Secretary of CRZZ), "Zadania ruchu związkowego w swietle uchwał XXI Plenum CRZZ," *Życie Partii*, April 1971, 20.

Workers saw trade union leaders not as their representatives but as allies of company management. This perception was not surprising, since unions focused primarily on maintaining workforce discipline and ensuring that enterprises met their production targets. To make unions more representative, they would now place emphasis on responding to workers' concerns and keeping workers informed about the actions taken by the unions on their behalf. Simultaneously, the party took steps to renew workers' identification with the PZPR. It instructed the CRZZ leadership to more closely coordinate activities between enterprise-level union and party organizations. At the same time the party encouraged workers' self-government organizations within enterprises to play a more constructive role. The party leadership felt that if workers came to see the former as representing workers' interests rather than those of management, workers' councils would contribute to easing tensions within enterprises.

The PZPR hoped that by being more attentive to workers' concerns and by promoting their political education, workers' councils would facilitate peaceful conflict resolution within enterprises and return workers to the party's support coalition. As one regional party newspaper put it, "The most important mission of trade unions, socialist state institutions and party organizations is to prevent conflictual situations."[16] Within a few years, however, it was clear that these measures did little to diffuse workers' grievances or to establish better control over labor.

In 1976, sparked by a new round of price hikes on basic commodities, protests erupted in Radom and Ursus. Although the regime harassed and prosecuted strike leaders, many within the party leadership felt that Gierek's relative tolerance of opposition groups was encouraging more "counterrevolutionary" activities rather than appeasing the protesters.[17] In fact, following the 1976 workers' protests, some within the opposition intelligentsia began forming closer ties with workers to more effectively pressure the regime to implement substantial political and economic reforms. They formed the Workers Defense Committee (KOR) to provide legal and financial assistance to workers prosecuted by the government. However, when a year after the Radom and Ursus strikes the government amnestied jailed workers, KOR did not disband but rather continued to support

16. *Trybuna Mazowiecka,* March 1971.
17. Gierek continued to maintain that the prosecution of workers following the 1976 protests in Ursus and Radom was not caused by any political activity on their part but because property damage resulting from the "disturbances" was very high. See a book-length interview with Gierek by Janusz Rolicki, *Edward Gierek: Przerwana dekada* (Warsaw: Wydawnictwo FAKT, 1990).

various civil society initiatives and established a thriving underground publishing network. Among these publications was *Robotnik* (Worker), a newsletter that became widely circulated in factories and maintained a link between workers and intellectuals. KOR also proved to be very successful in raising foreign funding and assistance, much of which it used to benefit prosecuted workers.[18]

In response to this challenge, the regime once again tried to reenergize the discredited workers' councils, hoping to diffuse growing labor discontent.[19] But workers showed little interest in these powerless councils and they soon began to disappear.[20] As the official unions became increasingly discredited, workers began establishing independent workers, organizations, fundamentally challenging the party's control over labor. In 1977 a free union was established in Radom. In 1978 the Free Trade Union of Silesia and the Committee for Free Trade Unions for the Baltic Coasts were created. They were followed in 1979 by the establishment of the Founding Committee of the Free Trade Unions of Western Pomerania. In establishing these independent organizations, workers explicitly criticized official unions and demanded better wages, free Saturdays, improved safety conditions, and promotions not dependent on loyalty to the party.[21] These ideas provided the basis for the most profound challenge to the PZPR's authority that erupted in the summer of 1980 and whose consequences for the relationship between organized labor and the state reverberated even once the Communist regime disintegrated in 1989.

## The 1980 Rise of Solidarity

The combination of economic difficulties and workers' anger at the lack of meaningful representation soon exploded again. As the economy slid deeper into recession, the regime again attempted to raise consumer prices. And once again the result was worker protests, this time at a much larger scale and with even more profound consequences for both intraregime dynamics and the state-labor relationship. In August 1980, strikes erupted in the Gdańsk shipyard, giving birth to what became an eighteen-month period of unprecedented

---

18. Michael Bernhard, *The Origins of Democratization in Poland* (New York: Columbia University Press, 1993), 125.

19. Alex Pravda, "Poland in the 1970s: Dual Functioning Trade Unions Under Pressure," in *Trade Unions in Communist States,* ed. Alex Pravda and Blair A. Ruble (Boston: Allen and Unwin, 1986), 131.

20. Kolankiewicz, "Employee Self-Management," 132.

21. Denis MacShane, *Solidarity: Poland's Independent Trade Union* (Nottingham, U.K.: Spokesman, 1981), 42–45.

political and social mobilization under the banner of Solidarity. Initially a labor organization, Solidarity soon became a political opposition movement with a membership of 10 million. Solidarity's demands included the establishment of independent trade unions, free speech, the dismantling of party members' privileges, and government respect for citizens' constitutional rights. The concessions that Solidarity eventually extracted had far-reaching consequences for the ability of organized labor to shape policy at both the national and enterprise levels and continued to shape state-labor relations after the 1989 transition to democracy.

The emergence of Solidarity posed a direct challenge to both the PZPR and the CRZZ, the latter headed by Politburo member Jan Szydlak. With the growth of a popular opposition movement, many officials within CRZZ began openly criticizing the federation's leadership and frequently sided with striking Solidarity activists. At the August 1980 CRZZ meeting, the unionists accused their leadership of having abandoned their responsibility of representing workers; called for internal reforms within the official unions; and, in particular, demanded that the right to strike, veto power over government decisions on wages and prices, more union democracy, and independence from the PZPR be granted to union organizations.[22]

The CRZZ leadership was deeply divided about how to respond to this challenge. One faction within the federation was unwilling to contemplate any changes in union structure. As its chairman, Szydlak, stated, "We shall not give up power and shall not share it."[23] Others, however, argued that to retain rank-and-file loyalty, the federation had to be reformed. As one party official commented, "If the public feels that the unions do not fulfill their function satisfactorily, and that this overgrown structure has become outmoded, then it must be changed."[24] The PZPR having decided that reform was necessary, expelled Szydlak from the Politburo. However, what other changes were needed was less clear to the increasingly divided party leadership.

Despite the call for the reform of CRZZ, more and more unions were leaving to establish themselves as independent organizations. Solidarity remained suspicious of this exodus, arguing that the defections were ordered by the PZPR to appropriate the mantle of independence and thereby defuse the challenge

22. *Trybuna Ludu,* August 27, 1980; September 1, 1980; September 6–9, 1980.

23. Anna Sabat and Roman Stefanowski, *Poland: A Chronology of Events, July–November 1980,* RAD Background Report 91, Radio Free Europe Research (New York, 1981), 13.

24. Cited in A. Kemp-Welsh, *The Birth of Solidarity: The Gdańsk Negotiations, 1980* (New York: St. Martin's Press, 1983), 41.

posed by the opposition movement.[25] The party therefore changed its strategy and on October 27 the CRZZ was dissolved and replaced by a new organization, the Coordinating Commission of Branch Trade Unions. Despite these reforms, the official unions continued to lose support and members to Solidarity. Corporatist labor institutions established by the party were disintegrating.

Solidarity, for its part, much more explicitly than previous worker opposition movements, framed its demands in terms of procedural rather than substantive issues. One of its central proposals concerned worker self-management within enterprises. The PZPR, mindful that it had few resources that would make possible material payoffs in exchange for renewed support, began considering procedural concessions in order to diffuse the political crisis. It formed a Government Economic Reform Commission to consider opposition movements' demands and recommended the establishment of employee councils with veto powers over the appointment and dismissal of enterprise directors. Before the commission's recommendations were made public, however, workers in many factories had already begun to set up their own self-management organizations, thereby creating facts on the ground. The regime was unable to stop or gain control over this process. In the long run, these changes in enterprise self-management would significantly reshape the balance of power between the regime and organized labor.

Solidarity's self-management proposals emerged out of an association established between seven major enterprises. The association known as Sieć (Network) met for the first time in mid-April 1981. As Kolankiewicz notes, "The Network rejected the idea of participation in management and stipulated that self-management must appoint the director. Self-management would allow Solidarity to take a more constructive part in economic 'renewal' without accepting the responsibility for macroeconomic decisions in which they had no say."[26] Founding Committees for Self-Management were to be set up in individual enterprises and would begin designing self-management proposals specifically tailored to each company.

Initially, the National Committee of Solidarity was ambivalent about the proposals put forth by Sieć, insisting that the movement should focus on establishing strong trade union organizations. Nevertheless, in many enterprises self-management structures began appearing anyway. In some cases Solidarity members cooperated with the old state-sponsored unions in setting them up.

---

25. See, for example, Ost, *Solidarity and the Politics of Anti-politics,* 94–97.
26. Kolankiewicz, "Employee Self-Management," 139.

By the summer of 1981, the pressure on Solidarity leadership from the rank and file to establish control over enterprise management increased. In June 1981 in an unprecedented move, Sieć sent a draft of a new state enterprise law to the Sejm (parliament) for consideration.[27] In July, Solidarity chairman Lech Wałęsa finally came out in support of worker self-management.[28] Although the parliament voted down the proposal, many within the regime recognized that at least some of the Sieć demands would need to be satisfied if the party was to regain political initiative.

The emergence of Solidarity intensified the internal conflicts within the PZPR. Those within the leadership who advocated economic and political reforms pushed for granting procedural concessions to labor. The reformist faction argued that in light of the growing economic crisis few material concessions could be granted to workers to bring them back into the party fold. At the same time, it viewed extending such procedural concessions as a means of bolstering public support for the reform party faction, thus strengthening its hand in internal party struggles. The reformers won the argument and the regime quickly prepared its own plan for restructuring enterprise management and by early fall 1981 the parliament began considering the government bill. Its proposal rejected, Solidarity shifted tactics and began lobbying deputies to ensure that a number of provisions, and especially the right of workers' councils to hire and fire enterprise directors, be included in the new legislation. In the end, the regime agreed to this concession and on September 26, 1981, the Sejm approved the law on state enterprises and worker self-management.[29]

The new law gave extensive powers to the workers' councils within enterprises. They now had control over general company activities. For example, they had the right to study and evaluate implementation of the annual plan and of contracts, analyze the annual report and budget, and evaluate all reports prepared by the director. The director also had to give the council access to all necessary company documentation so that the council could perform its oversight functions and be available to answer its questions about the state of the enterprise. In addition, the councils had the right to stop a director's decision if it was contrary to a prior council's decision, if it was taken without consulting the council when such consultation was required, or if it was taken without the council's approval when such approval was required. Finally, the council had

27. For a detailed account of Sieć history, see Marcin Chodorowski, *"Sieć"—81: Powstanie, struktura, działanie* (Warsaw: Instytut Studiòw Politycznych Polskiej Akademii Nauk, 1992).

28. *Niezależność,* July 24, 1981, no. 91, 1.

29. *Trybuna Ludu,* September 26–27, 1981, 2.

the right to hire and dismiss the enterprise director. These legal prerogatives of the workers' councils would give organized labor the resources necessary to shape privatization policies in the post-1989 period.

Once granted, the procedural concessions proved difficult to rescind. Unlike in earlier periods, by the 1980s the continuing economic crises had left the regime with few resources to grant substantive concessions while withdrawing procedural ones. Since it could no longer make material side payments, the party found it politically difficult to abrogate the powers of the workers' councils as it had two decades earlier. Hence, although the regime suspended workers' councils when martial law was imposed in December 1981, within a year they were reactivated. Studies conducted among workers at the time indicated tremendous interest in reviving self-management. According to one survey, more than 83 percent of workers viewed self-management as very important and believed that it should be reinstituted as quickly as possible.[30] In fact, by 1983, self-management was reactivated in 78.4 percent of enterprises, and by 1986 workers' councils were operating in 95 percent of companies. The councils had tremendous support among employees of state enterprises: 62.3 percent of workers wanted to have councils in their places of employment and a majority believed the councils would ensure that workers' interests were adequately represented. Most workers also thought that the councils should play a more important role in the decision-making process at the enterprise level and have a direct role in policy making at the national level.[31] Rather than attempting to take away these valued prerogatives, the regime sought to reduce the threat the councils posed to its monopoly on power.

To prevent the reemergence of an independent opposition network, the regime tried to prevent contact between councils in different enterprises. As a report prepared by the then illegal Solidarity trade union stated, "All attempts at communication and coordination between workers' councils in different enterprises are the subject of special interest to the security services. Seeking to atomize the self-management movement the regime blocks all independent activity of the workers' councils in this area."[32] This strategy was unsuccessful and workers' councils cooperated with each other, coordinated responses on issues affecting workers, and remained very popular among workers

---

30. Leszek Gilejko and Przemysław Wòjcik, eds. *Położenie klasy robotniczej w Polsce—potrzeby i aspiracje robotnikòw; Tom 7* (Warsaw: Akademia Nauk Społecznych i Instytut Badań Klasy Robotniczej, 1987), 410.

31. Gilejko and Wòjcik, *Położenie klasy robotniczej,* 426.

32. *Raport: Polska 5 lat po sierpniu* (n.p.: Międzyzakładowa Struktura "Solidarności," 1985), 66.

themselves.[33] In addition, the attitude of the underground Solidarity toward workers' councils began to change fundamentally. Although initially the union tried to boycott the councils, arguing that they were little more than another attempt by the regime to control workers, by 1985 the boycott was applied only selectively and in many enterprises that did not have workers' councils Solidarity activists tried to establish them.[34]

Although Solidarity was disbanded in 1982, the new trade union law adopted that same year reflected the regime's recognition that it had to extend far-reaching concessions to organized labor if it wanted workers to return to its support coalition. The new law had profound consequences for the ability of trade unions to influence policy. It gave trade unions more rights and greater independence from the state and from management within individual enterprises. These changes were a direct result of the demands that came out of the August 1980 strikes and the agreements between the government and Solidarity. The new law gave the unions the right to evaluate and give opinions on all legal acts and decisions that affected the rights and interests of workers as well as the right to participate in the process of formulating new legal acts and decisions. They also had the right to evaluate the wage policies and work environment.[35] These legal changes meant that trade unions had access to all relevant information about the socioeconomic situation in the country. On the enterprise level, trade unions now had the right to represent and defend workers on issues of wages and working conditions. In addition, the new law gave unions the right to sign collective work agreements on the national level. Finally, the law once again legalized strikes, albeit with restrictions. Along with the legal prerogatives that workers' councils acquired in this period, these legislative changes expanded organized labor's resources and significantly increased their capacity to influence policy making in the post-1989 period.

In other words, in many ways the imposition of martial law was not quite the victory for the regime as it first appeared. Initially, the jailing of many labor activists and the disbanding of Solidarity appeared to restore the PZPR's control over the political situation. Although during the first couple of years following December 1981 there were sporadic demonstrations and protests, with time these became less and less frequent and society as a whole withdrew from political activism. Yet not only were many of the procedural concessions granted during

---

33. "Opinia Środowisk Przemysłowych o Samorządzie Załogi," CBOS, March 1984.

34. *Raport: Polska 5 lat po sierpniu*, 70.

35. *Dziennik Ustaw*, no. 32, article 216, 1982.

the Solidarity period enshrined in law, but the inability of the party elite to devise a consensus concerning the political and economic course of action meant that the economic situation continued to deteriorate.

Ironically, Solidarity, which unlike other Eastern and Central European trade unions was never financially dependant on the state, was able to tap into additional financial resources after it was delegalized. Various organizations funneled money and equipment to the organization. For example, in 1986 alone, the New York–based Institute for Democracy in Eastern Europe in cooperation with the Soros Foundation offered two hundred thousand dollars in assistance to Polish intellectuals and activists. In 1982–83, the U.S. Central Intelligence Agency is estimated to have provided Solidarity with close to $8 million and the National Endowment for Democracy in 1989 provided about $1 million to help Polish workers. The American Federation of Labor and Congress of Industrial Organizations (AFL-CIO) was also one of Solidarity's biggest foreign supporters, providing large assistance programs.[36] Thus, although delegalized, Solidarity continued to increase its financial resource base.

The shift in the balance of power away from the regime was amply demonstrated by the embarrassing defeat in the fall of 1987 of a government-sponsored referendum on an economic restructuring program. How problematic any reform measures would be was further underscored when, after a number of years of industrial peace, strikes broke out again in the spring of 1988. Although the immediate cause of the strike was demands for wage increases, the protests quickly acquired a political coloring when activists from the disbanded Solidarity took charge over the strike. While these protests were defused, in August of the same year a new wave of strikes swept the country.[37] The growing worker unrest underscored what Wojciech Jaruzelski's more moderate PZPR faction had recognized for some time, namely, that without establishing a dialogue with the opposition there was little hope of bringing the country's economy around. Later that year, first discussions were held between Wałęsa and representatives of the regime, eventually leading to what became the Roundtable negotiations that laid the groundwork for Poland's political transition in the summer of 1989. As we shall see in Chapter 4, the contentious encounters between state and labor, which punctuated the country's post–World War II history, left organized labor with important recourse—legal, financial, and

36. Jan Kubik and Grzegorz Ekiert, "Civil Society from Abroad: The Role of Foreign Assistance in the Democratization of Poland," CIAO Working Papers (June 2001), 8.

37. Andrzej Stelmachowski, *Kształtowanie się ustroju III Rzeczypospolitej* (Warsaw: Wydawnictwo Ośrodek Doradztwa i Szkolenia "Tur," 1998), 40–41.

experiential—that allowed it to significantly shape economic reform policies in the years following the transition.

## Internal PZPR Dynamics

Conflicts between state and labor were a persistent feature of post–World War II Polish political dynamics. Workers took to the streets when living standards were threatened by deteriorating economic conditions and rising prices. More important, although the regime did not hesitate to repress these expressions of worker discontent, it also tended to fulfill many of the demands put forth by protesters. Initially, most of the concessions the regime offered were substantive in nature and entailed primarily wage and consumer subsidy increases. Later, it extended increasingly significant procedural concessions that weakened its control over organized labor and provided labor with important legal prerogatives as well as rich experience in successfully confronting the state. Thus, unlike its counterpart in neighboring Czechoslovakia, the Polish party elite struggled to maintain political control over organized labor, in the end failing to retain workers within its coalition of support. The internal dynamics of the PZPR shed light on why the party did not succeed in controlling and subordinating organized labor.

Following its establishment, the PZPR moved to suppress its political opponents while at the same time expanding party membership and presence within the country. Within a few years it had reached into every village and every industrial enterprise. Through control of the state administration, the media, and the educational system, the ruling party had numerous tools at its disposal to push through its policies, to control the flow of information, and to shape the ideological indoctrination of the public. The party harnessed labor activism by establishing a hierarchical labor confederation, the CRZZ. Most working Poles belonged to the CRZZ, whose primary mission was ensuring workers' compliance with the political and economic goals set by the party

Despite these control mechanisms, the PZPR found it difficult to subordinate workers to the party and to maintain their political support. The periodic eruptions of labor protest resulted from the regime's inability to improve living standards of workers in exchange for their political subordination. The PZPR's reactions to these expressions of worker discontent were colored by internal party dynamics. Starting with the strikes in Poznań in 1956, the regime's response was twofold. Although it tended to move swiftly and often brutally to quell the protests, it invariably gave in to many of the demands. And while the party elite usually backtracked on some of the concessions, it was never willing to abandon them wholesale. This pattern of labor protest and regime concessions reached a peak in 1980–81 when workers succeeded in forming and legalizing an independent trade union. Even when Solidarity was disbanded many significant Solidarity demands were enshrined in law, substantially strengthening the bargaining leverage of unions and workers' councils at both the national and enterprise levels. In other words, over time the composition of the concessions granted changed. While initially these concessions were primarily substantive, later they shifted toward procedural ones.

These concessions to organized labor seem surprising in light of the apparent asymmetry of power between labor and the state. As will be discussed in the following chapter, such worker protests also occurred in Mexico. Yet in the Mexican case, while the regime was willing to be responsive to some demands concerning wage levels, its reaction was harsh whenever protests threatened to undermine the regime's control over organized labor. In those instances, the PRI government did not hesitate to use force or mass layoffs. Similarly, the Czechoslovak regime succeeded in maintaining a quiescent labor force. What differentiated Polish state-labor relations from those that developed in Mexico and Czechoslovakia was a distinct pattern of intraparty dynamics. Unlike the PRI and the KSČ, the PZPR, throughout its existence, remained deeply torn by factionalism.

The PZPR, like other parties in Eastern Europe, was modeled on the Soviet Communist Party and had a hierarchical, pyramid-like structure. At the lowest level were party cells, or committees organized primarily in places of work, which were responsible for both oversight of workplace activities and for the political indoctrination of employees. Above them were local-level party units, which oversaw all party activities in a given village or city. Next were provincial party organizations, which ensured that the directives flowing from above were implemented by the local and workplace party committees. The Party Congress, which was composed of delegates from all the provinces and met about every four years, was theoretically the most important party institution. In practice, real power was vested in the Central Committee and the Politburo, which met regularly between the Party Congresses and set the policy agenda. Finally, at the very pinnacle of the party was the party's first secretary. The party was governed internally according to the principle of democratic centralism. This doctrine, developed by Lenin, encouraged discussion and the exchange of views and airing out disagreements during party meetings. However, once a decision was reached, all party members were expected to abide by it, not to question it in public, and to follow through with its implementation. All mass organizations, such as trade unions, youth leagues, and farmers' associations, were supervised by the party and served as channels for the political mobilization of the public.[38]

Alongside the party were the state administrative institutions. In theory, the government and its bureaucracy were independent of the party, and the council of ministers was the supreme executive agency. In practice, though, the separation between the party and the government was illusory, since the PZPR was explicitly empowered to provide the direction and maintain oversight over government administration. The hierarchical nature of the party, its presence at all levels of the political system down to village and state firms, as well as its dominance over the state administration, was to provide the PZPR leadership with the resources necessary for maintaining control over society. Nevertheless, in practice, the PZPR struggled to retain its dominance of Polish political life. The history of the PZPR is one of a continued struggle to establish effective control over the society and of continuous, ultimately futile efforts to create an effective, internally cohesive party organization that would enable the leadership to overcome factional struggles.

The party leadership was unable to devise mechanisms for resolving internal party disputes and disagreements and once the initial period of Stalinization was over, few incentives remained in place to reward loyalty to the party while making disloyalty costly. Although on occasion dissenters were expelled from the party, this penalty was applied only sporadically. The divisiveness of the party elite had two distinct but interrelated consequences. In the first place, it made the pursuit of coherent economic policies difficult, because various party factions pushed for different policies, thus contributing to reoccurring economic crises.[39] These crises in turn provided a trigger for labor mobilization, further exacerbating tensions within the PZPR. At the same time, the party's factionalism made it more susceptible to demands put forth by organized labor as party rivals appealed to workers for political backing. In this way, the divisiveness that hindered policy making also provided labor with a favorable opportunity structure for extracting concessions.

---

38. For more information about the internal structure of the PZPR, see Juliusz Wacławek, *Podstawowa Organizacja PZPR* (Warsaw: Książka i Wiedza, 1976); George Kolankiewicz and Paul G. Lewis, *Poland: Politics, Economics, and Society* (New York: Pinter, 1988), especially 66–69.

39. Maria Hirszowicz, *Coercion and Control in Communist Society: The Visible Hand of Bureaucracy* (Brighton, U.K.: Wheatsheaf Books, 1986), 20.

Although the party was continually torn by factionalism, the lines of cleavage shifted over time. During the 1950s, the deepest divisions existed between the Moscow-oriented faction, which wanted to replicate the Soviet model as closely as possible, and groups that pushed for a more indigenous road to socialism. The factions clashed for the first time following Stalin's death, when political repression eased and discussions of democratic reforms came to dominate party meetings. While conservatives sought to preserve Stalinist controls, the nationalist faction pushed for reducing ties with Moscow and for internal political reforms. The conflict came to a head following the brutally suppressed workers' protest in Poznań in 1956. The nationalist faction emerged victorious from this confrontation. Led by the politically rehabilitated Gomułka, it believed that the PZPR had to extend tangible benefits to social groups in order to consolidate the party's authority rather than relying primarily on suppressing dissent. This faction sought the support of peasants by advocating an end to the agricultural collectivization program and of the industrial workers by promoting wage increases and promising an improvement in their living standards.[40]

By the late 1960s, as the economy was running into trouble, another faction emerged. Led by first provincial party secretary Gierek, it advocated placing more emphasis on economic modernization. The emergence of this new faction signaled the deepening of internal PZPR conflicts. The conflict intensified with the eruption of workers' protests in December 1970 in the Baltic cities of Gdańsk and Szczecin that resulted in Gomułka's downfall. As the three factions battled one another, they sought to augment their political clout by appealing to disaffected social groups. The smallest, and in the end least influential, of these factions sought support among the intelligentsia by promoting political and economic liberalization. Another group, led by Edward Gierek, a party boss from the coal-mining region of Katowice whose power base lay among industrial workers, pushed for a major economic restructuring that would improve living standards. The most serious challenge came from a faction led by Mieczysław Moczar, deputy minister of internal affairs and Central Committee secretary in charge of internal security. This group also appealed to the increasingly dissatisfied workers, but unlike Gierek's faction, it sought to stir nationalist sentiments and place the blame for Poland's economic problems on minority groups and Jews in particular.[41] Edward Gierek edged out Moczar and took on the title of first party secretary. Despite taking over the top post, however, he was

40. For a good overview of the debates within the party in the 1953–56 period, see Roszkowski, *Historia Polski*, 218–36.
41. Roszkowski, *Historia Polski*, 273–84.

unable to secure a dominant position within the party and the state apparatus remained deeply divided. The prime minister's post, for example, went to Piotr Jaroszyński, widely believed to be closely aligned with Moscow.[42]

Given his still-weak position, Gierek sought to build a broad coalition of support for his policies among the public. Worried about his internal party rivals and having made pledges to disaffected workers that his economic policies would emphasize the supply of badly needed consumer goods, Gierek embarked on a spending spree. Lacking domestic resources, however, he resorted to borrowing from the West to finance growing import bills. Although these policies were aimed at securing workers' backing for the first secretary, they inadvertently intensified rifts within the party. In particular, the shift away from dependence on the Soviet Union galvanized the conservative faction, for whom reliance on capitalist credit was anathema.[43]

As tensions within the party mounted, Gierek's strategy of building his support coalition among industrial workers was proving unsuccessful. After a few years of calm, in 1976 labor protests erupted again. Discussions within the PZPR about an appropriate response to the unrest further exacerbated divisions within the party leadership. The conservative faction called for deploying more repressive measures against the striking workers and their increasingly assertive allies within the intelligentsia. Others within the leadership felt that full-scale repression would be counterproductive at a time when the regime was in the midst of debt-rescheduling negotiations with Western creditors.[44] Wanting to maintain a decent public image, this faction was therefore receptive to workers' demands and willing to extend substantive concessions and, in particular, to increase wage levels and consumer subsidies. Once again, internal party factionalism provided labor with an opportunity to expand its resources.

This liberal faction, however, thought that wage increases were at best a temporary solution and sought new strategies for extricating Poland from the growing economic crisis. To this end, it encouraged various groups within the party to explore possible reforms. In November 1978 a midlevel party group called Experience and Future was created to serve as a forum for examining potential reform strategies. Soon the group began publishing the results of its discussions, including calls for "reduced censorship, economic decentralization,

42. Alexander Muller, *U źròdeł polskiego kryzysu: Społeczno-ekonomiczne uwarunkowania rozwoju gospodarczego Polski w latach osiemdziesiątych* (Warsaw: Państwowe Wydawnictwo Naukowe, 1985), 92–95.

43. Kazimierz Z. Poznanski, *Poland's Protracted Transition: Institutional Change and Economic Growth* (New York: Cambridge University Press, 1996), 66.

44. Muller, *U źròdeł polskiego kryzysu*, 135–46.

limitation of the party's role, revitalization of representative organs and a new relationship between the rulers and the ruled."[45] Not surprisingly, these ideas exacerbated conflicts within the party leadership.

The conservatives were not the only PZPR leaders concerned about the group's proposals. Although the liberal faction was interested in reforms, it was not prepared to endorse these suggestions and withdrew its support for the forum. Nonetheless, responding to the growing support among the party's rank and file for implementing changes within the party, a number of Politburo members, and in particular Stafan Bratkowski and Stefan Olszowski, continued promoting the group's activities. More ominously for Gierek, in 1979 Olszowski began encouraging opposition figures to more forcefully criticize the party and helped provincial party leaders mount a letter-writing campaign criticizing Gierek's leadership.[46]

By early 1980, party meetings were increasingly raucous affairs. No longer willing to toe the party line, rank-and-file members began voicing open criticism of the leadership. Most criticized were the constant food shortages; the lack of accurate information about domestic economic and political developments; and the absence of any genuine representation of workers' interests at the enterprise level, where workers viewed both the workers' councils and trade unions as part of the management structure.[47] Dissident leaders quickly seized on the growing discontent among the PZPR rank and file. Some regime opponents began making direct appeals to party members and encouraged them to push for reforms from within the party.

By the summer of 1980, the PZPR was faced with an unprecedented challenge to its authority. As had also happened earlier, tensions within the party set off a vicious cycle. It made policy making more difficult, thus hindering crafting of responses to the economic crisis. The deepening economic crisis, in turn, sparked popular protests that further exacerbated factionalism with the PZPR. Growing factionalism then made it easier for labor to extract concessions from the regime.

Although the debates within the party were new and focused primarily on how to respond to Solidarity, the lines of cleavage reflected the long-standing differences between the conservative and the liberal, or "nationalist," factions.

45. Werner G. Hahn, *Democracy in a Communist Party: Poland's Experience Since 1980* (New York: Columbia University Press, 1987), 16.

46. Poznanski, *Poland's Protracted Transition*, 67.

47. Neal Ascherson, *The Polish August* (New York: Viking Press, 1981), 126–27; *Nowe Drogi*, 1983 (Kubiak report).

These divisions permeated all levels of the party apparatus from the Politburo to local offices. The splits immobilized the party, with most factions taking a wait-and-see attitude rather than responding to the growing public anger. The Solidarity period thus further exacerbated internal struggles within the PZPR.

The disunity and factionalism of the PZPR had far-reaching consequences for its effectiveness as a political party. During the Gomułka period, fear of showing party disunity led to strict control over information that was presented to the public and of communication within the party itself. The circle around Gomułka was concerned that open debate and discussion of policy options, instead of providing an opportunity to devise new and better strategies, would expose the thinly suppressed rifts within the party and the government and thus result in the weakening of social control. As Bielasiak notes, "On the one hand, these factions neutralized one another; on the other, hostility among them escalated. Since balancing these various factions tended to lead to no decisions at all on important issues—for fear that any innovation would damage the fragile 'checks and balances' system—social and economic problems were ignored and popular dissatisfaction increased."[48] Furthermore, although the power hierarchy was nominally well defined within the party and the government structures, the conflicts among party leadership led to weakened control over regional party centers. Local leaders, cognizant of the center's weakness, formed alliances to promote their own economic and political objectives and played various central factions off against one another to achieve these local goals.[49]

As the regional centers increasingly pursued their own policies without informing and often in contradiction of the center's directives, Gomułka, uncertain of other party bosses' support, increasingly bypassed institutional structures of the state. Toward the end of the 1960s the PZPR Politburo and the Central Committee for all intents and purposes stopped functioning as policy-making bodies. Most decisions were made by Gomułka and his closest advisors, without consultation with either the state or the party apparatus. The Politburo, nominally the highest policy-making body, was often unaware of directives being sent to the regional centers, while the provinces implemented Gomułka's instructions selectively.[50]

The PZPR leadership was aware that the constant factional battles undermined its ability to govern effectively and made it more vulnerable to workers'

48. Jack Bielasiak, "The Party: Permanent Crisis," in *Poland: Genesis of a Revolution,* ed. Abraham Brumberg (New York: Random House, 1983), 13.

49. Adam Bromke, "Beyond the Gomułka Era," 25–34.

50. Roszkowski, *Historia Polski,* 273–84.

demands, and on a number of occasions the party initiated internal structural reforms. The first round of these came after the 1956 workers' demonstrations, with the party's abandoning the repressive policies of the Stalinist era and shifting to a strategy of providing positive incentives to encourage and maintain public support. The most ambitious restructuring took place following the December 1970 clashes between the regime and striking workers. Gomułka, along with a number of other high-level party officials, was expelled from the party. Other leaders resigned on their own, taking personal responsibility for the crisis.[51] Gierek's faction, however, believed that the crisis was caused by more than poor judgment on the part of individual leaders and could be traced to the deterioration of effective channels of communication with the public. In their view the party no longer functioned as a political-mobilization organization and was increasingly alienated from society. Over the following two years, an animated discussion continued within the party about how best to establish constant and effective dialogue with social groups.[52]

As a result of these debates the Central Committee decided to expel from the PZPR those who belonged to the party for reasons other than political conviction. Unlike previously, when the party was primarily interested in expanding membership rolls, now it emphasized member quality rather than quantity. Extensive interviews were conducted with almost 50 percent of the party membership and an was effort made to improve member qualifications through more intensive political training and education. Finally, new internal party information and communication channels were put in place. The goal was to create a more coherent organization with new incentives to promote loyalty to the party and make it less susceptible to factionalism.

Improving the quality of party cadres was also designed to facilitate the reestablishment of the "party's leading role" within society. The party expected its staff at the provincial and enterprise-level committees to now become active promoters and educators of the party's political ideology, although how exactly they were to go about this was never made clear.[53] In particular, the party renewed its commitment to establishing better communication with workers, especially those employed in the large industrial enterprises, with the goal of enticing more workers to join the PZPR. Attracting more workers into the party was a priority because by the early 1970s, although the party claimed to be

51. "VII Plenum KC PZPR," *Życie Partii*, March 1971, 1–2.

52. For more on this discussion, see the party monthly *Życie Partii*, in particular for the period 1971–74.

53. *Życie Partii*, April 1977, 6.

a representative of the proletariat, the percentage of workers and peasants within its ranks was dwindling.

The next step in the far-reaching restructuring of the party-state apparatus was administrative reform. The new leadership believed that without putting an end to the factionalism of the Gomułka tenure it would be difficult to jump-start the economy.[54] The middle-level administrative units, the county (*powiaty*) committees, which previously exercised strong control over state administration, were eliminated and the number of provinces increased from twenty-two to forty-nine. Although the party argued that increasing the number of provinces was a way to decentralize administrative functions and bring citizens closer to the policy-making process, from Gierek's perspective a more crucial goal was to undercut the power of the provincial bosses. However, the two goals turned out to be incompatible. Gierek, interested primarily in consolidating his power, pushed the reforms through rapidly, with little preparation. Consequently, rather than professionalizing the administrative apparatus, the immediate result of the administrative reform was a very high turnover of staff and the loss of many experienced cadres with personal knowledge and established relationships with local social groups.[55]

Ironically, Gierek's attempt to attract and promote more qualified administrators exacerbated tensions within the party because it resulted in members of the nomenklatura gaining additional privileges and security of employment.[56] The proprietorial attitude toward occupied posts and the lack of effective control by the central leadership meant that over the course of the 1970s members of the nomenklatura began to engage in increasingly corrupt practices and more conspicuous consumption, which fostered growing public resentment.

One of the reasons for the lackluster results of the reform effort was that the internal party incentive structure remained intact. That is, the lack of sanctions for disloyalty to the PZPR continued to plague the party. Although following leadership turnovers individual high-level party officers would be removed from positions of power and sometimes expelled from the party itself, such punishment was rarely meted out on a wider scale. Regional party bosses who at best ignored party directives and often promoted policies at odds with those directives remained in office and continued to build up independent power bases. Even those who openly challenged the party leadership were not penalized.

54. Bielasiak, "The Party," 16.
55. *Życie Partii*, October 1977, 35; Paul G. Lewis, *Political Authority and Party Secretaries in Poland, 1975–1986* (New York: Cambridge University Press, 1989), 61.
56. Lewis, *Political Authority*, 42.

The period between the emergence of Solidarity and the transition to democracy nine years later had the most far-reaching consequences for the relationship between the party and organized labor. During this period, party factionalism intensified and the deepening economic crisis meant that the PZPR was increasingly forced to turn to procedural concessions to satisfy labor demands. Furthermore, unlike during previous rounds of conflict between the state and labor, by the 1980s the PZPR no longer had the material resources to abrogate procedural concessions once the immediate conflict was over by providing additional substantive concessions, as it had done in the preceding decades.

The worker mobilization that began in the summer of 1980 was triggered, as were previous such eruptions, by price increases, which were a part of an austerity package. Solidarity's unprecedented challenge to the PZPR's authority further deepened and publicly exposed internal party divisions. The main cleavages appeared between those pushing for far-reaching decentralization and liberalization of the party and state administration and saw in Solidarity a potential ally; those advocating taking a hard-line approach to the challenge posed by the Solidarity movement and who wanted to eliminate it, by force if necessary; and finally, those who wanted to implement some reforms but remained concerned about the politically destabilizing impact of Solidarity.[57]

Because supporters of different approaches to dealing with the opposition occupied positions in competing party and government agencies, the decisions emanating from these institutions, rather than reflecting a coherent policy, were expressions of specific individual and institutional preferences. The divisions came to a head after the court charged with legalizing the Solidarity labor union, contrary to party leadership's agreement with Solidarity, inserted a provision requiring Solidarity to recognize the supremacy of the party. The court's decision exposed the party leadership's lack of control over its own bureaucracy and sent a clear signal to the public about the disarray within the regime.[58]

The deep party factionalism provided Solidarity with the opportunity to extract concessions from the regime. In turn, the emergence of Solidarity also had a profound impact on the relationship between PZPR leadership and rank and file. The internal turmoil within the PZPR now took on new and, from the

57. They were concerned that the Soviet Union might not remain neutral if the PZPR disintegrated. By fall 1981 the Soviet army had begun military maneuvers on the Polish border, increasing fears of a potential intervention.

58. Jane Leftwich Curry, "The Solidarity Crisis, 1980–81: The Near Death of Communism," in *Poland's Permanent Revolution: People vs. Elites, 1956 to the Present,* ed. Jane Leftwich Curry and Luba Fajfer (Washington, D.C.: American University Press, 1996), 174–75.

leadership's perspective, more threatening overtones. The rank and file, whose dissatisfaction with the PZPR had been growing over the previous decade as the excesses of the privileged nomenklatura became more apparent, saw in the new dissident movement a potentially valuable ally in their quest to reshape the party. The growing visibility of Solidarity encouraged them to call for reform of the PZPR's electoral procedures. When these went unanswered, the lower-level echelons of the party began bypassing the vertical chains of command and forming horizontal ties between regional party organizations. More ominously for the party's cohesion, many members of the top leadership were being voted out by their primary party organizations in elections that were taking place prior to the Extraordinary Party Congress. As a result, nearly 80 percent of provincial committee members and more than sixty percent of lower-level committee members were replaced. Among the provincial leaders, forty-eight out of forty-nine were new following the elections.

With the rank-and-file members revolting and various institutions of the state administrative apparatus allying with Solidarity and supporting its proposals, or at least those that did not entail reforms in their own fiefdoms, the battle at the top intensified. Led by Stefan Olszowski, a faction opposing Gierek mounted an open challenge to his leadership, succeeding in pushing him out of the party at the December 1980 Party Congress and replacing him with Stanisław Kania.[59] Kania responding to the rank-and-file demands, promised to implement new, more democratic rules of internal party governance and, in particular, to institute term limits for elected officials and introduce secret balloting. To further bring the membership into his camp, he praised the previously criticized horizontal links that local party organizations had been establishing with one another.[60] At the same time, cognizant that despite Gierek's expulsion from the party, his own position was far from secure, Kania reached out to Solidarity in a bid aimed at weakening the conservative faction, calling for initiating negotiations between the PZPR and the opposition movement.[61]

This change in leadership and attempts at housecleaning that Kania undertook did little to put an end to the internal party struggle and, if anything, made the conservatives all the more determined to go on the offensive. The

---

59. Gierek and Prime Minister Jaroszewicz were also expelled. *Nowe Drogi,* October 1983, 14.

60. Speeches at the December party meeting can be found in *Nowe Drogi,* December–February 1981, and Kania's proposals for changes in the internal party organization in *Nowe Drogi,* December 1980.

61. Kania's statement at the meeting of the Politburo on January 17, 1981, reprinted in Zbigniew Włodek, ed., *Tajne dokumenty Biura Politycznego PZPR a "Solidarność," 1980–1981* (London: Aneks, 1992), 231.

opening salvo of this new round took place in March 1981, when police broke up a meeting of rural Solidarity leaders, beating participants, a move widely seen as orchestrated by the conservatives.[62] In response, numerous local party organizations joined forces with Solidarity in calling for the ouster of Olszowski, who was seen as the main instigator of the incident.[63] This support for Solidarity among the party rank and file posed an acute dilemma for the party leadership. It was unclear what the appropriate response was, since moving against the opposition movement would in effect also mean condemning and thus alienating party activists.[64]

The battle between conservatives and moderates continued at the July 1981 Party Congress, when the conservatives moved to oust Kania. This assault by the conservatives, however, only energized the moderates, who voted many conservatives out of office during party elections. The apparent shift in power toward the moderate faction and the growing independence of local party organizations seemed to present Solidarity with a new window of opportunity for extracting additional concessions from the regime. However, the organization's call to workers in other Eastern European countries to follow the Polish example and establish their independent trade union organizations, issued at the August 1981 National Congress of Solidarity, prompted the conservatives to mount a counteroffensive. Pointing to the threat of Soviet intervention if the political situation was not brought under control, they finally succeeded in ousting Kania and replacing him with General Jaruzelski.[65]

Only a few months later, on December 13, 1981, Jaruzelski declared martial law.[66] This event underscored the PZPR's paralysis. The party was not involved in the planning or execution of the countrywide military action. In fact, it was not even informed about the decision to impose martial law. Although martial law and the arrests of opposition activists managed to suppress the direct

62. This suspicion was further confirmed when the Politburo, with many of the more liberal members absent, issued a statement of support for the police. Stefan Bratkowski, chairman of the Journalists Union, distributed a letter to party organizations directly pointing to some members of the elite who were actively involved in undermining Kania's leadership by "attempting to place public order institutions in direct confrontation with society in order to justify the repressions and battle with that society." For the full text of this letter, see Alojzy Szudrowicz, *Solidarność: NSZZ Solidarność 1980–1981; Zarys działalności w swietle prasy i innych źródeł* (Bydgoszcz, Poland: Margrafsen, 1998), 146–47.

63. Hahn, *Democracy in a Communist Party*, 128.

64. See in particular, Dokument no. 47, Protokòł no. 79 z posiedzenia Biura Politycznego KC PZPR, March 21, 1981, in *Tajne dokumenty Biura Politycznego*, 286–99.

65. *Nowe Drogi*, November 1981.

66. For a detailed account of the events of December 13, 1981, see Gabriel Mérétik, *La nuit du général* (Paris: Edition Pierre Belford, 1989).

challenge to the PZPR's position posed by Solidarity, it did little to put an end to the factional struggles within the party or to make the party a more effective organization.[67] The PZPR's membership began declining rapidly as rank-and-file members began leaving in droves.[68] And despite calls from the Central Committee that the party would "fight the internal divisions and differences, cleansing the party of elements that had weakened it and restore party discipline," little was done to put these words into action.[69] Jaruzelski, a member of the reform faction, was reluctant to purge the party because of concerns that a full-scale assault on the democratic reforms introduced within the party during the Solidarity period would lead to a mass exodus of members, further weakening the organization. In other words, an incentive structure that would have promoted loyalty to the party and punished disloyalty, one that the party leadership recognized was essential if the PZPR had any hope of rebuilding itself as an effective organization, was not put in place. Jaruzelski's unwillingness to thoroughly purge the party quickly set him on a collision course with the conservative faction.[70] With internal party factionalism unresolved, Jaruzelski wanted to ensure that workers remained on the political sidelines. Many of Solidarity's demands, despite the union's dissolution, became law, thus significantly augmenting resources available to organized labor.

At the same time, the PZPR leadership decided that establishing a new organization was more likely to mobilize political support behind the regime and formed the Patriotic Movement of National Rebirth (PRON).[71] All political groups willing to declare their loyalty to the socialist system were invited to join.[72] PRON was to function as a new channel of communication between the regime and the society and facilitate the mobilization of public support behind government policies.[73]

---

67. The list of those whom the authorities were unable to find and who therefore were placed on a wanted list appeared in *Trybuna Ludu,* December 17, 1981. Those arrested, however, were not exclusively members of the opposition. Among those interned was the former PZPR first secretary, Edward Gierek.

68. Just a couple of months after the declaration of martial law, ninety-six thousand members had abandoned the party. Party membership declined from almost 3 million in July 1981 to just more than 2 million a year later. Karol B. Jankowski, *Polska, 1981–1989: Między konfrontacją a porozumieniem; Studium historyczno-politologiczne* (Warsaw: Wydawnictwo Naukowe SCHOLAR, 1996), 63.

69. *Trybuna Ludu,* February 27–28, 1982.

70. Hahn, *Democracy in a Communist Party,* 195–97.

71. The PZPR in the 1980s was an anemic organization. For example, an internal party survey found that in 1987 only about a quarter of the members could be classified as active, and about 15 percent of members did not even attend meetings or pay their dues. *Polityka,* May 30, 1987.

72. *Życie Warszawy,* July 21, 1982.

73. Jankowski, *Polska, 1981–1989,* 61.

By the second half of the 1980s, though, with the economy in a tailspin, Jaruzelski and his moderate faction within the PZPR realized that reform initiation required a broader national dialogue.[74] In December 1986, the Consultative Council was formed, bringing together fifty-six people of various political orientations, including Solidarity members, to begin formulating reform proposals.[75] Although the council did not have direct influence on policy making, its very establishment and inclusion of a broad cross section of political actors served to reenergize the more reform-minded faction of the PZPR. Thus, when a new wave of strikes swept Poland in 1988, demands for reforms coming from the disbanded Solidarity met with a positive reception among some regime groups. The strikes also provided new arguments for the intraregime reformers that an even more inclusive national dialogue was necessary if the country had any hope of extricating itself from the economic crisis. In late summer of 1988 General Kiszczak, one of the architects of the martial law, met with Wałęsa, the still-illegal Solidarity chairman. In exchange for pledges that preparatory meetings for what became known as the Roundtable negotiations would begin immediately, Wałęsa agreed to halt workers' protest actions.

The PZPR was far from unanimous about the wisdom of starting such direct discussions with the opposition. In fact, the announcement of the upcoming government-opposition discussions generated a wave of protests among party members.[76] Despite the opposition within the party to initiating the Roundtable negotiations, the pro-reform faction, having found a responsive partner in the opposition camp, succeeded in sidelining its internal party rivals. Through the spring of 1989, discussions between the two sides were held, culminating in the historic elections in the summer of that year and the transition to a democratic system in Poland.[77]

As we will see in Chapter 4, the organized labor that emerged following the 1989 political transition had important resources that allowed it to significantly

74. Andrzej Stelmachowki, *Kształtowanie się ustroju III Rzeczypospolitej* (Warsaw Wydawnictwo Ośrodek Doradztwa i Szkolenia "Tur," 1998), 40.

75. For a list of the most prominent members of the Consultative Council, see Jankowski, *Polska, 1981–1989,* 118.

76. As one party member expressed this disapproval, "For seven years we were being convinced that Lech Wałęsa is a dummy; now we have to ask did the dummy become wise or did the government become dumb." Cited in Stelmachowski, *Kształtowanie się ustroju,* 46.

77. For accounts of the Roundtable negotiations, see, for example, Peter Raina, *Droga do "Okrągłego Stołu," zakulisowe rozmowy przygotowawcze* (Warsaw: Wydawnictwo von borowiecky, 1999); Andrzej Paczkowski, *Pół wieku dziejòw Polski, 1939–1989* (Warsaw: Wydawnictwo Naukowe PWN, 1998), 566–83.

shape policy debates. These included important legal prerogatives, financial autonomy, and rich experience of successfully confronting the state. The availability of these resources was a consequence of the state-labor dynamics that evolved in postwar Poland, where internal party factionalism provided workers with a favorable opportunity structure to demand and extract significant substantive and, more important, procedural concessions from the state.

## The Czechoslovak Labor Movement

The state-labor dynamics in Czechoslovakia evolved along a very different trajectory. Here, the Communist Party, with the exception of the 1968 Prague Spring period, developed effective mechanisms for maintaining party cohesion and containing factionalism. The lack of party factionalism meant that the favorable opportunity structure that allowed Polish labor to extract important concessions from the state did not exist here and Czechoslovak organized labor was unable to acquire similar resources.

The postwar history of Czechoslovakia evolved in marked contrast to the turbulent history of Poland. Prior to the war, Czechoslovakia was one of the most industrialized European countries, with a long labor movement tradition. Unlike in Poland, where the prewar trade unions were affiliated with the Socialists, most unions were aligned with the Communist Party (KSČ). Prior to the war, about half the workforce in Czechoslovakia was unionized and with the end of the German occupation, unions were reestablished in both the Slovak and Czech republics. They soon merged and formed the Revolutionary Trade Union Movement (RUH), which in its heyday boasted more than 5 million members. The movement declared itself independent of all political parties but maintained a Communist orientation.

Following the war, the government in exile, led by Eduard Beneš, was allowed to return, but on Soviet insistence the Communist Party gained a prominent role in the cabinet. Although other parties were also represented, the Communists quickly moved to secure the most influential positions. The 1945 economic reforms left close to 70 percent of industrial production in state hands.[78]

Initially, the KSČ had broad popular support. In the first elections, which were generally seen as free and fair, the party garnered 38 percent of the vote,

---

78. Grzegorz Ekiert, *The State Against Society: Political Crises and Their Aftermath in East Central Europe* (Princeton: Princeton University Press, 1996), 127.

twice as much as the next political organization.[79] Many Czechs saw the KSČ as the alternative to the discredited, prewar political order. The party's strength was further bolstered by its takeover of confiscated German property, which it distributed in exchange for political support and by the complete disarray and infighting among the other parties, which failed to form a coalition capable of opposing the KSČ in the elections.

The period of political freedom did not last long. In 1948 the KSČ, led by its first secretary, Klement Gottwald, engineered a bloodless coup, bringing the pluralist experiment to an end and initiating one of the most repressive periods in Eastern Europe.[80] A new constitution was adopted in May 1948 establishing a "people's democracy" in Czechoslovakia. With the takeover, the regime quickened the pace of nationalization, initiated the collectivization of agriculture, closed down independent newspapers, disbanded or purged all political organizations, and introduced centralized planning. Labor unions lost their independence from the state and the regime abolished workers' councils set up in 1945.[81]

The party conducted a thorough reorganization of the RUH, turning it into a hierarchical and centralized organization, administered through eighteen Czech and eighteen Slovak sectoral unions.[82] Although technically a labor union, the RUH was not an exclusively workers' organization and included enterprise managers among its members.[83] As with CRZZ in Poland, the main function of this reconstituted trade union confederation was the administration of various social programs and the ideological education of workers in order to turn them into a secure base of support for the regime. The center of RUH's mission, the labor code explicitly stated, was to "reinforce and fulfill national economic policy goals."[84]

79. Juan J. Linz and Alfred Stepan, *Problems of Democratic Transition and Consolidation: Southern Europe, South America, and Post-Communist Europe* (Baltimore: Johns Hopkins University Press, 1996), 317.

80. For a more thorough discussion of the coup, see Ivo Duchacek, "The February Coup in Czechoslovakia," *World Politics* 2, no. 4 (1950): 511–32.

81. John N. Stevens, *Czechoslovakia at the Crossroads: The Economic Dilemmas of Communism in Postwar Czechoslovakia* (Boulder, Colo.: East European Monographs, 1985), 162.

82. Joseph L. Porket, "Czechoslovak Trade Unions Under Soviet-Type Socialism," in *Trade Unions in Communist States*, ed. Alex Pravda and Blair A. Ruble (Boston: Allen and Unwin, 1986), 90.

83. For a discussion of the various methods employed by the Communist Party, through trade union organizations, to control the working class during the first two decades of its rule, see Robert K. Evanson, "Regime and Working Class in Czechoslovakia, 1948–1968," *Soviet Studies* 37, no. 2 (1985): 248–68.

84. Jiri Valenta, "Czechoslovakia: A Proletariat Embourgeoise?" in *Blue-Collar Workers in Eastern Europe*, ed. Jan F. Triska and Charles Gati (London: George Allen and Unwin, 1981), 213.

Although over the next few years there were occasional outbursts of worker protests, in contrast to their Polish counterparts the Czechoslovak workers did not mount any overt challenges to the regime. On the few occasions when strikes erupted, for example, in 1948 in response to consumer goods shortages and in 1953 at the Škoda factory in Pilsen, where workers stormed the city hall in reaction to a currency devaluation, they tended to be localized and easily dealt with by the security forces.[85] After 1953, although worker dissatisfaction with the political and economic situation could be deduced from the quiet resistance on the shop floor, usually in the form of workplace discipline violations, open confrontations between the regime and the workers ceased.[86]

It was not until the Prague Spring of 1968 that organized labor attempted to carve out an autonomous existence. The crisis was precipitated by mounting economic problems that produced tensions within the KSČ. The previously disciplined and united party began to fracture, with the reformist wing gradually gaining the upper hand. The emerging party factionalism had consequences strikingly similar to those in evidence in Poland. Sensing that a window of opportunity was opening, in March 1968, the usually compliant RUH leadership "demanded a new role [for the unions] as the main representative of workers' interest."[87] The reformist wing of the KSČ, wanting to see organized labor firmly in its camp, was more than willing to respond positively to these demands and to consider making both substantive and procedural concessions. In April 1968 the new party leadership published the Action Program, which among other changes proposed establishing new, more autonomous trade unions and reactivating democratically governed workers' councils within enterprises.[88] For proponents of reform, the reactivation of enterprise councils served to involve workers more directly in the process of change and provided a counterbalance to conservatives opposed to initiating reforms.[89] Both unions and workers

85. For an account of these events, see Otto Ulc, "Pilsen: The Unknown Revolt," *Problems of Communism* 14, no. 3 (1972): 46–49.

86. See, for example, Edward Taborsky, *Communism in Czechoslovakia, 1948–1960* (Princeton: Princeton University Press, 1961), 375–78.

87. Kieran Williams, *The Prague Spring and Its Aftermath: Czechoslovak Politics, 1968–1970* (New York: Cambridge University Press, 1997), 181.

88. For more detailed discussion of the proposed reforms, see Otto Ulc, "Political Participation in Czechoslovakia," *Journal of Politics* 33, no. 2 (1971): 422–47; Stevens, *Czechoslovakia at the Crossroads*, 161.

89. See Vladimir Fisera, *Workers' Councils in Czechoslovakia, 1968–69: Documents and Essays* (London: Allison and Busby, 1978); Valenta, "Czechoslovakia: A Proletariat Embourgeoise?" especially 214–19.

approved these changes, and in July 1968 experimental enterprise councils were set up. The councils were to participate in the daily management of companies. While the union local would organize elections to the councils and could send representatives to council meetings, it would not control them.

With these new pledges formalized, the trade union confederation began testing the limits of their newfound independence. Enterprise-level unions began making decisions without prior consultations with local party committees and in a number of instances successfully opposed attempts to close loss-making enterprises. The newly energized unions also scored a victory when in the summer of 1968 they extracted wage concessions from a reluctant government.[90]

However, while union leaders were pushing for political and economic changes most workers remained disengaged. They were suspicious of the reforms and concerned about their potential impact on their standard of living.[91] Conservatives within the regime exploited workers' well-grounded fears of potential job losses as they pushed to reverse these policies.[92] The trade union leadership had to therefore convince the rank and file that the changes being advocated by reformers would be beneficial to workers.

The Warsaw Pact invasion in August appeared to shake away workers' apathy and pushed the RUH to become even more politically engaged. Immediately following the invasion, the confederation called for a nationwide, one-hour general strike and began preparing for union and workers' councils elections. Union elections were free and fair and resulted in a huge turnover of officers with 85 percent of the incumbents losing their seats.[93] Thanks to this electoral success, the proponents of reforms within the unions became more vocal in their support for Alexander Dubček and in their willingness to publicly condemn the invasion.[94]

While the unions continued to support reforms, their allies within the regime were becoming more reluctant to push for Action Program's implementation. Not only was the threat of a second Soviet invasion looming, but the conservative faction, emboldened by this outside support, was beginning to reassert itself. Fearing more strikes and protests, Dubček appealed to organized labor to forgo

90. Williams, *The Prague Spring*, 181.

91. Alex Pravda, "What About the Workers?" in *Czechoslovakia: The Party and the People*, ed. A. Oxley, Alex Pravda, and Andrew Ritchie (Princeton: Princeton University Press, 1976), 579–85.

92. Stevens, *Czechoslovakia at the Crossroads*, 150.

93. Vladimir V. Kusin, *From Dubcek to Charter 77: A Study of "Normalization" in Czechoslovakia* (New York: St. Martin's Press, 1978), 93.

94. Williams, *The Prague Spring*, 182.

such confrontations.[95] By the time Dubček was replaced as the head of the KSČ by Gustav Husák, a representative of the more conservative faction of the party, the RUH, abandoned by its elite allies, did not voice any opposition. Shortly afterward purges of the party began. As reformers were being pushed out of the KSČ, a similar purge of trade union activists began and workers' councils in enterprises were abolished.[96]

With the conservative faction once again in control, the KSČ moved to abrogate procedural concessions that had been granted to unions during the Prague Spring. The June 1972 Eighth Trade Union Conference, now controlled by conservatives, denounced workers' councils as an attempt by counter-revolutionary forces to create economic chaos. The KSČ nullified all measures that had been adopted in the 1968–69 period and restored the previous "transmission belt" function of the unions, and unions returned to their previous focus on administering social, recreational, and cultural programs for their members.[97] While the RUH continued to boast a membership of more than 5 million workers, or about 80 percent of the working population, it remained politically compliant.[98] Over the course of four decades of KSČ rule, the trade unions became increasingly subjugated to the state. In contrast to the situation in Poland, organized labor in Czechoslovakia on the eve of political transition in 1989 had few resources. The legal prerogatives it acquired during the brief Prague Spring interlude were withdrawn once the KSČ reestablished its cohesiveness; it was financially dependent on the state and, unlike Solidarity, never gained access to monetary support from abroad; and it lacked the rich experience of successfully confronting the state enjoyed by its Polish counterpart. This lack of resources, as we will see in Chapter 6, made it difficult for organized labor to effectively insert itself into policy-making processes following the transition to democracy.

*Internal KSČ Dynamics*

Like the PZPR in Poland, the KSČ was modeled on the Soviet Communist Party. It had a hierarchical structure with party committees present in all villages, towns, and workplaces. At the pinnacle of the hierarchy was the Party Congress,

95. Williams, *The Prague Spring,* 208.
96. J. Svejnar, "Workers' Participation in Management in Czechoslovakia," *Annals of Public and Cooperative Economy,* April–June, 1978, 193.
97. Martin Myant, "Czech and Slovak Trade Unions," in *Parties, Trade Unions, and Society in East-Central Europe,* ed. Michael Waller and Martin Myant (Portland, Ore.: Frank Cass, 1994), 60–61.
98. Williams, *The Prague Spring,* 181.

which met every four years and set the policy agenda. However, as in Poland, it was the Politburo, which met more frequently, that had real influence over charting policy direction. The party incorporated various social organizations, such as trade unions, as a means of establishing channels of communication between the party and the public, mobilizing and controlling the political activism of these groups and promoting political and ideological education.

As in Poland, the state administration was nominally independent from the party, with the president and the council of ministers designated by the constitution as the highest executive authority. In practice, however, state administration was subordinate to the ksč. This allowed the party to dominate policy making, thanks to the widespread practice of dual office holding. Members of the council of ministers as well as other high government officials tended to hold high party posts simultaneously. Furthermore, the hierarchical structure of the party and its presence at all levels of government administration and in industrial enterprises made it possible for the ksč to ensure that policies set by the party leadership would be implemented.

However, these particular features of the party—the party's relationship to the state administrative institutions and the party's relationship to social groups—did not necessarily translate into a conflict-free party apparatus, the ability to implement decisions, or the capacity to subdue interest groups. Unlike its Polish counterpart, however, the ksč accomplished these tasks most of the time. It managed to do so as a result of the party's ability to breathe life into the concept of democratic centralism, which remained little more than a theoretical proposition in case of the pzpr.

As the Polish experience suggests, democratic centralism as an approach to elite conflict resolution may well be good in theory, but its implementation is fraught with difficulties. In the Polish case, decisions made by the leadership were frequently ignored by regional party bosses and many top party officials did not hesitate to voice concerns about them in public. What differentiated Polish and Czechoslovak political dynamics were the different incentive structures that the two elites faced. In Czechoslovakia, the ruling elite managed to devise powerful incentives that ensured that politically ambitious individuals were likely to follow the party line. In Poland such an incentive structure remained underdeveloped. The punishments and costs of disobeying the party were less onerous and were applied sporadically and selectively. Loyalty to the party was therefore not a prerequisite for political success. Rather, building up one's own power networks and resources and cultivating clients remained a viable and profitable path toward advancement.

This lack of effective elite conflict resolution mechanisms, as we have seen in the Polish case, had consequences that reached beyond internal party dynamics. The existence of competition within the party elite created an opportunity structure that allowed organized labor to extract more concessions from the state by allying itself, whether formally or tacitly, with one of the competing factions. In the Czechoslovak case, the ability of the KSČ to build into the system incentives that promoted loyalty and punished disloyalty meant that such a favorable opportunity structure did not exist. It made little sense for those within the party elite in Czechoslovakia to look to social groups as a means of building alliances for promoting their careers. If anything, such attempts would undermine their ability to move up in the power hierarchy. This conclusion is further reinforced by the very different dynamics during the brief period when the Czechoslovak elite did begin to fracture and the existence of factions became obvious to the broader public. In this new context, it did make sense to look for allies outside the elite to promote one's views and positions, and look to such allies they did. With the opportunity structure so changed, organized labor was able to not only verbalize demands but also extract concessions from the state. The events of the Prague Spring also underscore the challenges of maintaining elite cohesion over time as the external political and economic environment changes. Maintaining effective elite dispute resolution mechanisms and enforcing consensus is thus an ongoing task of any political party. Creating incentives that promote loyalty and penalize disloyalty therefore becomes crucial.

The incentive structure created by the KSČ relied primarily on making defection extremely costly. The Stalinist period in Czechoslovakia was marked by more intense repression than in Poland and lasted longer than anywhere else in the Soviet bloc, continuing even after the death of Stalin. Following the coup, Gottwald initiated an extensive purge of the party ranks. Some were expelled from the party. Others were tried and executed. At the same time, the KSČ expanded the secret police apparatus and political arrests took place on a massive scale. While in 1956 Poland was rocked by worker demonstrations and the Hungarian Revolution was brutally crushed by the Soviet Army, the Czech leadership staunchly resisted initiating political reforms.

The expulsion of close to 550,000 members from the KSČ made the party ideologically homogenous and demonstrated that dissention was extremely costly.[99] Thus, although many individual tragedies unfolded during the 1950s, the

99. David W. Paul, *Czechoslovakia: Profile of a Socialist Republic at the Crossroads of Europe* (Boulder, Colo.: Westview Press, 1981), 62.

purges created a much more unified party. Even revelations of Stalin's crimes did not lead to any significant reevaluation of political developments, as happened in both the Soviet Union and other Eastern European countries. The memory of the Stalinist period and the terror that it unleashed made the party elite reluctant to tamper with the status quo. As Taborsky points out, "Lively memories of the changes from above coupled with the fear of ever-lurking dangers from below cause them to stick together rather than fall apart into small cliques."[100] Hence, although disagreements no doubt existed among the Politburo members, the public only saw a fully unanimous leadership, in agreement on all decisions, large and small. Those whose loyalty became suspect were quickly purged.

## The Party Fractures

While the party maintained its unity, organized labor remained quiescent, but when this unity began to break down, workers' demands grew. For a brief moment in the late 1960s it seemed that Czechoslovak organized labor might succeed in extracting substantive and procedural concessions from the state and shift the balance of power between the unions and the party. However, with party factionalism brought under control and with internal cohesion reestablished, organized labor lost the concessions it had acquired during the so-called Prague Spring and once again became subordinate to the regime.

After 1960 the economic situation began to deteriorate, ethnic tensions between the Slovak and the Czech republics grew, and party intellectuals began demanding a reevaluation of Stalinism. Repression weakened and, consequently, the party's incentive structure, which had relied primarily on heavy penalties for disloyalty, became less effective. The once unified KSČ began to splinter.

The main conflict within the KSČ concerned the appropriate response to the failing economy. The conclusions of a special commission set up to study possible reform measures further exacerbated the intraregime tensions. Although reformers within the party supported the commission's recommendations to inject some market mechanisms into the planned economy, the conservative faction resisted implementing any changes and was especially infuriated by proposals to introduce democratic procedures into the party's governance structures.[101] Younger members of the party, lacking firsthand experience

---

100. Taborsky, *Communism in Czechoslovakia,* 117.
101. Gordon Wightman, "The Changing Role of Central Party Institutions in Czechoslovakia, 1962–67," *Soviet Studies* 33, no. 3 (1981): 412–13.

with the brutality of the Gottwald period, were especially willing to advocate reforms more openly.

Tensions between the Czech and Slovak branches of the KSČ also intensified. Slovaks, who always felt like the junior partner within the party, began pressing for more autonomy for the republic. The disputes within the party leadership soon spread to lower levels of the party hierarchy and to the state administration. Antonín Novotný's inability to prevent the nomination as Slovak KSČ first secretary of one of his staunchest critics, Alexander Dubček, in April 1963, signaled that Novotný's power base had significantly eroded.[102]

By 1967, the opposition to Novotný had intensified and during the Central Committee meeting in October that year, he was no longer able to prevent open criticism of his administration. The Politburo and the Central Committee became increasingly divided between those who continued to support him and those who were interested in pushing him out and pursuing reforms more vigorously. As in Poland, as the leadership fractured, its various factions began seeking backing from outside the party, with reformers increasingly turning to the intelligentsia for support. Suddenly, the press became very attentive to the Central Committee's struggles and articles critical of Novotný's policies began making their way past the censors.[103] In January 1968, Dubček replaced Novotný as party leader, although the latter retained his position as president of Czechoslovakia.

The removal of Novotný from the top party post did little to alleviate divisions within the leadership, and the flood of contradictory policy statements issued by the Politburo added to confusion and paralysis within lower party ranks. At the same time, the attempts by the two warring factions to seek allies outside the upper party echelons intensified. Novotný and his supporters crisscrossed the country promoting their views at party meetings, mass rallies, and factory visits, appealing to workers who, they correctly sensed, were apprehensive about the economic restructuring advocated by the reform wing of the party.[104] Dubček and his supporters, by contrast, made appeals to the intelligentsia as well as to organized labor. Although rank-and-file members were reluctant to give full backing to the reformers, the union leadership proved very receptive

102. Joseph Rothschild, *Return to Diversity* (New York: Oxford University Press, 1989), 167.
103. As Renner notes, this "critical attitude of mass media that did not meet immediate counter measures would have been totally unthinkable only a few months earlier." Hans Renner, *A History of Czechoslovakia Since 1945* (London: Routledge, 1989), 43. This suggests, in view of the very tight control over dissemination of information that the party had previously exercised, that someone from the highest levels of the party was allowing these articles to appear.
104. Stevens, *Czechoslovakia at the Crossroads*, 135.

to these overtures and quickly formed an alliance with the intelligentsia. Together the two groups began working on reform proposals.[105]

For Novotny, the strategy of going directly to the public with appeals of support backfired. As public criticism mounted, Novotny's supporters in the party leadership began to abandon him, and he resigned in March 1968 and the reformers won party elections. An Extraordinary Party Congress was scheduled for September 1968 and was expected to finalize internal party democratization.

Political tensions increased with the publication in June 1968 of a joint statement by Czechoslovak intellectuals and unionists, titled "Two Thousand Word Manifesto," which harshly criticized the party's leadership of the previous decades. The manifesto called for an acceleration of the reform process and demanded the resignation of party officials who were opposed to reforms. Although intended to bolster the reforming wing of the party, it alarmed the conservatives, the Soviet Union, and other Eastern European countries. In July 1968 the Warsaw Pact members, with the exception of Romania, called for halting the liberalization policies. Prague ignored the ultimatum and instead drafted a law on a new party system that was to be adopted at the Extraordinary Party Congress in September. The new law, which provided for the election of party delegates by secret ballot, proved too much of a challenge for the Warsaw Pact and on August 20 the Soviets and pact troops invaded Czechoslovakia, ostensibly at the invitation of the Czech party leadership. Unlike in Hungary a decade earlier, both the invasion and the clampdown that followed were relatively bloodless. Although initially there was public opposition to the invasion, resistance quickly began to dissipate.[106]

### The Party Reestablishes Internal Unity

Dubček hung onto power for a few more months following the Warsaw Pact's invasion. By April 1969, however, he was increasingly isolated within the party, and with the threat of another Soviet intervention he was replaced as the first party secretary by Gustav Husák, an opponent of the liberalization program. With the conservative faction once again in power, the process of reintroducing an incentive structure that would facilitate elite cohesion began. As earlier, the primary mechanism through which loyalty to the party was promoted was by

105. Evanson, "Regime and Working Class," 256–57.
106. For a more extensive discussion of the Prague Spring, see Williams, *The Prague Spring*; Karen Dawisha, *The Kremlin and the Prague Spring* (Berkeley and Los Angeles: University of California Press, 1984).

making dissent extremely costly. The purges began at the top, with reformers removed from all leadership party positions.

Eventually, the purges also affected the rank and file of the party and political screenings for positions of any influence were initiated and continued through the early 1970s. The "purification" of the ranks was accomplished through the exchange of party membership documents. Those who sided with the reformers in 1968 faced a choice of either publicly repenting or being expelled from the KSČ.[107] Those who were involved in the events of the Prague Spring were not the only ones punished, primarily through loss of employment; repercussions were directed at their families as well. For example, children of those deemed politically unacceptable were barred from higher education.[108] Through these measures, the incentives to remain loyal to the party were once again reintroduced. The cost of dissension became extremely high and entailed not just the loss of access to information and power but also a direct threat to the economic well-being of those deemed to be disloyal. The political purges were accompanied by the growth of the police apparatus, curtailing of free speech and media, and the reinstitution of strict central economic planning. A flurry of new laws strengthened the ability of the regime to arrest suspects without a warrant and new punishments were added to the criminal code, including banishment from one's place of residence for up to five years.[109] To underscore that the regime was serious about implementing these laws, in the summer of 1972 political trials were held. Forty-seven reform Communists were found guilty and sentenced to a total of 718 years.[110]

A particularly harsh policy was pursued against the intelligentsia. In September 1970 minister of education Jaromir Hrbek demanded that all university personnel who had signed the Two Thousand Word Manifesto repudiate it publicly or lose their jobs. The threat was carried out, and hundreds of employees were dismissed from universities and whole departments shut down.[111] Contacts with the West were curtailed. The crackdown was facilitated by the exploitation of anti-Czech sentiments in the Slovak Republic, which made the unification of opposition more difficult. The Slovaks were willing to forgo all reforms, whether political or economic, as long as the autonomy they gained during the Prague

107. Edward Taborsky, "Czechoslovakia: The Return to 'Normalcy,'" *Problems of Communism* 19, no. 6 (1970): 33.
108. Vlad Sobell, "Czechoslovakia: The Legacy of Normalization," *East European Politics and Society* 2, no. 1 (1988): 40–41.
109. "Czechoslovak Situation Report," *Radio Free Europe Research* 29 (July 17, 1970).
110. Kusin, *From Dubcek to Charter 77,* 160.
111. Taborsky, "Czechoslovakia: Return to Normalcy," 36.

Spring was preserved. In fact, the only remnant of the reforms became the institutionalization of the country's federal structure.

In 1971 Dubček and other reformers were officially condemned and in 1975 Husák took over the presidency, thereby consolidating his position within the party-state. Whatever differences continued to exist within the elite were resolved internally and not allowed to be aired in public. Those whose actions were deemed threatening to the elite consensus forged during this period of "normalization," either because they built personal power bases or promoted policies that were at odds with the prevailing elite agreements, were quickly pushed out.[112]

The process of normalization thus succeeded in reunifying the party and effectively silencing dissenting voices. Although in the late 1970s Charter 77 was created by ex-Communist reformers and dissident intellectuals looking to expose the regime's human rights violations despite its signing of the Helsinki Accord in 1975, the group was small and confined to the intelligentsia of large cities. The KSČ, through direct attacks on the group in the media and through making collaboration with the Charter extremely costly, successfully marginalized the organization.[113] Organized labor, by contrast, with its Prague Spring concessions withdrawn, remained disengaged from politics and was not prepared to challenge the state.

Ironically, the cohesiveness of the party elite became a liability in the second part of the 1980s. The Husák regime found it difficult to respond to the policies of glasnost and perestroika advocated by the new Soviet leader, Mikhail Gorbachev. At the same time, economic problems began to reemerge. The lack of reformers within the party elite made it difficult for the regime to respond to the fast-changing international environment. In quick succession, the Communist governments in Poland and Hungary negotiated themselves out of power and in November 1989 the Berlin Wall came down. None of these events promoted a response from the Soviet Union. Emboldened, students and intellectuals came out onto Prague streets, calling for political liberalization. The brutal response of the regime only energized the protesters, who expanded their demands to include ending KSČ dominance. The party was not able to respond to this unexpected challenge, since all reformers had been so effectively purged from the party. By December 1989, what came to be called the Velvet Revolution succeeded in pushing the KSČ out of power. Unlike their counterparts in Poland, where organized labor was a key actor in the transition to democracy,

112. Kusin, *From Dubcek to Charter 77*, 191.
113. Skalnik Leff, *The Czech and Slovak Republics*, 61–63.

Czechoslovak workers, although they staged a two-hour general strike on November 27, 1989, played only a minor role during the Velvet Revolution. This relatively minor role was a reflection of organized labor's lack of resources and high levels of dependence on the KSČ.

## Conclusion

The very different intraregime dynamics in Poland and Czechoslovakia profoundly influenced the relationship between the state and organized labor. In Poland, the PZPR never succeeded in containing and managing party factionalism. The continuing conflicts within the elite and the lack of incentives to remain loyal to the party provided labor with the opportunity to more effectively press its claims. As the various party factions battled for control, they looked outside the regime for support. Organized labor, with its large membership base and strategic location, was an attractive ally. As a result, by the 1980s unions and workers' councils possessed legal prerogatives that gave labor a decisive voice over company policies and allowed it to participate in decision making at the national level. Organized labor could also draw upon years of experience in successfully confronting the state. Finally, Solidarity, which was never dependent on the state for financial resources, also had access to foreign funding. Consequently, when the new democratic government began reforming the Polish economy, organized labor had significant resources that enabled it to shape the process of public sector reform design and implementation.

The posttransition Czechoslovak government did not have to contend with powerful organized labor as it sought to privatize state enterprises. Unlike the PZPR, the KSČ was able to create effective mechanisms for containing party disputes. Not only was the party thoroughly purged of dissenters on two occasions, but the KSČ crafted powerful incentives that promoted loyalty to the party. The costs of insubordination, unlike in the Polish case, were extremely high and entailed removal from the party ranks and the loss of professional opportunities. For politically ambitious individuals it made little sense to look to social groups outside the regime as a means of shoring up the former's power. In other words, the internal cohesion of the party elite foreclosed opportunities for labor unions to extract concessions from the state. Rather than continually challenging the regime, as happened in Poland, the Czechoslovak trade unions, with the brief exception of the Prague Spring, remained subordinated to the KSČ. As a result, when the democratic government of Vaclav Klaus initiated economic reforms, including the privatization of the public sector, Czech unions lacked the legal prerogatives, financial autonomy, or experience of successfully challenging state policies that Polish organized labor could draw upon. As a result, as we will see in Chapter 6, they found it difficult to shape public sector reform policies.

RULING PARTIES, ORGANIZED LABOR, AND
CONTINUED AUTHORITARIANISM

*Egypt and Mexico*

Unlike Poland and Czechoslovakia, neither Egypt nor Mexico experienced a
political transition as it initiated economic reforms. As we will see in the chapters
that follow, the persistence of authoritarianism in these two latter cases shaped
the strategies that organized labor used to influence public sector reform policies.
The effectiveness of the strategies, however, was shaped more by the legacies of
the pre-reform period than by the nature of the political regime. As in Poland,
Egyptian organized labor was able to significantly influence reforms because in
the years prior to reform initiation, through numerous contentious encounters
with the state, it succeeded in extracting important resources, including legal
prerogatives, greater financial autonomy, and experience of successfully confronting the state. As in Czechoslovakia, the official unions in Mexico did not
extract such resources and at the time when structural adjustment policies were
initiated was highly dependent on the regime, thus hindering their ability to
shape reforms. This chapter will explore why corporatist labor institutions proved
so durable in Mexico and why they were weakened in Egypt.

## Labor Movement in Postrevolutionary Egypt

The military officers who overthrew the Egyptian monarchy in July 1952 came
to power with only a limited political blueprint. What united them was the
narrow goal of freeing Egypt from foreign domination and deposing the much
despised King Faruq. Although they had a similar socioeconomic background,
coming primarily from the urban and rural middle class, their political ideologies

varied. Among the Free Officers were supporters of the Muslim Brotherhood, Marxists and socialists, democrats, and advocates of military rule.

Lacking a common ideology or program, the Revolutionary Command Council (RCC) limited itself to issuing fairly broad principles that were to guide the revolution. They were (1) an end to imperial control, (2) an end to feudalism, (3) the termination of monopoly capitalist influence, (4) a strengthening of the national defense, (5) greater social justice, and (6) return to parliamentary rule. The sixth principle was quickly discarded and the RCC concentrated on implementing the other five goals with varying degrees of commitment.

The initial economic program they advocated was far from radical. The regime sought to revitalize the economy through the promotion of market mechanisms, concentrating state resources on providing infrastructural projects and a number of large-scale industrial enterprises. Most Free Officers valued private property and expected the national bourgeoisie to become the driving force behind economic development. The only major reform initiated shortly after the revolution was land reform. Although issues of social justice were not absent, they were not the primary motivation behind promulgating this initiative. Rather, the RCC, fearful of the potential threat from the old political elite and, in particular, the aristocracy, which was still seething after Faruq's exile, wanted to dispose of these potentially threatening challengers. Land redistribution did occur but only members of the royal family saw their holdings expropriated.[1]

Looking to private capital as the driving force behind economic development, the Free Officers were interested in subduing the labor movement, which had become increasingly militant during the decades preceding the revolution. The first confrontation between the new regime and workers had occurred already in August 1952 when security forces moved to crush a strike that had broken out at the textile factory in Kafr al-Dawwar. Twenty-nine workers were tried in connection with the strike, two of whom received death sentences for their involvement.[2] A purge of Communist leaders from trade union ranks quickly followed.

Despite this initial harsh response to workers' demands, the RCC remained deeply divided about the appropriate policy toward trade unions. Some wanted

---

1. Joel Beinin, MERIP, 1982, 24–25. The group that benefited most from the land reform were not landless peasants but the rural middle class.

2. For a further discussion of events at Kafr al-Dawwar, see Mahmoud 'Abbas, ed., *Niqabat wa al-'amaliya al-Misriya*, Kirasat Ishtirakiya, no. 3 (n.d.), especially 52–54; Joel Beinin and Zachary Lockman, *Workers on the Nile: Nationalism, Communism, Islam, and the Egyptian Working Class, 1882–1954* (Princeton: Princeton University Press, 1987), 421–31.

to provide workers with more benefits to ensure labor's support for the regime. The more conservative faction, however, pushed in the opposite direction, fearing that too many concessions would have a negative impact on investment.[3] A compromise was eventually hammered out. While job security guarantees were expanded and limits placed on employers' ability to dismiss workers, measures that limited unions' ability to disrupt industrial production were also included. Most important, the right to strike was suspended.[4]

### Establishment of Corporatist Institutions

The relationship between state and organized labor began changing, however, as a consequence of the power struggle between President Muhammad Naguib and Gamal 'Abd al-Nasser. The conflict came to a head in March 1954, ostensibly over the issue of the restoration of parliamentary life. Naguib, who spent much of his time traveling across the country, was immensely popular with the public. Nasser, by contrast, worked primarily behind the scenes, building up his authority within the security forces and various state institutions. As a result, when the final showdown between the two occurred, few groups outside the ruling elite came out to back Nasser. The only group that unequivocally supported him was organized labor, in particular, the transport workers' union.[5] This assistance, however, came at a price. By backing Nasser at this crucial juncture, organized labor expected that many of its long-standing demands would be fulfilled. Nasser, for his part, was aware that if union backing was to be sustained, labor's loyalty would have to be rewarded. Following the March 1954 crisis, therefore, he met repeatedly with union leaders, promising to improve workers' living standards and to establish mechanisms for more formal future consultations on issues of mutual concern.[6]

Yet while Nasser was interested in establishing firmer state control over trade unions and creating corporatist institutions based on the Yugoslav

3. For a discussion of the debates and compromises that were made within the RCC about policy toward trade unions in this period, see Marsha Pripstein Posusney, *Labor and State in Egypt: Workers, Unions, and Economic Restructuring* (New York: Columbia University Press, 1997), 46–53.

4. Joel Beinin, "Labor, Capital, and the State in Nasserist Egypt, 1952–1961," *International Journal of Middle East Studies* 21, no. 1 (1989): 74.

5. Khalid Muhiddin, among others, argues that the demonstrations were far from spontaneous and that in fact Nasser paid four thousand pounds to ensure that the workers did come out to back him up. See also 'Abd al-'Zim Ramadan, *Al-sira' ijtima'iya wa siyasiya fi Misr munthu qiyam thawra 23 yuliu ila nihaya azmat maris 1954* (Cairo: Maktabat Matbuli, 1994), especially 195–209.

6. Beinin and Lockman, *Workers on the Nile,* 440–43.

model, he remained concerned about the potential consequences of such an arrangement, viewing the creation of a centralized union organization as a double-edged sword. On the one hand, it could facilitate monitoring and greater control over labor. On the other, it could result in the development of a powerful institution that could be used to challenge his position.[7]

Consequently, the establishment of corporatist labor institutions proceeded in a piecemeal fashion. Although a trade union confederation was created in 1957, organized labor remained highly fragmented.[8] Only about half the existing unions chose to affiliate themselves with the new umbrella organization. The task of bringing more unions into the fold proved difficult. Some within organized labor were unenthusiastic about the idea and many ruling elite members opposed such centralization, fearing it would give trade unions undue influence.[9] The situation began to change following the 1956 Suez crisis. As a result of the war, relations between Egypt and the West soured. The foreign assets nationalized during the war remained in state hands following the conflict. The regime established Ministries of Public Enterprise and Planning and charged them with developing a three-year plan, for which Soviet financing was secured.[10]

The reorientation in economic and foreign policies generated tensions within the regime. As its internal dispute over the course of domestic policies intensified, Nasser looked to ensure continued labor loyalty by extending further substantive and procedural concessions to the trade unions. At the same time, he came to view a centralized union federation as the most effective means of ensuring political control of organized labor. In 1959 the regime adopted a new labor code and modified other legislation governing labor affairs. In particular, to ensure that labor was firmly behind him as he moved against the more conservative regime faction, Nasser conceded to trade union activists' demand that closed-shop provisions be scrapped.[11] The regime adopted additional laws with

7. Robert Bianchi, *Unruly Corporatism: Associational Life in Twentieth-Century Egypt* (New York: Oxford University Press, 1989), 79.

8. Al-Sayyid, for example, estimates that even toward the end of the decade there were about five hundred unions. See Mustafa Kamel al-Sayyid, *Al-mujtama' wa al-siyasa fi misr: Dur jama'at al-masalih fi al-nizam al-siyasiy al-misri, 1952–1981* (Cairo: House of the Arab Future, 1983).

9. Pripstein, *Labor and the State*, 65; Fathi Kamil, *Ma'a al-harakah al-niqabiya al-Misriyya fi nusf al qarn* (Cairo: House of the Arab Future, 1985), 193–94.

10. For a discussion of the regime's motivations behind this change in orientation, see, for example, John Waterbury, *The Egypt of Nasser and Sadat: The Political Economy of Two Regimes* (Princeton: Princeton University Press, 1983), 73–99; Raymond William Baker, *Egypt's Uncertain Revolution Under Nasser and Sadat* (Cambridge: Harvard University Press, 1978), 188–90.

11. For a discussion of the labor legislation during this period, see F. J. Tomiche, *Syndicalisme et certains aspects du travail en République Arabe Unie (Égypte), 1900–1967* (Paris: G.-P. Maison-neuve and Larose, 1974), 49–67.

the goal of raising workers' living standards and ensuring that the private sector respected the labor code, raised minimum wages, shortened the work week, and set up a new social insurance program. In 1961 the regime extended additional procedural concessions with the introduction of Law 114, which granted workers representation on management boards of state firms. Two years later, worker representation on the boards of directors of public sector companies was raised from two to four. The regime also made dismissing workers more difficult, requiring the approval of a committee composed of unionists, company management, and Ministry of Labor representatives.[12]

The changes in economic policies and the growing power of the military also persuaded Nasser that a more viable political organization was needed to better mobilize political support, resulting in the creation in 1962 of the Arab Socialist Union (ASU).[13] Workers and peasants were to form the core of the organization and were guaranteed 50 percent of positions within the ASU and the parliament. At the same time, a special office was created within the party with the sole aim of devising strategies to bring unions under ASU control.[14]

In 1964 the regime reduced the number of federations from the original sixty-five to twenty-seven. The new trade unions had a hierarchical structure, with enterprise-level unions grouped into industrial federations, which in turn were assembled into an umbrella confederation (ETUC). The federations had increased powers in collective negotiation of work contracts and became responsible for the disbursement of monies for health, social, cultural, and professional services; and the establishment of savings funds, cooperatives, and athletic and cultural clubs for members, partially financed through membership dues. Each federation was also guaranteed monopoly status.[15] This state control was further reinforced by a number of provisions in the 1964 labor law, which facilitated government interference in internal union affairs and required the confederation to submit, on a regular basis, financial reports.[16] Nasser and his faction hoped that the hierarchical structure would ensure better state control of lower union levels.

---

12. Assef Bayat, "Populism, Liberalization, and Popular Participation: Industrial Democracy in Egypt," *Economic and Industrial Democracy* 14, no. 1 (1993): 68.

13. Corporate groups—peasants, workers, businessmen, intellectuals, and the military—were to be represented within the party.

14. Waterbury, *Egypt of Nasser and Sadat*, 321–23; Joel Gordon, *Nasser's Blessed Movement: Egypt's Free Officers and the July Revolution* (New York: Oxford University Press, 1992), 39–59.

15. Robert Bianchi, "The Corporatization of the Egyptian Labor Movement," *Middle East Journal* 40, no. 3 (1986): 432.

16. Pripstein, *Labor and the State*, 26.

By the beginning the 1960s, corporatist labor institutions were finally in place and organized labor seemed firmly under regime control. Organized labor was willing to extend its support to the regime. Thanks to the shift in Egypt's domestic and foreign policies and the support that organized labor threw behind the "socialist" regime faction, it succeeded in fulfilling many, if not most, of its major demands. These included both substantive gains, primarily in the form of higher wages and benefits, and a number of procedural ones that gave the union leadership significant authority over the administration of internal union affairs and finances as well as political access to the top decision-making circles through its membership in the ASU.

However, it did not take long for the conditionality of labor support for the regime to become clear. As would happen again in the future, when the economic situation deteriorated the regime attempted to withdraw some substantive concessions it had earlier extended to organized labor. This in turn would set off workers' demonstrations and protests and further intensify intra-elite conflict. The protests generally subsided when organized labor secured concessions it demanded. As in Poland, initially substantive concessions in the form of higher wages, benefits, and consumer subsidies were sufficient to placate workers. With time, as recurring economic crises depleted regime resources, the regime increasingly relied on procedural concessions. These gradually tilted the balance of power between state and organized labor.

The first wave of workers' protests following the establishment of corporatist institutions swept Egypt in the mid-1960s. Workers, government employees, and shopkeepers demonstrated in Cairo. In Dimyat police clashed with students, peasants, and workers. In Kafr al-Shaykh, Dissuk, and Damahur peasants organized protest marches and hunger strikes to protest the government decision to increase the prices of some basic commodities. Workers staged slowdowns and destroyed machines at their places of employment.[17] The loss of the Sinai to Israel in the June 1967 war sparked even more protests among workers and students.

The economic crisis also intensified conflicts within the regime, with the conservative faction more assertively calling for initiating reforms. As the conservative faction began making appeals to the business community, ASU's chairman, 'Ali Sabri, moved against Nasser, appealing to the increasingly disaffected workers. These elite conflicts emboldened the ETUC to press for more concessions. Sensing that Nasser was concerned both about the growing assertiveness of the

---

17. Mahmoud Hussein, *Class Conflict in Egypt, 1945–1970* (New York: Monthly Review Press, 1973), 231–35.

conservative faction and about Sabri's ambitions, the confederation demanded that the 1964 trade union law be modified, that the prerogatives of the Ministry of Labor to interfere in internal union affairs be curtailed, and that some of the ministry's functions be transferred to the confederation.[18] Nasser, under pressure to respond, promised workers that reforms, and in particular that new, free elections to the ASU and ETUC, would be held.[19]

Elections to the ASU were held and the Ministry of Labor was placed under the ETUC's control. However, trade union elections did not go forward. Although Nasser was anxious to extend additional concessions in order to maintain organized labor within his base of support, his rivals were equally keen on preventing this alliance from solidifying. Sabri, whose relationship with the unions had always been tense, saw such elections as directly threatening his attempts to establish firmer ASU control over organized labor.[20] Nasser found it difficult to move forward over Sabri's objections.

## Organized Labor and Sadat

Although organized labor did not win all the procedural concessions it sought from Nasser, the power struggle within the elite that followed Nasser's death in September 1970 created a favorable environment for the ETUC to press additional demands and assert greater independence from the regime. Over the course of the next few years, as the new president, Anwar al-Sadat, fought to consolidate power, organized labor succeeded in extracting significant procedural concessions from the state. By the end of the decade, the ETUC had won important legal prerogatives that gave it a voice in policy making, acquired significant financial autonomy of the state, and gained experience from successfully confronting the state. When Sadat's successor, Hosni Mubarak, initiated a new round of economic reforms in 1991, organized labor had resources that allowed it to shape the design and implementation process of public sector reforms.

Following Nasser's death most trade union leaders were happy to see ASU leader Sabri removed from power and were willing to support Sadat. However, this backing came at a price. The confederation mounted pressure to curtail government interference in internal union affairs. Sadat, struggling to consolidate his position and anxious to retain the ETUC within his coalition of

---

18. For a discussion of the demands and the regime's response, see Pripstein, *Labor and the State*, 84–85.

19. These promises were encapsulated in the March 30 Declaration.

20. Joel Beinin, "Labor, Capital, and the State," 81.

support, was willing to acquiesce to many union demands. And indeed the union elections held in July 1971 were generally regarded as free and fair. Shortly afterward, the president of the ETUC was named minister of labor.[21]

These concessions ultimately proved insufficient in bringing organized labor firmly into Sadat's support coalition. With economic problems mounting in the fall of 1971, strikes broke out at Helwan Iron and Steel as well as other factories and Cairo was paralyzed by taxi drivers' strike.[22] Protests and strikes continued through 1972.[23] Adding fuel to the fire was the continuing no-war, no-peace, situation with Israel. Sadat never ceased promising that Egypt was on the verge of restoring Egypt's dignity (and the Sinai) but as time went on and nothing happened, dissatisfaction both in the army and among civilians grew. Even the normally quiet People's Assembly (parliament) chimed in, in 1972 openly criticizing the government's assertions that Egypt was finally ready to take on Israel.

While the regime freely deployed repression to silence critical voices and used force to quell strikes and demonstrations, Sadat recognized that given his still-shaky political position he could not afford to antagonize too many social groups. Although he was not prepared to extend procedural concessions to labor, many of its substantive demands were met. In particular, the regime raised minimum wages and increased pensions and sick leave benefits.[24] These substantive concessions, however, proved insufficient, and workers again protested in February, March, and April 1972.[25]

The success of the October 1973 war provided a brief respite for the regime. However, by 1974 workers were protesting again, staging about 400 work stoppages and minor strikes.[26] On New Year's Day 1975 riots shook Cairo and a strike erupted in Helwan. In March 1975, thirty-three thousand workers staged a strike at Mahalla al-Kubra.[27] The strike turned violent when security forces

21. Pripstein, *Labor and the State,* 97.
22. John Waterbury, *Burdens of the Past, Options for the Future* (Hanover, N.H.: American Universities Field Staff Reports, 1977), 7
23. Lafif Lakhidar, "The Development of Class Struggle in Egypt," *Khamsin: Journal of Revolutionary Socialists of the Middle East* 5 (1978): 67.
24. *Middle East International,* January 1972, 17. Minimum wages were raised from 84 pounds a year to 108 pounds; workers were to get full pay, rather than 70 percent of pay, when they fell sick; and pensions were raised by 10 percent.
25. The overall political situation was tense, since there were also growing problems within the armed forces, with protests erupting in February, July, October, and November 1972 and again in February 1973, prompting rumors of an impending coup. At the same time, student demonstrations were becoming more frequent.
26. David Hirst and Irene Beeson, *Sadat* (London: Faber and Faber, 1981), 231–32.
27. Lakhidar, "Development of Class Struggle," 69–70.

were sent in to put it down and the whole city exploded in protest.[28] Strikes continued in 1976 with clashes between workers and security forces taking place in August and September in 'Amariyya.[29]

This growing worker restlessness came at an inauspicious moment for Sadat, who was attempting to consolidate his position both through reforming the ASU and by redirecting Egypt's economic policies in order to attract more foreign and domestic private investment. Both moves set him on a collision course with organized labor.

The collapse of the ASU, while opposed by unionists, provided the ETUC with the opportunity to reassert its independence from the regime. In November 1976 it announced that it would not align itself with any of the newly established three political platforms.[30] Many within the labor movement began advocating the creation of an independent workers' party.[31] The growing assertiveness of the unions was also evident in the inroads that the new opposition parties, and in particular the left-wing Tagammu' party, made in local trade union elections.

The disbanding of the ASU and the redirecting of economic policies thus proved to be a watershed in state-labor relations. Given the changing political and economic environment, the contract between the regime and trade unions underwent significant modifications that would prove to have far-reaching consequences for organized labor's ability to influence policy making. Most significant, from the late 1970s on, labor no longer flexed its political muscle only through the staging of strikes and protests, although these tactics remained important. Rather, the procedural concessions Sadat felt compelled to make in order to retain organized labor within his coalition of support and make it unavailable to other elite factions meant that the ETUC acquired important legal prerogatives that allowed it to directly participate in decision making.

The first sign of the concessions Sadat was willing to make to ensure that the ETUC would not abandon him politically was his offer to the confederation leadership prior to the 1976 elections. Fearful that the ETUC would make good on its pledge not to back any of the newly created political platforms, Sadat promised to place unionists in leadership positions in his ruling party, soon named the National Democratic Party (NDP), in exchange for abandoning

28. Al-Sayyid, *Al-mujtama' wa al-siyasa,* 76.

29. Kirk J. Beattie, *Egypt During the Sadat Years* (New York: Palgrave, 2000), 160.

30. Al-Sayyid, *Al-mujtama' wa al-siyasa,* 83.

31. Huwaida 'Adli, *Al-'ummal wa al-siyasa: Al-dawar al-siyasiy li-l-haraka al-'ummaliya fi misr min 1952–1981* (Cairo: Ahali Books, 1993), 169.

their idea of an independent workers' party.[32] Over time, the ruling party and the ETUC leadership developed a close relationship. Senior unionists traditionally belong to the NDP, and the regime continually sought to isolate ETUC leaders from the rank and file and bind them closely to the ruling party, a strategy that produced decidedly mixed results.

At the same time, to put an end to industrial unrest and convince the ETUC to support his economic policies, he extended additional substantive and procedural concessions. As usual, substantive concessions entailed increases in wages and in subsidies for consumer goods. In addition, the revised trade union law gave the ETUC the right to participate in all government discussions concerning any policy changes that would have an economic or social impact on workers, to have input into designing such policies, and to assist in their implementation.[33]

In a move that also proved to have far-reaching consequences, Sadat encouraged the union leadership to look beyond the public sector and expand their business activities. As Bianchi points out, the confederation was granted powers to "expand the existing system of cooperatives and to use a combination of public funds and compulsory worker contributions in establishing its own economic enterprises."[34] During this time the confederation established its own bank, university, and vacation resorts, becoming one of the wealthiest interest groups in Egypt. While Sadat's goal in promoting these union activities was to soften the union's opposition to economic liberalization (infitah) policies, their long-term effect was the growth of the ETUC's financial independence from the state.

Like its Polish counterpart, the Egyptian regime was loath to make such far-reaching concessions, and once the immediate crisis was over, it attempted to rescind them. The conflict that erupted between the regime and organized labor over this attempt and its eventual resolution indicated how much the balance of power between the state and labor had shifted.

The substantive concessions granted to labor, especially the expanded subsidies program, provided the regime with breathing room. However, by the latter part of the 1970s they became increasingly difficult to maintain. Despite rumors that belt-tightening measures were in the offing, the introduction of an austerity package in January 1977 caught most Egyptians by surprise. Historically, whenever economic conditions deteriorated, workers tended to organize protests, strikes, and demonstrations, most often without ETUC approval or support. Nevertheless, the protests that erupted in response to subsidy cuts

32. Pripstein, Labor and the State, 109–11.
33. 'Adli, Al-'ummal wa al-siyasa, 172.
34. Bianchi, Unruly Corporatism, 49.

were unprecedented in scope. The riots spread from Alexandria to Cairo and then to other urban areas. Clashes between the demonstrators and security forces left an estimated eight hundred dead. The specter of these events continues to haunt Egyptian policy makers.[35] Although Sadat described the events as an "uprising of thieves," subsidies were quickly restored and the salary increases for public sector workers and government employees that went into effect to compensate for the subsidy cuts were left in place.[36]

At the same time, the ETUC's response to the January events made clear that the confederation was now willing to publicly oppose government policies. Although the ETUC did not approve of the protesters' tactics, it also strongly condemned the price increases pushed through by the government. The events of that January also underscored that the ETUC took seriously the concessions the regime granted the previous year in exchange for organized labor backing *infitah* policies. The ETUC pointed out that the implementation of the subsidy cuts was in direct violation of the amended labor law that gave the confederation the right to be consulted on decisions such as the one taken by the regime.[37]

At the same time, organized labor, taking advantage of political liberalization, began resorting to the courts to challenge policies it saw as threatening the interests of the rank and file. In 1980, for example, the Federation of Electrical, Engineering, and Metal Workers brought a case before the administrative court to nullify a decision allowing the merger between the British company Chloride with its Egyptian counterpart, which would have resulted in the closure of one of the three companies that were part of Chloride Egypt.[38] The ETUC also established a secretariat whose job was to oversee union relations with the parliament and, when necessary, to introduce amendments to existing legislation.[39] The ETUC's political visibility was also bolstered by its presence in the People's and Consultative Assembly, company management boards, and various policy-making committees.[40]

How significant these procedural concessions were became clear during the 1980s when President Mubarak came to power following Sadat's assassination.

35. Author interview with a World Bank official, Cairo, August 25, 1998.
36. Thomas W. Lippman, *Egypt After Nasser: Sadat, Peace, and the Mirage of Prosperity* (New York: Paragon House, 1980), 114–17.
37. Al-Sayyid, *Al-mujtama' wa al-siyasa*, 75–76.
38. While the court ruled that the case was beyond the scope of its jurisdiction, in the end the union prevailed and the company remained open. See *Rose al-Youssef,* June 9, 1980, and June 23, 1980; Pripstein, *Labor and the State,* 189–90.
39. 'Adli, *Al-'ummal wa al-siyasa,* 172.
40. Bianchi, "Corporatization of the Egyptian Labor Movement," 433.

As Chapter 5 will explore in greater detail, when in response to mounting economic problems, the regime sought to cut subsidies and restructure public sector enterprises, it faced stiff opposition. Organized labor, drawing on the legal prerogatives it had acquired during the 1970s and on the long experience of challenging the state and bolstered by greater financial autonomy from the regime, proved very capable in shaping pubic sector reform strategies.

## Dynamics Within the Regime

While labor sought to increase its voice in policy decisions affecting workers, the regime struggled to create a coherent political organization that would institutionalize public support. The postrevolutionary Egyptian regime quickly moved to disband political parties and silence the opposition. Repression was readily deployed against those who sought to challenge the Revolutionary Command Council (RCC). Within a few years following the overthrow of King Faruq, after two lackluster attempts at forming a political party, the regime created the ASU. At the same time, it centralized labor organizations and created corporatist institutions, thus subordinating unions to the state. However, as we saw earlier in this chapter, over time organized labor acquired increased autonomy from the state.

As in Poland, the ability of organized labor to transform itself into an important political actor was facilitated by the inability of the Egyptian regime to create effective mechanisms for elite conflict resolution. As a consequence, over time organized labor acquired important resources that allowed it to shape public sector reform policies. Throughout the postrevolutionary period, the ruling elite remained deeply divided over the direction of policies that the regime should pursue. The successive ruling parties reflected this hetero-geneous nature of the elite and lacked a coherent program or ideology. Lack of unifying ideology does not need to be detrimental to the establishment of an effective political party. As we will see later on in this chapter, the Mexican ruling party was also an organization in which very different political philosophies were represented. What matters more than the internal differences within a political party is how these differences are managed and how internal conflicts are resolved. Unlike the Mexican PRI, the successive Egyptian ruling parties did not create effective mechanisms for elite conflict resolution. In particular, they put in place few incentives to promote elite loyalty to the party and penalize disloyalty. In both Mexico and Czechoslovakia, dissension among elite members was dealt with quickly and often harshly. At the very least, a politician who openly challenged regime decisions could expect to be expelled from the ruling party, thus putting an end to his or her political ambitions. In the Egyptian case, rarely was such a severe punishment meted out. In fact, by the 1980s, it seemed that for politically ambitious individuals a more certain path toward advancement lay not in toeing the party line but rather in challenging it, since the NDP was quite willing to offer plum posts to elected opposition and independent candidates.

In the Egyptian case, open conflicts between factions within the ruling elite were common. These conflicts, in turn, pushed the various factions to build personal fiefdoms within state bureaucracy as a way of amassing resources that could facilitate successful confrontations with other elite factions. At the same time, this elite competition created a window of opportunity for interest groups to more effectively press their claims. As elite factions battled for control they often looked for allies outside the regime to bolster their intraregime position. The backing of these external allies could be secured in exchange for promises of future concessions. Over time the type of concessions offered to organized labor changed. Although initially organized labor's demands could be satisfied primarily with substantive concessions and in particular wage increases, as economic crises became more severe the resources available to the regime declined. With fewer material resources to offer, the regime had little choice but to increasingly rely on granting organized labor procedural concessions. While these seemed less costly, over the long term they significantly shifted the balance of power between state and organized labor. As a consequence, corporatist labor organizations that had been established following the revolution did not perform the mobilization and control functions that the regime anticipated. Rather, over time they carved out significant autonomy from the state.

Although the postrevolutionary elite was always characterized by factionalism, the lines of cleavage shifted over time. Nonetheless, there has been a persistent split between the more conservative and the more left-leaning factions. During the first years following the revolution, the conservative faction pushed for maintaining a market economy and relying on the private sector as the primary engine of growth. The leftist faction promoted a more state-centered and state-planned development path and saw the creation of an industrial public sector as the best means of ensuring sustainable growth. In the 1970s, when the United States supplanted the Soviet Union as Egypt's patron, the leftist faction remained critical of Sadat's *infitah* policies, his close ties with the West, and the peace treaty with Israel, while the conservative faction supported these policies. During Mubarak's tenure, and especially once the structural adjustment program began in earnest, the conservative faction embraced the economic reform program and pushed for quick liberalization, while the leftist faction remained skeptical of these policies and resisted attempts to shrink the public industrial sector.

The ruling elite was aware that factionalism had detrimental consequences for its ability to devise a coherent economic program and build stable public support for the regime and that it afforded interest groups the ability to extract concessions from the state. It therefore periodically embarked on restructuring the ruling party to transform it from a factional battleground into an effective political organization that would ensure broad popular support and mobilization during electoral contests and would serve as a vehicle for the political education and recruitment of members and as a means of both forging elite consensus and ensuring that the decisions taken by the elite would be implemented by the lower levels of the party and state administrative apparatus. Despite these attempts, however, the successive ruling parties proved ill equipped to perform these functions.

## The Nasser Years

Since the first days of the revolution, relations within the RCC were contentious. The first couple of years witnessed a major dispute over the issue of restoring parliamentary life. The controversy became intertwined with the power struggle between Nasser and Naguib. It was during this crisis that organized labor for the first time made its support of Nasser explicitly dependent on guarantees of future concessions. Once Naguib was removed from office and the March 1954 crisis was diffused, in June 1954 a new constitution was adopted. With the new legal framework in place, the RCC was dissolved and Nasser became president, following a referendum, with most members of the RCC taking over ministerial positions. With Naguib removed and with political parties disbanded, it did not take long for the Free Officers to realize that some sort of organization was needed to fill the political vacuum and help solidify the regime's base of support among the public.[41] However, the divisions among the Free Officers had profound consequences for their ability to construct such an organization. On the

---

41. Leonard Binder, *In a Moment of Enthusiasm: Political Power and the Second Stratum in Egypt* (Chicago: University of Chicago Press, 1978), 35–36.

one hand, they recognized that in order to consolidate and strengthen their power, they needed to routinize political participation. On the other, because there was no agreement within this core group about policy direction, it was difficult to create a tight, coherent organization.

The divisions at the top presented two additional problems for party formation. Creating a programmatically coherent party was perceived by Nasser and others within the elite as implying that certain groups would have to be excluded from participation. This would mean, however, that those excluded would become available to political competitors. At the same time, creating a cohesive political party was perceived as a potential threat to those within the elite who would not control the organization. They therefore had powerful incentives to minimize its effectiveness. Consequently, the first political organizations that were established were designed more to occupy political space and forestall the formation of competitor political groups.[42]

The first incarnation of the political party, the Liberation Rally (LR), established in December 1952 with Nasser as its secretary general, reflected this ambivalent attitude. The LR lacked any clear ideology beyond a nationalist call to unite behind the RCC in its struggle to bring independence from foreign domination. The only prerequisite for joining was the "expression of loyalty to the Free Officers."[43] Since the goal of the LR was to create as broad based a coalition as possible, discussions of ideology or detailed political program were carefully avoided.[44]

The LR's life was short-lived. With the adoption of a new constitution in the summer of 1956 it was replaced by the National Union (NU). Like the LR, the NU welcomed anyone who wished to join and its membership quickly swelled to 6 million. Furthermore, because the regime remained ambivalent about the role that a mobilizing party should perform, it allocated few resources for training party cadres and establishing channels for two-way communication between the leadership and the rank-and-file members.[45]

42. See, for example, Shahrough Akhavi, "Egypt: Diffused Elite in a Bureaucratic Society," in *Political Elites in Arab North Africa*, ed. I. William Zartman, Mark A. Tessler, John P. Entelis, Russell A. Stone, Raymond A. Hinnebusch, and Shahrough Akhavi (New York: Longman, 1982); Mark N. Cooper, *The Transformation of Egypt* (London: Croom Helm, 1982).

43. Iliya Harik, "The Single Party as a Subordinate Movement: The Case of Egypt," *World Politics* 26, no. 1 (1973): 80–105.

44. Kirk J. Beattie, *Egypt During the Nasser Years: Ideology, Politics, and Civil Society* (Boulder, Colo.: Westview Press, 1994), 80.

45. Leonard Binder, "Political Recruitment and Participation in Egypt," in *Political Parties and Political Development*, ed. Joseph LaPalombara and Myron Weiner (Princeton: Princeton University Press, 1966), 219.

One of the main factions within the elite was the military. During Nasser's presidency, Field Marshal 'Amer succeeded in building an impressive fiefdom. What made 'Amer's empire so powerful and threatening from Nasser's perspective was that it expanded beyond the army into various bureaucratic institutions, the public sector, and land reclamation projects.[46] 'Amer placed officers loyal to him in various positions within the public sector and forged close ties with members of the bourgeoisie who were interested in the lucrative contracts he could provide. He thus further bolstered his position by making alliances with influential groups and individuals from outside the regime. By the early 1960s, 'Amer could and did ignore many of Nasser's directives.[47]

The growing clout of the military convinced Nasser and his faction that a more tightly organized political party could serve as a counterweight to the field marshal. At the same time, with the move toward greater state intervention in the economy and more widespread state ownership of the means of production, the regime became aware of the need to articulate a more coherent ideology in order to bolster public support. Nasser and his faction also came to believe that the best means of institutionalizing organized labor support and making it unavailable to other elite factions was through the creation of a centralized corporatist labor organization.

The National Congress of Popular Working Forces convened on May 21, 1962, and negotiations over the political platform began. Ironically, while the National Charter was to spell out the principles unifying the ruling elite, the discussions concerning the formation of the ASU revealed how deeply divided the elite was on even the most fundamental issues. Most important, while some wanted to see Egypt move firmly in the socialist direction, others were deeply suspicious of nationalization policies and concerned about the close relationship between Egypt and the Soviet Union. Unable to reach a compromise and to maintain a semblance of unity in the face of evidence that the prerevolutionary elites were trying to reassert themselves, these disagreements were quietly swept under the rug.

The party was to be an alliance of all working forces: peasants, workers, intellectuals, soldiers, and national capitalists. Workers and peasants were guaranteed 50 percent of representation in the party and the parliament. The

---

46. For a discussion of 'Amer's involvement in nonmilitary pursuits, see, for example, Robert Springborg, "Patrimonialism and Policy-Making in Egypt: Nasser and Sadat and the Tenure Policy for Reclaimed Lands," *Middle East Studies* 15, no. 1 (1979): especially 56–60.

47. Beattie, *Egypt During the Nasser Years*, 161.

various groups were thus to be brought under ASU control. Through the establishment of such corporatist arrangements, the regime hoped that labor and peasants could be more effectively mobilized in support of its policies. However, because of the deep divisions concerning the political platform of the ASU, its overall mission remained vague. It did not take long for the negative consequences of this lack of consensus to become clear.

The regime decided that membership in the ASU would not be automatically conferred. Rather, a more careful screening of candidates was to be put in place to ensure that only those committed to the ASU platform would be allowed to join. Given the vagueness of the platform, however, fulfilling this objective proved difficult, since it was unclear what criteria were to be used to prevent people from joining. In addition, because the negotiations over the ASU platform and the establishment of the new political party did little to address the problem of elite factionalism, Nasser, who had hoped to consolidate his power through the ASU, became concerned that by excluding certain groups and individuals he would make them politically available to his rivals.

Consequently, the ASU's membership rolls quickly expanded to almost 5 million by 1963. The results were predictable. The party cadres were a hodgepodge of differing ideologies and the loyalty of many members of the party to the regime was at best suspect. Furthermore, although the party had branches in villages and factories, few resources were channeled to these party cells and the party remained dependent on the traditional power structures already in place. This meant, among other things, that the regime's penetration of the countryside remained limited.[48]

As long as the economy was growing, these internal tensions in the regime and the ineffectiveness of the ASU did not present significant problems. However, with the first sign of economic trouble, both issues resurfaced. The deterioration of the economy in the mid-1960s contributed to shifts in the balance of power within the ruling elite. Although Nasser succeeded in pushing out some of the more influential representatives of the conservative faction, many others remained.[49] As the economy began to falter they became more critical, and to bolster their position within the ruling elite, they began to look outside the

---

48. In his study of the ASU, Binder quite starkly demonstrates that for all its socialist rhetoric the party was dominated by rural notables and that to a great extent the party did the bidding of this group rather than promoting regime policies. See Binder, *In a Moment of Enthusiasm*, 303–25.

49. Among them were members of the former RCC Husayn Shafa'i, Abd al-Latif Boghdadi, Zakariyya Muhyi al-Din, and Anwar Sadat.

regime for potential allies, finding many willing partners within the private business community.[50]

As the conservative faction sought allies in the business community to increase pressure for implementing economic reforms, those within the ruling elite who were opposed to abandoning socialism began looking for their own supporters. Recognizing that public sector workers were angry about deteriorating living standards and the government's attempt at belt tightening, ASU leader Sabri and his backers within the elite tapped into this frustration and helped organize protests against the government over wage increases. By mobilizing workers Sabri hoped that he could more successfully challenge Nasser while at the same time acquire greater control over organized labor. With contradictory pressure coming from the various factions in the regime and with social groups more visibly mobilized, Nasser attempted to ensure that none of them could pose a real challenge to his position. In particular, to counter Sabri's overtures to the workers, he extended substantive concessions to labor and promised procedural ones.[51]

As discussed earlier in the chapter, Nasser pledged that some of the Ministry of Labor's responsibilities would be transferred to the ETUC and that new free elections to the ASU and ETUC would be forthcoming, thus assuring the confederation that, despite his ambitions, Sabri would not be allowed to take firmer control over labor organizations. In other words, the intensifying tensions within the ruling elite and in particular the growing conflict between the conservative and the socialist factions offered organized labor the opportunity not only to extract more concessions but also to successfully defend and strengthen its organizational prerogatives.[52]

The already tense relations within the ruling elite became all the more acrimonious with the June 1967 debacle.[53] While the army was in disarray, public criticism of economic policies and political repression became more intense. These intra-elite tensions and Nasser's much more precarious position meant that he was willing to respond positively to these demands. The protests by workers and students that followed the light sentences meted out to army officers

50. Yahya Sadowski, *Political Vegetables? Businessman and Bureaucrat in the Development of Egyptian Agriculture* (Washington, D.C.: Brookings Institution, 1991), 100–103.

51. Beattie, *Egypt During the Nasser Years*, 194.

52. Bianchi, *Unruly Corporatism*, 80.

53. 'Ala 'Abd al-'Aziz Abu Zeid, *Haqiqat al-tu'addidiya al-siyasiya* (Cairo: Matbuli Books, 1990), 72–73.

who were deemed to be responsible for the military failure also made clear to Nasser that the ASU had to be restructured to more effectively control popular mobilization. Further underscoring the need to restructure the party was the strong circumstantial evidence that some within the regime, and in particular those associated with Sabri, were instrumental in instigating the protests.[54]

The outcome of the ASU restructuring program was disappointing and did not result in the creation of a more coherent organization. Rather, the reforms exposed the deep divisions within the elite and encouraged various factions to establish competing patron-client networks.[55] At the same time, Sabri, rather than turning the ASU into an organization that could bring the masses firmly into the regime's fold, began to turn the party into his own political fiefdom, staffing it with his cronies and moving it in a more leftward direction.

## The Sadat Years

With Nasser's death in 1970, the presidency passed to Anwar al-Sadat. Seen as weak and lacking his own power base, Sadat agreed to not act unilaterally without consulting other members of the ruling elite. Soon, however, a power struggle between Sadat and Sabri and Sabri's allies in the ASU intensified. Although the conflict was ostensibly over the issue of bringing Egypt into a federation with Libya and Syria, in fact, the struggle was over who would wield the ultimate authority within the Egyptian polity, the state and the president or the ASU. The conflict came to a head in April 1971 when Syria and Libya officially announced their agreement to join the federation. With the army's backing Sadat relieved Sabri of his vice presidential post and dismissed the minister of interior, Sharawi Gumma. Members of the Sabri camp tendered their resignations and were arrested on Sadat's orders.[56]

Although the ASU was neutralized as a source of opposition to Sadat, dissatisfaction with the party did not go away. Sadat was interested in seeing the ASU restructured in such a way as to prevent it from becoming a potential challenger

---

54. For a discussion of this circumstantial evidence, see Waterbury, *Egypt of Nasser and Sadat,* 329–32.

55. Akhavi, "Egypt," 232–33; Beattie, *Egypt During the Nasser Years,* 169, 195–97; Robert Springborg, "Patterns of Association in the Egyptian Political Elite," in *Political Elites in the Middle East,* ed. George Lenczowski (Washington, D.C.: American Enterprise Institute for Public Policy Research, 1975), 83–108.

56. The period became known as the May 15 Corrective Movement.

to his authority, as had happened at the end of Nasser's rule.[57] Furthermore, the ASU, although purged, was not an organization that Sadat could use to build a support coalition. He was especially interested in the backing of the increasingly assertive bourgeoisie. Like him, this group was interested in economic liberalization. However, it was also suspicious of the ASU and eager to dismantle the one-party system. Although Sadat was not willing to contemplate the establishment of democracy, he was eager to bring the bourgeoisie into his support base.[58] Consequently, another round of party restructuring culminated in the formation of political platforms within the ASU in March 1976.

As we saw earlier, the reform of the ASU, as well as the initiation of *infitah* policies, while appealing to the business groups Sadat was courting, put the president on a collision course with organized labor. Although he was interested in broadening his support base to business groups, he was loath to make organized labor available to his political rivals. At the same time, the continuing worker unrest made reestablishing good relations with the ETUC all the more imperative. Sadat therefore extended significant procedural concessions to the confederation, granting it the right to participate in government policy making, weakening the corporatist labor institutions significantly. These procedural concessions significantly altered the balance of power between the state and organized labor and in the 1990s allowed labor to significantly shape structural adjustment policies.

To Sadat's consternation, after his call for ASU reform, there was an immediate proliferation of platforms that exposed the deep ideological divisions within the elite. To prevent the political liberalization experiment getting out of control, in the end only three platforms—right, center, and left—were permitted to compete in the elections of 1976. For the first time, independents were allowed to run, and they won 14 percent of the vote.[59]

The establishment of three separate platforms, which were officially transformed into political parties following the 1976 parliamentary elections, presented an opportunity for creating a more cohesive ruling party. In the new environment, those whose ideological leanings were different from those of the program advocated by the center platform identified with Sadat could simply move

57. Abu Zeid, *Haqiqat al-tu'addidiya al-siyasiya,* 73.

58. Raymond A. Hinnebusch, "The National Progressive Unionist Party: The Nationalist-Left Opposition in Post-populist Egypt," *Arab Studies Quarterly* 3, no. 4 (1981): 327.

59. El-Mikawy, for example, attributes this good showing of independent candidates to the "clear disapproval of the arbitrary decision to allow three platforms only." Noha El-Mikawy, *Building of Consensus in Egypt's Transition* (Cairo: American University in Cairo Press, 1999), 31.

to the other organizations. As happened during previous rounds of party reforms, however, the incentive structure that would have promoted loyalty and punished disloyalty to the dominant party remained underdeveloped. No attempt was made to ensure that those who disagreed with the party's policies would no longer be welcomed within its ranks. No mechanisms for screening members were introduced. The underlying assumption was that those with differing worldviews would leave Sadat's center party voluntarily. However, given the dominant position that Sadat's new political organization was assured of playing, those with political ambitions had few reasons to migrate to the other two parties, which would play, at best, supporting roles. Both political advancement and access to state patronage would continue to flow through Sadat's party. The lack of ideological commitment became especially clear once Sadat abandoned the center platform, known as the Misr Party, in favor of the NDP in July 1978.[60] Within a short period of time, members of the Misr Party, sensing where the political center of gravity was shifting, migrated to the NDP. New elections were held in 1979 in which the NDP won an overwhelming majority, thanks to widespread vote rigging and the party's superior resources. However, the party lacked cohesiveness and any discernible ideology and, while it took over the physical property of its predecessor, its presence was barely felt outside its Cairo headquarters.[61]

The ineffectiveness of the NDP in mobilizing and controlling political support at a time when economic policies were shifting and Sadat had signed a peace treaty with Israel created a new set of problems. Both policy changes met with widespread opposition. Since these changes were taking place in a context of political liberalization, those disenchanted with Sadat's policies could potentially become available to his political rivals. Lacking an effective political organization, Sadat was forced to make side payments to those groups to maintain their backing. As was discussed earlier in this chapter, it was during this time that organized labor successfully extracted numerous substantive and procedural concessions that significantly expanded its resource base and consequently its ability to influence economic reform processes.

As Sadat's control over the political apparatus became more tenuous and factions and cliques with access to resources proliferated, decision making became both more complex and less coherent, with more groups having the

---

60. The party's program was published in *Al-Ahram al-Iqtisadiy* on September 1, 1978.
61. El-Mikawy, *Building of Consensus,* 46.

ability, through alliance making with elite members, to influence and veto policies.[62] At the same time, Sadat's preoccupation with the emergence of centers of power that could challenge his authority meant that governments were constantly reshuffled. These frequent reorganizations did little to strengthen the president's positions. Rather, as Waterbury points out, they allowed "some parts of the bureaucracy to behave like private fiefdoms, ignoring directives coming from above and imposing their own decisions."[63]

In the end, the lack of an effective political organization capable of mobilizing popular support behind Sadat left him with few tools to resolve social conflicts and respond to growing opposition activism, forcing him to increasingly rely on repression. In October 1981, he was assassinated by Islamic militants.

## The Mubarak Years

Mubarak, who took over the presidency following Sadat's assassination, recognized that the patronage system and corruption that had blossomed under his predecessor made policy making and implementation difficult and contributed to undermining the public's backing for the regime. To rebuild broad-based support, Mubarak replaced some of the more notorious figures of the Sadat era with more reform-minded, young technocrats; initiated regular consultations with the opposition; and permitted greater press freedom.

Although the relationship between the regime and the opposition became more cordial during the first years of the Mubarak presidency, a similar detente proved more difficult to engineer within the ruling elite itself. The NDP remained split into a number of factions that continued to battle for control over the organization. The conservative faction of the party, which included many private businessmen and government technocrats—among them Samir Tubar, the NDP's Economic Committee chairman; Muhammad 'Abdallah, head of the party's International Relations Committee; Suliman Nur al-Din, the leader of the NDP's parliamentary delegation; and Youssef Wali, the party's general secretary and minister of agriculture—pushed for accelerating economic liberalization. The left-wing faction, which included the Speaker of the parliament, Rifa'at al-Mahgub, and 'Atif Sidqi, prime minister between 1986 and 1996, by contrast, fought to preserve subsidies and the social benefits of the

---

62. Springborg, "Patterns of Association in the Egyptian Political Elite," 92–93.
63. John Waterbury, "Egypt: The Wages of Dependency," in *The Middle East: Oil, Conflict, and Hope*, ed. Abraham L. Udovitch (Lexington, Mass: Lexington Books), 1976.

public sector workers.[64] Finally, the Sadatist faction, which included close associates of the former president and was prominently represented in the media as well as economic and government institutions, sought to prevent any tinkering with *infitah* policies and worried about a possible return to Nasserism while fighting proposals from the conservative faction for privatizing the public sector.[65] Members of these various factions, thanks to their control of vast resources, were not only difficult to dislodge but also had the means to pursue policies that were at odds with those envisioned by Mubarak. As the future minister of the economy, Youssef Boutros Ghali remarked some years later, "Ministers controlled political fiefdoms which made them reluctant to countenance change. The Minister of Construction used to be a tsar. He presided over an empire worth zillions of pounds. The same goes for the Minister of Industry—112 companies close to $30 billion in assets under his control."[66]

Divisions within the ruling party were reflected in disputes among government officials, which became increasingly pronounced as the economy began sliding into trouble in 1984.[67] As a result, the government often had difficulties in formulating policies and when decisions were made, they rarely had the backing of the full cabinet. Moreover, the government had few tools for ensuring that decisions, once taken, would actually be implemented by the appropriate state agencies. These, in turn, were often unwilling to put these directives into practice, especially when the policies were deemed to threaten the interests of the institutions and their constituencies.[68] Consequently, if it encountered strong opposition from groups affected by the decision, the government tended to back down and retreat, since more often than not, the protesting interest groups were assured that there were regime members who were fully prepared to support their cause.[69] As we will see in Chapter 5, these internal divisions facilitated organized labor's ability to effectively block various privatization

64. El-Mikawy, *Building of Consensus*, 64–65.

65. Ayubi, *The State and Public Policies Since Sadat* (Ithaca: Reading, 1991), 228–29; *Rose al-Youssef,* August 28, 1989, 5.

66. *World Link,* January/February 1994, 222.

67. For examples of these intragovernment disputes, see *Financial Times,* June 5, 1985, D2 and April 8, 1986, 3; *Business Monthly,* April 1986, 21; *Rose al-Youssef,* August 21, 1989, 16.

68. For a discussion of policy consequences of these territorial battles between state agencies as they played out in the agricultural sector, see, for example, Denis J. Sullivan, "The Political Economy of Reform in Egypt," *International Journal of Middle Eastern Studies* 22, no. 3 (1990): 317–34.

69. Ayubi, *State and Public Policies,* 221–23. As Keinle notes, "Institutional complexity actually assisted in this appropriation of state agencies from below." Eberhard Keinle, *A Grand Delusion: Democracy and Economic Reform in Egypt* (London: I. B. Tauris, 2001), 10.

proposals that the government contemplated during the 1980s. In blocking public sector reform projects, the ETUC drew upon the legal resources it had acquired during Sadat's tenure and on its growing financial autonomy from the state. Its ability to rely on elite allies, for example, the minister of industry Muhammad 'Abd al-Wahab, further bolstered its ability to shape policy making.

Despite these disputes within the elite, Mubarak remained ambivalent about the role that the dominant party should play in Egypt's political life as well as its relationship with the state.[70] The NDP continued to lack any coherent ideology and sought to incorporate as many social groups as possible, including private businessmen and the urban working class. This lack of any discernible platform and programmatic initiatives resulted in the party's inability to recruit and train new crops of political leaders.

Although the NDP resorted to intimidating opposition candidates and rigging and occasionally tinkering with the electoral system, each parliamentary contest, notwithstanding continued crushing victories of the NDP, exposed the inability of the ruling party to attract broad-based support.[71] Most revealing was the high voter abstention rate during the elections, reaching more than 50 percent of the electorate in the country as a whole, with the highest occurring in the urban areas.[72] Furthermore, each parliamentary election brought to the public's attention the deep factionalism that plagued the NDP and the tensions that existed between the party's top leadership and local party bosses.[73]

The weakness of the NDP was further reinforced by the lack of internal mechanisms within the party that would promote the loyalty and punish the disloyalty of its members and leaders. Not only did various prominent party figures publicly criticize party and state policies with no discernible consequences, but the party in effect rewarded this lack of loyalty. Among the

70.  Richard U. Moench, "The May 1984 Elections in Egypt and the Question of Egypt's Stability," in *Elections in the Middle East: Implications and Recent Trends,* ed. Linda L. Layne (Boulder, Colo.: Westview Press, 1987), 50–51.

71.  The most extensive changes in the electoral system were made prior to the 1984 parliamentary contest when the majoritarian system was scrapped in favor of a proportional one, which made it impossible for independent candidates to stand in elections and created difficulties for the smaller opposition parties. The changes were eventually declared unconstitutional by the courts. For a discussion of these changes, see, for example, Bertus Hendriks, "Egypt's Elections, Mubarak's Bind," *MERIP,* January 1985, 11–12.

72.  Alexandre Buccianti, "Les elections legislatives en Egypte," *Maghreb-Mashrek* 106 (October/November/December 1984): 54–70.

73.  See, for example, Dina al-Khawaga, "Le parti national-démocrate et les élections de 1995: La conjonction de nombreuses logisques d'action," in *Contours et détours du politique en Égypte: Les élections législatives de 1995,* ed. Sandrine Gamblin (Cairo: CEDEJ, 1997), 83–99.

frequently employed tactics of the NDP was the practice of inviting opposition party members and independents who had defeated NDP candidates in particular districts to join the ruling party, often by offering them prominent positions within the NDP.[74] Similarly, the NDP had difficulty enforcing internal party discipline during electoral campaigns. For example, in the November 1990 parliamentary contest, 60 percent of candidates were independents. Most of them, in fact, were members of the NDP who were not chosen to run in their constituencies by the party.[75] Those former NDP members who won were routinely invited back into the party fold.

The relationship between the NDP and the government was also often strained, and the disagreements between the two sides frequently spilled out into the public arena. Unlike in Mexico, where the PRI and the state administration worked in a symbiotic relationship, the ruling party in Egypt could not be relied upon to back the government it was supposedly heading.[76] Throughout the 1980s, the regime, rather than relying on the NDP to shepherd its proposals through the parliament, spent energy ensuring that its own party did not embarrass the government. On many occasions the government and the party openly clashed. In the mid-1980s, for example, NDP parliamentary delegates attempted to engineer the fall of the cabinet.[77] There were also frequent disagreements between the NDP and the regime over economic policies and local administrative issues.[78] Similar conflicts erupted between state and party representatives at the local level.[79] These persistent conflicts within the ruling elite and the continuing economic crisis made it difficult for the regime to abrogate the procedural concessions won by organized labor during the previous decade. Rather, as we will see in Chapter 5, during the 1980s the legal prerogatives and financial autonomy that the ETUC acquired in the 1970s facilitated its ability to block the government's privatization proposals. The long experience of successfully confronting the state further bolstered organized

---

74. Robert Springborg, *Mubarak's Egypt: Fragmentation of Political Order* (Boulder, Colo.: Westview Press, 1989), 160–61.

75. Iman Farag, "Le politique a l'égyptienne: Lecture des élections législatives," *Maghreb-Mashrek* 133 (July/September 1991): 25.

76. For a discussion of episodes of such conflicts between the NDP and the government, see various issues of *Taqrir al-Istiratiji* (annual publication of the Al-Ahram Center for Political and Strategic Studies, Cairo).

77. *Taqrir al-Istiratiji, 1985,* 331.

78. See, for example, *Taqrir al-Istiratiji, 1987,* 491; *Taqrir al-Istiratiji, 1989,* 407.

79. For an example of such clashes, this one involving the NDP chief in Alexandria and local representatives of the Ministry of Interior, see Springborg, *Mubarak's Egypt,* 145–46.

labor's ability to shape economic policies. In particular, the fear of repeating the events of 1977, when social unrest swept the country, constrained the regime's policy options.

## The Mexican Labor Movement

In contrast to what occurred in Egypt, the Mexican revolution was a long, bloody, and protracted struggle that involved large segments of the population. While the diverse groups engaged in the conflict agreed on the need to end the Porfirio (1884–1911), there was little consensus among them about how Mexico's society and polity should be transformed.[80] The existence of these factions and differing blueprints for the future, as well as power struggles between the various revolutionary armies, prolonged the revolution's duration as these groups battled for control.

The revolutionary period produced a much more militant and organized labor movement than had previously existed in Mexico and the increasingly vocal demands emanating from trade unions posed a dilemma for the "revolutionary family." The man who took over the reins of government once Porfirio Díaz was deposed, Francisco Madero (1911–13), as well as other revolutionary leaders, proclaimed the need to bring about greater social justice in Mexico. Despite this, with the possible exception of Pancho Villa and Zapata, these leaders did not propose any fundamental restructuring of the economy and society. Most came from the middle and upper middle class. They wanted private property respected and envisioned a state-led but capitalist road to economic development.

The revolutionary turmoil led to massive capital flight and the Madero administration saw the continuing labor unrest as discouraging investors from returning, thus retarding economic growth. If organized labor was to cease its protests and be brought into Madero's coalition of support, however, some concessions would have to be granted. Over the next couple of decades successive Mexican administrations sought to consolidate power and bring organized labor under regime control. In the initial years following the revolution, because of the intense conflicts and divisions within the revolutionary family, organized labor was able to extract numerous concessions. Various elite factions saw it as an attractive ally as they vied for control of the state. The process of establishing corporatist labor institutions was therefore a long one and it was

80. *Porfirio* refers to the rule by longtime Mexican dictator Porfirio Díaz.

only in the 1930s that organized labor was brought firmly under regime control and lost the political influence it had wielded in the immediate postrevolutionary period. The subordination of organized labor was predicated not only on the creation of new labor institutions but also on the establishment of mechanisms for effective management of intra-elite conflicts. Once such mechanisms were devised, organized labor lost one of its most potent weapons—the ability to play various elite factions off one another in order to extract concessions. Over the long term, the state succeeded in subordinating organized labor, leaving it with few resources to challenge government policies. Labor's inability to resist policies it opposed became particularly clear during the second half of the 1980s when the Mexican government initiated a fundamental restructuring of the economy.

### The Establishment of Corporatist Labor Institutions

As the postrevolutionary elite sought to consolidate power, organized labor became an attractive coalition partner. Both Venustiano Carranza and Álvaro Obregón looked to unions as they battled rival factions within the revolutionary family. The revolution produced an unprecedented mobilization of both workers and peasants and Carranza sought to harness that mobilization and bring the two groups into his support coalition. In 1914, he struck a deal with the Casa del Obrero Mundial, which fielded Red Battalions on his behalf in exchange for promises of future concessions to labor.[81] In the Decree of December 12, 1914, Carranza (1914–20) acknowledged that the revolution's original goals were too narrow and called for adopting progressive labor laws.[82]

Once fighting stopped in 1916 these promises were quickly forgotten and Carranza moved in an increasingly conservative direction. Yet although armed hostilities had ceased, challenges to Carranza's position did not. It was largely thanks to the efforts of one of these challengers, the more liberal-minded Obregón group, that the Constitutional Convention of 1917 produced a document with the most progressive labor legislation anywhere at the time. Article 123 of the Constitution guaranteed the right to strike and to organize trade unions, limited the workday to eight hours, introduced gender equality in pay, and placed limits on child labor.[83] These laws, however, did little to change

---

81. Casa del Obrero Mundial was the largest worker organization of the period. Frank Tannebaum, *The Mexican Agrarian Revolution* (New York: Macmillan, 1929), 168–70.

82. Judith Adler Hellman, *Mexico in Crisis* (New York: Holmes and Meier, 1985), 18.

83. Hellman, *Mexico in Crisis,* 20.

labor's situation, because Carranza had little interest in their implementation. Disappointed by the broken promises, organized labor was therefore more than willing to throw its support behind Obregón (1920–24), who was championing reforms. Obregón's reliance on labor, and in particular on the Regional Confederation of Mexican Workers (CROM), quickly resulted in the splintering of the elite faction that had originally backed his presidential campaign, at one point leading to armed confrontations.

Despite the CROM-Obregón alliance, as Obregón's presidency wore on and he struggled to enlarge his base of support, reaching out to more conservative factions, the relationship began to cool.[84] As had happened toward the end of Carranza's tenure in office, when Obregón began to distance himself from the CROM, organized labor began looking for other partners, finding a willing one in Plutarco Elías Calles, who was beginning to position himself to take over the presidency after Obregón. As the battle for succession heated up and the "revolutionary family" began once again to splinter, Calles's reliance on labor grew. This dependence on the CROM was amply demonstrated when workers formed armed militias to back Calles in his conflict with another presidential contender, Adolfo de la Huerta.

The Calles presidency (1924–28) was a watershed in Mexican politics. It was during Calles's term in office that the ruling party began to take shape and the relationship between state and labor was institutionalized. Calles saw in the establishment of a political party a way to end the intense conflicts that had accompanied each presidential succession. The party would not only provide the institutional means of resolving elite disputes, but in Calles's visions would also serve as a forum for bringing various social groups into a permanent base of support for the regime.

Along with creating a political party, Calles forged a close relationship with the CROM. Labor leaders joined the government, supported the president's nationalist economic policies, and ensured that industrial peace prevailed as Calles sought to chart a new economic course for the country.[85] As a result, as Collier and Collier point out, "politically labor provided legitimacy and supported the government. Economically, a potentially radical and oppositionist

---

84. David Collier and Ruth Berins Collier, *Shaping the Political Arena: State-Labor Relations and Regime Change in Mexico* (Berkeley and Los Angeles: University of California, International and Area Studies Series, 1992), 208.

85. Marjorie Ruth Clark, *Organized Labor in Mexico* (Chapel Hill: University of North Carolina Press, 1973), 119–20.

working class was converted into a cooperating labor movement that supported capitalist reconstruction and modernization."[86]

The close relationship that developed between Calles and organized labor, however, created opposition within the business community. Although business groups were never formally incorporated into the new political party, their support, or at least their willingness, to invest was crucial, given the ambitious economic development goals of the regime. As his term came to a close, Calles therefore decided that a more moderate successor would be a better choice and would diffuse the intensifying political conflict. The succession, however, generated controversy when former president Obregón decided to run for office one more time. Although he won the election he never assumed office. Shortly before his term was to begin, he was assassinated.

The assassination ignited a period of political turmoil, with three men occupying the presidential post over the course of what was supposed to be Obregón's term. This period, known as the Maximato, saw a reversal of Calles's populist policies.[87] In particular, the relationship with organized labor began to be restructured, with focus shifting away from politically mobilizing labor to establishing firmer state controls over trade unions.[88] The changes in the federal labor code, enacted in 1931, instituted substantially enhanced powers of the state to intervene in industrial conflicts. At the same time, because labor issues were now placed under federal jurisdiction, state governors' authority was substantially curtailed.[89]

The most important institutions providing the state with authority to intervene in labor affairs were the tripartite conciliation and arbitration boards. The boards were responsible for registering and enforcing collective labor agreements and had substantial powers to regulate union formation. According to the federal labor code, workers were free to establish trade unions without first seeking state permission. However, to legally represent workers in for example collective bargaining, the unions needed to be officially registered with the conciliation and arbitration boards. In practice, this provision meant that the state was able to curtail the formation of independent union organizations. Similarly, although

---

86. Collier and Berins Collier, *Shaping the Political Arena,* 217.

87. The three men who held the presidency during this period were Emilio Portes Gil (1928–30), Pascual Ortíz Rubio (1930–32), and Abelardo Rodríguez (1932–34).

88. Collier and Berins Collier, *Shaping the Political Arena,* 225.

89. Kevin J. Middlebrook, *The Paradox of Revolution: Labor, the State, and Authoritarianism in Mexico* (Baltimore: Johns Hopkins University Press, 1995), 60.

the constitution guaranteed the right to strike, the conciliation and arbitration boards had the power to declare a strike illegal or nonexistent, thereby making work stoppages more difficult to organize. Finally, a number of reporting requirements provided the state with the means to directly intervene in internal union affairs.[90] As the government began distancing itself from organized labor, the CROM, already discredited in the eyes of many workers because of its corrupt practices, began losing members, and a new labor organization, under the leadership of Lombardo Toledo, was formed.

The gap between the regime and organized labor did not last long. With the Lázaro Cárdenas presidency (1934–40), more populist policies were restarted and the incorporation of labor began in earnest. Between 1930 and 1940 "the number of unionized Mexican workers tripled from 294,000 or 5.6% of the active labor force, to 878,000 or 15.4%."[91] Simultaneously, Cárdenas restructured the ruling party, renaming it the Party of the Mexican Revolution (PRM). The new party was organized along corporatist lines with four sectors represented: peasant, labor, popular, and military.[92] The labor movement was also reorganized. In 1936 Cárdenas assisted in the creation of the Mexican Labor Federation (CTM) under the leadership of Toledo and labor became the most influential sector within the PRM.[93]

Cárdenas's close relationship with labor had at its roots in his struggle to consolidate power and distance himself from Calles, who wanted to control the regime from behind the scenes as he had done during the Maximato. Since the Calles faction was more conservative, labor and peasant groups appeared to Cárdenas as the most attractive coalition partners. Although initially organized labor was uncertain about Cárdenas, as the power struggle between Calles and Cárdenas intensified, labor moved more firmly to back the latter, fearing that its position would deteriorate if Calles gained the upper hand.[94] Organized labor was concerned about Calles's close association with business groups and

90. For example, Middlebrook finds that unions were required to provide state authorities with reports on their activities upon request. They had to report within ten days any changes in their leadership or statues, and changes in membership had to be reported every three months. Middlebrook, *Paradox of Revolution,* 67.

91. Howard Handelman, "The Politics of Labor Protest in Mexico," *Journal of Interamerican Studies and World Affairs* 18, no. 3 (1976): 268–69.

92. The military was eventually discarded as one of the sectors incorporated into the party.

93. With the creation of the CTM, the CROM lost its status as the "official" labor confederation. However, the CROM, while the smaller of the two labor organizations, continued to function.

94. Nora L. Hamilton, *The Limits of State-Autonomy: Post-revolutionary Mexico* (Princeton: Princeton University Press, 1982), 109–12.

attracted by Cárdenas's economic policies, which called for greater national control over industry and for promoting the public sector.[95] Finally, in 1935 Cárdenas expelled Calles from Mexico.[96]

During the Cárdenas presidency, the CTM abandoned its position of political neutrality, openly proclaimed its support for his policies, and pledged to limit the number of strikes.[97] In addition, it decided to directly participate in the political party's activities and elections. As a result the CTM gained representatives in the national congress and occupied many high-level government posts.[98] The Cárdenas government also began extending financial support to the CTM. This close relationship with the regime significantly benefited organized labor. It gained political influence, and access to policy making, and expanded its organizational base. Such close association with the regime, however, had negative long-term consequences for labor, as became apparent during the more conservative administrations that followed Cárdenas's populist interlude. The close association with the regime, the incorporation of the CTM within the dominant party structures, and the increasing financial reliance of the CTM on the regime meant that labor organizations lost much of the political and economic independence that they previously enjoyed.[99] This loss of independence in turn meant that organized labor had few resources it could draw upon to successfully oppose policies the government was committed to implementing.

The prominence that labor played during the Cárdenas presidency ended during the more conservative administrations of Manuel Ávila Camacho (1940–46) and Miguel Alemán (1946–52), who placed less emphasis on social reform and more on accelerating industrialization through import-substitution policies. To attract investments, both Camacho and Alemán sought to ensure industrial peace. Strikes, which had become so common under Cárdenas, now declined and more open repression of labor protests became common. The Camacho administration made important changes in the federal labor code that undercut some of the gains workers had made following the revolution. The revised code placed additional restrictions on strike activity and made laying off

95. Middlebrook, *Paradox of Revolution*, 93.

96. Frank Brandenburg, *The Making of Modern Mexico* (Englewood Cliffs, N.J.: Prentice Hall, 1964), 80.

97. While labor pledged to curtail strike activity, in fact, the number of strikes during the Cárdenas period grew, with industrial disputes encouraged by Cárdenas himself.

98. Collier and Berins Collier, *Shaping the Political Arena*, 240–41.

99. Joe C. Ashby, *Organized Labor and the Mexican Revolution Under Lazaro Cárdenas* (Chapel Hill: University of North Carolina Press, 1967), 287–88.

workers easier. At the same time, Camacho initiated a campaign to marginalize leftist elements within the labor movement to make it more willing to cooperate with government policies. Although this strategy precipitated tensions and conflicts within organized labor, in the end it proved quite successful. The CTM in particular moderated its rhetoric and abandoned its socialist ideology.[100] Toledo was pushed out of the CTM and replaced by Fidel Velázquez, who was much less willing to challenge the regime.

Alemán moved even more forcefully than Camacho to ensure government's control over organized labor. In particular, he initiated a policy of directly intervening in internal union affairs to ensure that dissident voices within the labor movement were quickly silenced and, if necessary, sidelined and replaced with more compliant leaders. This new strategy, known as *charrismo*, proved very successful in preventing the emergence of independent-minded union leaders, with the result that, as Collier and Collier point out, "labor support for the government was now unconditional and uncritical and was granted without extracting anything in return in way of guarantees."[101] Along with greater government interference in internal union affairs, the CTM's financial dependence on the regime grew substantially with state subsidies to the confederation reaching, by some estimates, more than 60 percent of its monthly income by the 1950s.[102] Organized labor was unable to regain much political influence during the successive administrations. The administrations of both Adolfo Ruiz Cortines (1952–58) and Adolfo López Mateos (1958–64) forcefully repressed the rank and file's opposition to the "official" union leadership.

### Unsuccessful Challenges to State-Labor Relations

The establishment of labor organizations subordinated to the regime and the incorporation of the CTM within the structures of the Institutional Revolutionary Party (PRI) meant that organized labor largely lost the ability to influence regime policies. It also provided the regime with legal, financial, and political tools to regulate labor activity. This does not mean that there never were challenges from dissident labor activists and organizations to this state-labor relationship. While on the whole, labor remained supportive of the regime and did not oppose government policies, on a number of occasions groups calling for both greater internal union democracy and greater union autonomy from the state

---

100. Handelman, "Politics of Labor Protest," 269.
101. Collier and Berins Collier, *Shaping the Political Arena*, 416.
102. Middlebrook, *Paradox of Revolution*, 101.

did emerge. The durability of the relationship between state and labor and of the institutions that supported that relationship is attested by the inability of these challengers to have significant impact on internal union affairs or on state policies regarding labor. A couple of examples of such challenges can best illustrate the strategies employed by the regime in dealing with labor protests. What is striking about these examples is that while dissident labor groups have on occasion sought to press their demands, often quite aggressively, they proved unable to sustain such challenges once the regime decided that the demands fell outside the acceptable rules of the game. These challengers were unable to find elite allies to support them. Other allies, for instance, intellectuals, tended to abandon them in the face of regime repression.

The experiences of these challenges reveal the regime's strategies for controlling labor and its ability to withstand and put down overt challenges to the status quo. While the regime was willing to accommodate what it decided were reasonable and justifiable substantive demands when these did not conflict with other policies, it expected that labor groups would abide by the rules of the game and not go beyond the established boundaries of state-labor relations. When these boundaries were crossed and the demands that were made shifted from substantive toward procedural, the regime did not hesitate to respond with repression.

Labor groups challenging the status quo in an overt fashion were handicapped by three factors. One was the lack of consensus among left-wing opposition groups on goals and strategies. Although the Right was fairly well organized around the National Action Party (PAN), it was not an attractive ally for labor groups, since it represented the conservative, private business sector of the society. Second was workers' reluctance to join opposition movements. This reluctance to oppose the entrenched "official" union leadership was well founded. The leadership had access to preferential welfare benefits that it could distribute to union members. It also had sanctions it could use against those challenging the *charrismo*. The 1931 Federal Labor Law included a number of provisions that while ostensibly designed to protect laborers, in practice gave union leadership access to powerful weapons with which to regulate rank-and-file behavior. The code contained both exclusion and separation clauses. Exclusion clauses, if included in a collective agreement (and they generally were), stipulated that only union members could be hired by employers; separation clauses required that employers dismiss any worker who had been expelled from the union.[103] The

103. Middlebrook, *Paradox of Revolution,* 96–98.

latter allowed union leaders to have opponents fired. Union leaders often did away with the secrecy of the ballot as well as resorted to using thugs during union elections to ensure that votes would be cast that were to their liking.[104] Third, labor groups challenging the status quo were unable to bolster their bargaining position vis-à-vis the regime by making common cause with factions within the ruling elite. Such regime allies were simply unavailable.

Two of the most significant challenges to the status quo in state-labor relations came in 1958–59, when protests erupted among railroad workers, and in 1971–72, when an internal union challenge to the CTM emerged among workers in the electrical industry.

The strike among the Mexican Railroad Workers Union began as an internal revolt by disaffected workers against the union leadership, which was closely aligned with the regime. Initially, the movement limited itself to work slowdowns, but as wages declined and with them workers' standard of living, the dissidents began staging strikes. As the number of strikes climbed from 193 in 1957 to 740 in 1958, workers began leaving the CTM-affiliated union in droves and forging alliances with disaffected workers in other industries.[105] Other sectors joined the movement and attempted to remove regime-allied union leadership. However, it was the railroad workers under the leadership of Demetrio Vallejo whom the regime viewed as the most disruptive because of their ability to effectively paralyze the country.

The Cortines administration's response was typical of the way the regime handled such labor disputes. It promised striking workers limited wage increases with the understanding that although they were not as high as the workers demanded, the government, having shown its understanding of the problem and its willingness to address it, now expected workers to return to their jobs. When this did not happen and workers continued to demand wage increases and Vallejo began making accusations in the press that the government was subsidizing private industry, the government quickly changed tactics and launched its own media campaign depicting Vallejo and his supporters as Communist subversives.[106] When the campaign convinced many Vallejo allies in other industries and within the circles of the intelligentsia to abandon him, but did not deter railroad workers from threatening another strike, the regime took off

104. Dan La Botz, *Mask of Democracy: Labor Suppression in Mexico Today* (Boston: South End Books, 1992), 47.

105. Handelman, "Politics of Labor Protest," 273.

106. Handelman, "Politics of Labor Protest," 277.

its gloves. Mass arrests of union leaders and strikers as well as their supporters in other industries took place. Thousands of workers who participated in the movement were fired. With Vallejo and his supporters behind bars, the old union leadership once again took charge of the Railroad Workers Union.[107]

The other large-scale protest action took place in the early 1970s, when the government attempted to force the merging of the three separate union organizations that represented workers in the electrical industry and bring them under the control of Sindicato Nacional, or National Engineers Union (SNE), the CTM-affiliated union. The move sparked a wave of mass demonstrations throughout the country and quickly evolved into a full-blown attack on the *charrismo*. When the government agreed that the smaller, independent union led by Rafael Galván would have parity on the governing boards of the newly merged union organization, it seemed that the tactic of staging mass protests was successful. This agreement proved to be little more than the calm before the storm. By June 1974 the two unions were once again locked in a struggle when workers, unhappy about a contract that had just been negotiated, struck. Galván, rather than backing the union leadership, sided with the striking workers. In response, he and his supporters were expelled from the union and then fired by the employers. Undeterred, Galván proceeded to form the Democratic Tendency (TD), which called for union democracy and social reforms that had been promised during the revolution. To make its demands clear, the TD organized mass demonstrations during the spring and summer of 1975. The government expressed a willingness to reinstate workers who had been fired by the electrical companies during the previous months but did not follow through, and mass demonstrations continued. The government of President Luis Echeverría proposed that negotiations begin between parties on condition that the strike threatened by the TD was postponed. When this conciliatory strategy proved unsuccessful, the army was called in to crush the movement.[108]

Although the electrical industry workers' protest movement was the largest during the Echeverría years (1970–76), workers in other industries, and in particular textiles and automobile, prompted both by the deteriorating economic situation and by dissatisfaction with the lack of internal union democracy, also staged strikes during this period. The protests generally followed a similar pattern. As Collier and Collier point out, "Typically, the movement within each

---

107. For a more extensive discussion of this episode, see La Botz, *Mask of Democracy*, 70–71; Middlebrook, *Paradox of Revolution*, 190–205.
108. La Botz, *Mask of Democracy*, 72–74.

union started with economic demands and broadened as the existing union leadership came to be seen as an obstacle. It came to take on dimensions of rejecting the existing union structure and advocating a more militant, representative, democratic form of unionism and thus took on a political coloration."[109] The regime's strategy for dealing with these challenges also unfolded in a similar way. The regime would be inclined to negotiate some of the economic demands and, in particular, was willing to grant wage increases. If the strikers did not desist after these small substantive concessions were granted and continued to protest, the regime's tactics shifted. In particular, once the political demands attacking the CTM's control over the labor movement became more explicit, the regime would abandon negotiations and concessions in favor of repression.[110]

Thus over time Mexican trade unions gradually lost their independence and became increasingly subordinated to the state. While the official labor unions gained important substantive concessions from the regime that made them more than willing to support the PRI, the ruling elite also made clear that when labor demands shifted from what were regarded as reasonable and substantive toward the procedural, the willingness of the regime to respond positively would cease. Consequently, by the time the structural adjustment program began in the 1980s, the CTM had few resources, whether legal prerogatives or financial autonomy, at its disposal to ensure that its views would be taken into account when the public sector reform program was being considered. Neither could Mexican labor draw on the experience of successfully challenging the state. The official unions did not engage in open protests and the independent trade unions were small and unable to mount effective campaigns to challenge regime policies. When they attempted to do so, they were easily crushed by the PRI.

## Internal Regime Dynamics

How were the successive Mexican governments able to maintain control over organized labor? The first years following the revolution did not bode well for the ability of the elite to establish such control. Workers mobilized on an unprecedented scale during the revolution and the divisions within the "revolutionary family" provided organized labor with the opportunity to further advance its goals as it made its support for particular elite factions dependent on concession guarantees. Yet beginning in the 1930s, the regime began to slowly

---

109. Collier and Berins Collier, *Shaping the Political Arena*, 602.
110. See, for example, Hellman, *Mexico in Crisis*, 125–72.

bring labor firmly under its control. Although the following decades witnessed waves of labor protest and the appearance of dissident labor organizations that challenged both the official labor unions and the regime itself, all these eruptions of labor unrest were quickly quelled and the opposition voices silenced. In none of these instances did the position of the official labor unions become seriously threatened, and more important, at no time was the position of the regime weakened. Furthermore, while the regime would offer some substantive concessions to labor, most demands emanating from the dissident labor movements were simply ignored and the movements themselves would quickly fade into obscurity.

Studies of Mexican labor point to a number of reasons for the inability of labor to seriously challenge the government. Among the more important of these explanations is that unlike its Egyptian counterpart, the Mexican regime did permit a measure of pluralism within organized labor. While the CROM (and later the CTM) was the most important labor confederation, it was by no means the only significant workers' organization. The existence of numerous labor associations allowed the regime to deploy divide-and-rule tactics, playing the various confederations off one another. The fragmentation of the labor movement also contributed to its overall weakness, since often, rather than presenting a unified front in confrontations with the regime, labor organizations competed with one another for state favors and resources. The incorporation of most labor confederations within the PRI structures, moreover, ensured that labor leaders would be able to channel their demands in politically controllable ways, provided them with an arena where bargaining could take place and where two-way lines of communication between labor and the regime could be maintained.

The Mexican regime also proved adept at responding to the always evolving political environment. When various side payments were considered insufficient to maintain control over labor organization, the regime set up new institutions that could facilitate incorporation. The creation of the Labor Congress (CT) should be seen in this light. The CT, established in the mid-1960s, was a means by which to overcome the increasing fragmentation of organized labor and bring trade unions that were dissatisfied with the CTM into an umbrella organization that could be controlled by the PRI.[111] Over time, unlike in Egypt, organized labor became increasingly dependent on the regime and less able and less willing to openly challenge it. Even when the rank and file were dissatisfied, official unions were not willing to oppose the regime. The *charrismo*

---

111. Middlebrook, *Paradox of Revolution,* 275–76.

system, by providing material benefits to union leaders, made them reluctant to tinker with the status quo. While these explanations are important, they do not present the full picture of the political dynamics that allowed the regime over a period of seven decades, despite challenges from dissident labor groups, to maintain its control over trade unions and ensure that with time unions were less and less able to press their demands on the state. Their inability to do so became especially manifest during the structural adjustment reforms initiated during the de la Madrid presidency.

To complete the picture, it is necessary to turn now to the other side of state-labor dynamics—the state. The Mexican regime, unlike the Polish or the Egyptian, succeeded after an initial period of intense intra-elite conflict, in establishing effective mechanisms to resolve these intra-elite disputes in a constructive rather than a destructive manner. As noted in Chapter 1, conflicts and disputes within the ruling elite are unavoidable. What is significant, however, is how they are managed. As we have seen, in Poland and Egypt mechanisms for elite conflict resolution were underdeveloped and ineffective. The lack of such mechanisms in turn had profound consequences for how policies were pursued and what role interest groups were able to play. A divided elite creates the opportunity for interest groups in society to more effectively press their claims, since they are more likely to find elite allies willing to make common cause with them than they are in cases in which elites are cohesive.[112] Thus even groups that may possess few resources are more likely to be in a position to extract concessions for the regime. The reverse also holds. In a situation in which the elite maintains cohesion and disputes are managed internally without spilling out into the public arena, interest groups are hard pressed to find elite allies willing to collaborate with them. Hence, even if groups manage to mobilize and press their claims, their demands are more likely to fall on deaf ears. Unable to find elite supporters for their positions, they are more likely to fall prey to repression, to disintegrate, or both.

Although the initial period following the revolution did not bode well for the ability of the Mexican elite to construct such effective mechanisms for conflict resolution, over time it did construct them. Hence, when interest groups challenged the regime, their task was much more difficult, since there were no elite allies that could be counted on to champion their cause. In the case of

112. See, for example, Doug McAdam, "Conceptual Origins, Current Problems, Future Directions," in *Comparative Perspectives on Social Movements: Political Opportunities, Mobilizing Structures, and Cultural Framings,* ed. Doug McAdam, John D. McCarthy, and Mayer N. Zald (New York: Cambridge University Press, 1996), 23–40.

labor organizations, once institutions of elite conflict resolution were devised, unions' ability to extract concessions declined. In the first years following the revolution, when struggles for power were intense within the "revolutionary family," labor was able to present itself as a valuable ally in these struggles. Or put differently, seeking to extract concessions for itself, organized labor was able to look to various elite factions to form a common front. Elite factions, by contrast, were interested in making such alliances even at the cost of future concessions because they recognized that mobilized workers were an important source of support. However, once mechanisms for elite conflict resolution were institutionalized, the dynamics between the state elite and labor changed. For ambitious politicians looking to advance their careers, it no longer made sense to seek allies outside the elite. The changes in incentives meant that party loyalty rather than the ability to bring workers out onto the street offered the best chance for securing promotions. Those within the labor movement who sought to extract more concessions from the state found their options limited. Although the regime was willing to negotiate and offer some compromises and inducements for cooperation, and often preferred this strategy, when demands went beyond the established rules of the game, it did not hesitate to deploy repression. Often, once repression was used, whatever initial substantive concessions had been offered were withdrawn.

The recognition that an official political party could play an important stabilizing role in Mexico first came about during the presidency of Álvaro Obregón (1920–24). Obregón saw in the establishment of a political party a way to integrate the variety of groups that had been mobilized during the revolutionary struggle and bring an end to the continuing battles. The destructiveness of these battles was further reinforced when Obregón, after winning reelection to the presidency, was assassinated before taking office. Faced with this crisis, Obregón's successor, Calles, saw in the establishment of a political party a means of bringing about stability.[113] The National Revolutionary Party (PNR) was created in 1929, with the goal of facilitating the resolution of the succession crises and bringing together regional leaders.[114] The party proved to be more effective in centralizing authority than in facilitating mass political mobilization and control.

113. John Bailey and Leopoldo Gomez, "The PRI and Political Liberalization," *Journal of International Affairs* 43, no. 2 (1990): 295.

114. Evelyn P. Stevens, "Mexico's PRI: The Institutionalization of Corporatism?" in *Authoritarianism and Corporatism in Latin America,* ed. James M. Malloy (Pittsburgh: University of Pittsburgh Press, 1977), 230.

Cárdenas introduced some innovations into the way the party was organized in order to expand its mass mobilization and incorporation functions
and to bring workers and peasants firmly into the organization. In 1938 the
party was renamed the Party of the Mexican Revolution (PRM) and reorganized along territorial lines, and collective rather than individual membership
was introduced.[115] Furthermore, because of the conflict surrounding Obregón's
return to the presidency, the principle of no reelection to that office was
adopted. At the same time, state governors and national legislators also became
limited to one term.

The creation of the Institutional Revolutionary Party (PRI) in 1946 by
Camacho and Alemán marked the final consolidation of the ruling party. The
PRI, like its Egyptian counterpart, was characterized by a vague ideological
platform, and membership requirements were far from stringent. As Anderson
and Cockcroft note, "Membership required no specific ideological commit-
ments. Marxists and other socialists became members, as did traditional liber-
als and people without any coherent beliefs at all. The party has by and large
continued to be pragmatic and ideologically vague."[116] The intention behind
this ideological vagueness was to incorporate as many groups as possible within
the framework of the PRI. The expectation was that by channeling the demands
of these various groups within the party, social peace and overt challenges to the
regime from politically dissatisfied groups could be minimized. While divergent
views were welcomed, however, there was little tolerance for open dissension or
attempts to build independent centers of power within the party. Although
repression and even assassination was used to enforce compliance, cooptation
was the preferred strategy.[117] Generally, in exchange for their loyalty, various
side payments were made to groups to bring them into the PRI fold. The hope
was that by addressing the main economic demands of these groups their
political quiescence if not their full political support, could be secured.

How did this cooptation work? As we have seen, the Egyptian regime used
tactics similar to those of its Mexican counterpart. The political parties that
were created were also ideologically and programmatically vague, to ensure
that groups and individuals from all over the political spectrum could find a

115. In other words, a person became a party member through his or her affiliation with an
organization or a union that was a member of the official party.

116. Bo Anderson and James D. Cockcroft, "Control and Cooptation in Mexican Politics," in
*Latin American Radicalism: A Documentary Report on Left and Nationalist Movements*, ed. Irving
Louis Horowitz, Josue de Castro, and John Gerassi (New York: Random House, 1969), 376–77.

117. Anderson and Cockcroft, "Control and Cooptation," 379.

home within the dominant party. The reasons behind this inclusiveness were similar as well. Elites in both states saw the inclusion of these diverse political forces within an organization over which the regime had control as the best means of neutralizing their potential opponents and challengers to their rule. Yet in the Egyptian case the results were starkly different from what they were in Mexico.

One explanation that a number of scholars of the PRI point to as the reason for its success at containing elite factionalism is the legacy of the destructiveness of the revolution and the years that followed it. A fear of disorder pushed elites to cooperate with one another and refrain from mobilizing social groups outside the party structures.[118] Although this fear may be a necessary, it is certainly not a sufficient condition to explain the Mexican regime's stability. As numerous examples of reignited civil wars indicate, the knowledge of the carnage that may ensue if a peace agreement is broken has not stopped contending factions from resuming the bloodletting. In other words, fear needs to be accompanied by appropriate incentives for that cooperation to come about. In the Mexican case, the regime, in fact, relied on more than fear of returning disorder to ensure that the elite maintained cohesion and that factions within the elite were not tempted to step outside the established boundaries of political conduct to pursue their interests.

Several factors contributed to the creation of a stable political regime. The elite's cohesiveness was enhanced by shared class and geographical background, familial ties, and common educational experience.[119] Most members of the elite attended the National University of Mexico (UNAM), and most government and political leaders at some point in their careers taught there, making the university campus one of the main recruiting grounds for new crops of political leaders. The fact that there was little intermixing between the political and the economic elites further contributed to the cohesiveness of the former.[120]

118. Kenneth M. Coleman and Charles L. Davis, "Preemptive Reform and the Mexican Working Class," *Latin American Research Review* 18, no. 1 (1983): 5.

119. Most elite members came from the urban middle class and primarily from the northern states and the Federal District.

120. For a detailed discussion of the elite recruitment patterns, see Roderic Ai Camp, *Mexico's Leaders: Their Educational Background and Recruitment* (Tucson: University of Arizona Press, 1980); Kevin J. Middlebrook, "Dilemmas of Change in Mexican Politics," *World Politics* 41, no. 1 (1988): 120–41. Beginning in the 1980s, these recruitment patterns began to change. For discussion of these changing patterns and their consequences, see David Ronfeldt, "Prospects for Elite Cohesion," in *Mexico's Alternative Futures*, ed. Wayne A. Cornelius, Judith Gentleman, and Peter H. Smith (San Diego: Center for U.S.-Mexican Studies, University of California, San Diego, 1989), 435–51; Rogelio Hernandez Rodriguez, "The Partido Revolucionario Institucional," in *Governing Mexico: Political*

While the shared socioeconomic background of the political elite helped foster cohesiveness, the establishment of institutional incentives that rewarded loyalty and penalized dissent allowed the elite to effectively manage internal disagreements over the long term. The destructiveness of intra-elite conflicts in the years immediately following the revolution convinced Obregón and Calles that a political party needed to be established as a way of providing a forum for mediation among the various factions while at the same time institutionalizing and thus controlling mass mobilization. The dominant party, then, was a state creation, and as such was subordinate to the state. However, the relationship between the state and the political party was a symbiotic one. Both performed distinct but complementary functions that were essential to the stability of the regime. While the state was responsible for policy design and implementation, the political party was charged with recruiting and organizing the political elites; ensuring that voters were mobilized during electoral campaigns; and providing, through the establishment of corporatist institutions that aggregated peasants, workers, and the popular sectors, a means of two-way communication between state elites and citizens. Finally, the party was the primary vehicle through which elite cohesiveness was maintained.[121] The official party thus played an important stabilizing role and aggregated diverse interests within it.[122]

The PRI ensured elite conflict resolution through mechanisms that injected flexibility into the system while creating powerful incentives to remain loyal to the party. One of the most important innovations that contributed to both goals was the principle of no reelection to the presidency as well as to most other contested offices. As Middlebrook points out, "Regular personnel changes and the prospects of future success are powerful stimuli for loyalty to the established system. . . . The possibility that former officials might one day return to office gives them strong incentives to avoid an irreparable break with the regime and emphasized loyalty as the essential rule of behavior for Mexican politicians."[123]

For those competing for state governor or congressional posts, the prohibition against immediate reelection meant that for politically ambitious individuals it made little sense to devote energies and resources to building up their own power bases, since the way to promote their careers did not depend on the

---

Parties and Elections, ed. Monica Serrano (London: Institute of Latin American Studies, 1998), 71–94; Miguel Angel Centeno and Sylvia Maxfield, "The Marriage of Finance and Order: Changes in the Mexican Political Elite," Journal of Latin American Studies 24, no. 1 (1992): 57–85.

121. Bailey and Gomez, "PRI and Political Liberalization," 292.

122. Martin C. Needler, "Political Development of Mexico," American Political Science Review 55, no. 2 (1961): 308–12.

123. Middlebrook, "Dilemmas of Change," 125.

control of a particular district or constituency but rather on the establishment of relationships with higher-ranked party members who controlled the promotions process.[124] In most cases, these incentives were sufficient to ensure that politicians remained loyal. When individuals did attempt to break ranks, the reaction from the elite was swift. For example, in 1930 Cárdenas "expelled several senators from the party for criticizing finance minister Luis Montes de Oca."[125] In 1965, Carlos Madrazo, then head of the PRI, attempted to push through internal party reforms that were perceived by other elite members as undermining the supremacy of the president within the system and hence as undercutting the state's control over the party. He was promptly forced to resign.[126] Likewise, attempts by some PRI deputies to permit reelection in the late 1960s were quickly quashed.[127] A similar approach was taken toward what was perhaps the greatest internal challenge to elite unity, when in the 1980s Cuauhtémoc Cárdenas and Muñoz Ledo began pushing for democratization of the presidential-candidate selection process. When internal party discussion about possible compromise failed and Cárdenas and Ledo made their opposition to the prevailing rules public, they were summarily expelled from the party.

Although the principle of no reelection to the lower-level posts created strong incentives for politicians who were interested in advancing their careers to remain loyal to the system, the single six-year presidential term further bolstered the system's stability while at the same time injecting flexibility. Changes, at regular intervals, in the administration and government of the country made it easier to initiate new policies and correct any problems that may have arisen during the previous administration. Moreover, these six-year changes ensured that all factions represented within the PRI, advocating often very different policy preferences, would have their chance to rotate in and out of power. At the same time, because of the ideological vagueness of the PRI, any changes could be framed in terms of fulfilling the goals of the revolution, thereby not abandoning the principal ideological glue that held the political system together.[128] Thus, Cárdenas, López Mateos, and Echeverría's populist policies as well as the pro-business tilt of Camacho, Alemán, and Díaz Ordaz

---

124. See, for example, Susan Kaufman Purcell, "Decision-Making in an Authoritarian Regime: Theoretical Implications from a Mexican Case Study," *World Politics* 26, no. 1 (1973): 34–36.

125. Sylvia Maxfield, *Governing Capital: International Finance and Mexican Politics* (Ithaca: Cornell University Press, 1990), 58.

126. L. Vincent Padgett, *The Mexican Political System* (Boston: Houghton Mifflin, 1966), 56–57.

127. Kaufman Purcell, "Decision-Making in an Authoritarian Regime," 36.

128. John W. Sloan, "The Mexican Variant of Corporatism," *Inter-American Economic Affairs* 38, no. 4 (1985): 12–14.

could all be cloaked in the myth of the revolution.[129] The regular turnover at the top provided strong incentives for the factions that existed within the PRI to maintain loyalty to the system because they had the assurance that if they played by the rules of the game, their turn to assume the highest positions within the political structure were fairly certain.[130] As Sloan explains, "Losers in one administration can always hope their horizons will brighten under the next president, who is never more than six years away."[131]

Furthermore, because with each incoming president most high-level administrative posts were also rotated, it provided an additional tool of elite control.[132] Because the president thus controlled the career prospects of those within the bureaucracy, they tended to be responsive to his policy priorities.[133] Additionally, the central role that incumbent presidents played in the selection process of his successor meant that members of the political elite more generally were unwilling to publicly oppose him. Doing so would effectively destroy any hopes of these elites' potential designation to the highest office. Since traditionally the next president was chosen from among the cabinet members, those politicians with the greatest political and financial resources at their disposal were precisely those least likely to ignore the president's wishes. In fact, those cabinet members perceived as carving out too much independence from the president and eclipsing the latter in the mass media were most likely to lose in the competition for succession.[134] The consequences of these effective elite conflict management mechanisms for organized labor were profound. In an environment where the incentive structure encouraged loyalty to the ruling party and discouraged the mobilization of social groups to advance one's career, organized labor lacked intra-elite allies willing to promote its demands. Although the regime sometimes extended

129. For a discussion of populist policies, see, for example, Steven E. Sanderson, "Presidential Succession and Political Rationality in Mexico," *World Politics* 35, no. 3 (1983): 315–34.

130. For a more extensive discussion of the way presidents were chosen, see, for example, Roderic Ai Camp, "Mexican Presidential Candidates: Changes and Prospects for the Future," *Polity* 16, no. 4 (1984): 588–605; Jorge G. Castaneda, *Perpetuating Power: How Mexican Presidents Are Chosen* (New York: New Press, 2000).

131. Sloan, "Mexican Variant of Corporatism," 14.

132. Kaufman Purcell, for example, estimates that up to forty-three thousand positions were filled by presidential appointment. As cited in Collier and Berins Collier, *Shaping the Political Arena*, 591.

133. Merilee S. Grindle, "Policy Change in an Authoritarian Regime: Mexico Under Echeverria," *Journal of Interamerican Studies and World Affairs* 19, no. 4 (1977): 527.

134. See, for example, Jorge Castaneda's discussion of the failed presidential candidacy of Silva Herzog, de la Madrid's minister of finance. Castaneda argues that what pushed Herzog out of competition was the fact that he began eclipsing the president in the media. Castaneda, *Perpetuating Power*, 64–67.

substantive concessions to labor, it refused to grant procedural concessions that could have affected the balance of power between the state and labor.

## Conclusion

In Egypt, the ruling elite never succeeded in turning the successive ruling parties into organizations that could provide mechanisms for containing, if not resolving, elite conflicts. In fact, rather than serving as a means of facilitating elite consensus, the successive ruling parties themselves became yet another faction involved in elite power struggles. This inability to create a viable party organization had profound consequences for both policy making and the ability of social actors to assert their independence from the state. Unlike in Mexico, where the PRI and the state worked in tandem, focusing on different activities but with an eye toward achieving a common goal, in Egypt the government and the dominant party were often at loggerheads. This resulted in cumbersome policy making, as the regime was often immobilized by internal disputes and unable to formulate a coherent program or implement decisions. At the same time, internal regime factionalism and conflict created opportunities for interest groups, including organized labor, to extract ever more concessions from the state.

The Mexican regime, by contrast, when it began its structural adjustment program, did not face a labor movement that was in a position to influence economic policy debates and decisions. The official labor movement remained firmly under PRI's control and was far more financially dependent on the state by the 1980s than it had been in the first years following the revolution. This unwavering control of the party over trade unions and the continuing coordination between the PRI and the state administration was the result of the PRI's ability to create an effective party organization. Unlike in Egypt, the PRI devised powerful incentives that put a premium on loyalty to the party and the state for politically ambitious individuals and thus was able to establish effective mechanisms for elite conflict resolution. The lack of elite factionalism meant that, unlike in Egypt, organized labor could not extract concessions by making alliances with competing elite groups. On the contrary, the elite cohesion resulted in an increasing subordination of the unions to the state.

The significantly different dynamics in the years preceding the beginning of economic restructuring meant that trade unions in Egypt and Mexico had different resources at their disposal as the transition to a market economy began.

As we will see in later chapters, these differing resources affected the ability of organized labor to shape economic reform policies. Egyptian organized labor, thanks to the legal prerogatives it had extracted from the regime, significant financial autonomy from the state, and long experience of successfully challenging state policies, was able to have significant input into the process of public sector restructuring both at the design and implementation phase. Mexican trade unions lacked these resources when the structural adjustment program began. Consequently, they found it very difficult to insert themselves into policy-making processes and were ineffective in shaping privatization strategies.

# 4 LABOR AND PRIVATIZATION IN POLAND

The Roundtable discussions that took place in 1989 between opposition forces and General Jaruzelski's Communist regime laid the foundation for a transition to democracy and market economy. Although the displacement of the Communist ruling elite was not the intended goal of the agreement, the first partially free elections made clear that Polish United Workers Party's (PZPR's) hold on power had crumbled. With the party unable to form a government, the responsibility for forming a coalition passed to the opposition.

The reform program adopted by the new government sought to stabilize the macroeconomic environment and to begin moving the country toward a market economy. Although initially the economy went into a deep recession, by 1992 growth resumed. By the end of the decade the Polish economy was one of the fastest growing in Europe, with an average rate of growth of 6.5 percent between 1995 and 1997 and 4.5 percent between 1998 and 1999, and Poland was seen as the most successful of Central European countries that had embarked on similar political and economic transitions in 1989. In 1999 Poland joined the North Atlantic Treaty Organization (NATO) and in 2004 entered the European Union, thus completing its international political realignment.

One of the central components of the economic reform program was the privatization of the vast public sector. As the first posttransition government began debating how best to design and implement the sale of state enterprises, organized labor emerged as one of the main participants in this debate. Over the following decade, organized labor succeeded in significantly shaping both the design and the implementation phase of the privatization program, drawing on the resources it had acquired during the previous decades. Legal prerogatives and long experience of successful confrontations with the state proved to be especially important in giving organized labor the tools to influence policy debates and the process of implementation. As we saw in Chapter 2, organized labor acquired those resources in the years prior to the 1989 political transition. Although the establishment of democracy meant that organized labor would now employ very different strategies in challenging government policies from those extant during the Communist era, the resources it acquired proved very durable. Despite the turmoil of the early posttransition years, organized labor continued to use them to shape policy debates.

## Organized Labor

The organized labor that emerged in Poland following the political transition was highly fragmented. The number of trade unions expanded after a new law was adopted in 1991 guaranteeing the right to form unions and removing them from state control. In addition, each enterprise had a workers' council. The two labor institutions were independent of each other, although they frequently cooperated. However, their rights and legal prerogatives differed. Trade unions were empowered by law to sign collective agreements and negotiate specific provisions of social pacts within enterprises, work conditions as well as layoffs. The new law maintained the right of unions to participate in national policy debates that they had won in the 1980s and they could present opinions to the government and parliament concerning issues that affected the rank and file.[1] The legal prerogatives of workers' councils, acquired in the pre-transition period, were concentrated at the enterprise level. Councils had the right to evaluate the annual enterprise development plan and its implementation and had oversight over all management activities and decisions. Most important, their voice was decisive in decisions concerning the hiring and dismissal of company directors.

Although there were more than two hundred independent unions, it was the two largest union federations, the OPZZ and Solidarity, that played the central role in Polish political and economic life during the first decade following the 1989 transition. The two were frequently in conflict, at least at the national

---

1. For a discussion of union prerogatives, see Janusz Michalski, *Restrukturyzacja i prywatyzacja: Pozycja i zadania związków zawodowych* (Poznań, Poland: Oficyna Wydawnicza Sami Sobie, 1997), especially 11–21.

Table 3    Membership in the largest Polish trade unions in 1993

| Union | Membership |
| --- | --- |
| OPZZ | 4 million |
| Solidarity | 1.7 million |

level, and pursued different strategies in confronting the changing political and economic environment. Each of the federations, and especially Solidarity, also frequently experienced internal tensions, which were most often the result of the divergent preferences of federation leadership and enterprise-level union activists.[2] The OPZZ, established in 1984 following the disbanding of Solidarity, was not opposed to the reform effort, but at the same time refused to champion economic restructuring. It fielded candidates in parliamentary elections and, after the 1993 contest, became part of the Social Democratic Left–Polish Peasant Party (SLD-PSL) governing coalition. However, unlike Solidarity, it chose not to play a prominent role in the government, remaining very much the junior partner within the political alliance. This allowed it to maintain a distance from the policies pursued by the government. Solidarity had a much more difficult time resolving issues of its identity in the first posttransition decade. The main point of tension within this union was whether the organization should function as a traditional trade union, become a political party, or be both. During the first decade of reforms (1989–99), three stages of different involvement can be discerned.

The first stage, lasting from 1989 to approximately 1991, was a period when the lines between its trade union and its political functions were to a large extent blurred. Although formally the union did not participate in government, many of its leaders and advisors did, and the union extended what became known as a "protective umbrella" over the reform effort. The second phase, lasting from approximately 1991 to 1993, saw Solidarity moving into opposition and openly criticizing the Solidarity-affiliated government. The shift in strategy was a direct response of Solidarity's trade union leadership to mounting tensions within the organization. As its social position began to weaken because of its close identification with the governing coalition and under pressure from its rank-and-file members, the union began focusing its activities on enterprise-level

---

2. See, for example, Włodzimierz Pańkow, "Funkcje związków zawodowych w zakładach pracy," in *Rozpad bastionu? Związki zawodowe w gospodarce prywatyzowanej*, by Juliusz Gardawski et al. (Warsaw: Instytut Spraw Publicznych, 1999).

issues and taking a more confrontational stance toward government policies. The third phase began with the reassertion of the post-Communist parties during the 1993 parliamentary elections. Shocked by the loss and believing that the political parties it had backed failed to pursue policies that reflected its goal and preferences, Solidarity moved to combine the functions of a trade union and a political party more explicitly. Rather than forming an alliance with a political party, it chose to establish its own, winning the 1997 parliamentary contest and forming a government.

## The 1989 Reform Program

Roundtable negotiations between the opposition and the PZPR were held in 1989. The agreement that came out of these talks provided for only a partial opening of the political process, with parliamentary elections scheduled for June that year not yet fully competitive. Although all seats in the newly created Senate were to be contested, in the more powerful lower house 65 percent of seats were reserved for the PZPR and its smaller satellites.

Solidarity swept the Senate, winning all but one seat (which went to an independent) and all 35 percent of the contested seats in the lower house. General Jaruzelski was elected president by the two chambers, thanks to Solidarity delegates voting for his candidacy in order to uphold the provisions of the Roundtable agreement. However, the PZPR's ability to govern quickly unraveled. General Kiszczak, one of the architects of martial law, was entrusted by Jaruzelski with forming a government. His efforts were unsuccessful and after discussions with Solidarity leader Lech Wałęsa, Tadeusz Mazowiecki, an independent opposition figure, was asked to head the new government.

Prime Minister Mazowiecki's primary concern as the new government took office was restoring macroeconomic stability. Accordingly, the initial plan presented to the Sejm in October 1989 argued that the first priority was to tackle inflation and the budget deficit and to resolve the issue of foreign debt.[3] The shock therapy program, designed by finance minister Leszek Balcerowicz, went into effect in January 1990 and entailed freeing most commodity prices; eliminating many subsidies; devaluing the currency, the zloty, and initiating

---

3. The proposal became known as the Balcerowicz plan after its main architect, minister of finance Leszek Balcerowicz. Ewa Łukawer, "Poglądy polskich ekonomistów na ogólne założenia tranformacji systemowej," *Ekonomista 6* (1994); Leszek Balcerowicz, "Albo szybko albo wcale," *Polityka,* no. 48, 1989.

its convertibility; adjusting interest rates; liberalizing trade policy; and clamping down on government spending and investment.[4]

Although the new government's main priority was to stabilize the macro-economic environment, it also assumed that the shock therapy program would have an immediate impact on the behavior of state firms. Increased market competition and stricter limits on public sector financing were expected to force state enterprises to behave more like private firms, eliminating inefficient ones that were not able to adjust to the new economic environment. These assumptions soon proved to be unwarranted and the industrial mammoths found ways of staying afloat, whether through not paying taxes or through running up intercompany debts they could not repay. This lack of expected response from the public sector pushed the issue of privatization to the top of the government's agenda.

The task of reforming the state industrial sector was enormous. At the time of the transition the state sector produced 80 percent of gross national product (GNP) and employed close to 90 percent of the workforce outside agriculture. Furthermore, the industrial sector was dominated by about three hundred large companies.[5] Already in October 1989 a special office, the Government Plenipotentiary for Ownership Transformation (Biuro Pełnomocnika Rządu do Przekształceń Własnościowych), with Krzysztof Lis as its director, was established and charged with preparing privatization legislation.

The government completed its proposal in the spring of 1990 and submitted it to the parliament for discussion. The program envisioned two main privatization strategies: capital privatization and privatization by liquidation. Capital privatization would entail first turning state firms into joint-stock companies, restructuring, valuating, and then selling them through auction and public offers. All joint-stock companies would have to be sold within two years and three months from the date of their registration as a joint-stock firm. Privatization through liquidation, by contrast, would involve the selling of all or part of the company assets or leasing them with the clause that the company would eventually be purchased by the lease. Although the government also envisioned a mass privatization program for the largest enterprises, how vouchers would

---

4. Simon Johnson and Marzena Kowalska, "Poland: The Political Economy of Shock Therapy," in *Voting for Reform: Democracy, Political Liberalization, and Economic Adjustment,* ed. Stephan Haggard and Steven B. Webb (New York: Oxford University Press for World Bank, 1994), 193.

5. Dennis Rondinelli and Jay Yurkiewicz, "Privatization and Economic Restructuring in Poland: An Assessment of Transition," *American Journal of Economics and Sociology* 55, no. 2 (1996): 146.

be distributed to adult citizens and how they would be managed was left for future consideration.

Finally, because the government was determined that the issue of internal enterprise control be resolved and, most important, the new private owners' decision making not be hampered, workers were not given an opportunity to participate in the design process of the enterprise privatization plan. While they would be eligible to purchase up to 20 percent of shares in their companies on a preferential basis, they and company managers had few avenues open to them to initiate privatization procedures. In the government proposal, the responsibility for initiating the privatization process rested with the state and the founding bodies of enterprises. Similarly, the parliament was to play a limited role during the public sector sell-off process, with oversight of the program resting with state agencies. In offering its proposal to the Sejm, moreover, the government took great care to distance itself from the political undertones of privatization and presented the process of state divestiture in the language of economic efficiency.[6]

Even before the government submitted its proposal to the Sejm, as more information began trickling out about the direction of cabinet discussions, there was growing public concern and criticism of the divestiture program. Labor organizations in particular were not pleased that companies in the government's proposal would be available to any investors with adequate capital while workers were limited to only 20 percent of shares. They also criticized the lack of provisions ensuring the participation of labor groups in the process.[7] In March, right before the parliamentary debate on the government's privatization program was to begin, the Workers Self-Management Conference came out with a strongly worded statement opposing the government's plan. The conference demanded that employees have a role in choosing privatization strategies at the enterprise level. It also warned that given the lack of worker support for the government proposal, it was likely to meet with stiff resistance.[8] Trade union and workers' council representatives who came to testify before the parliament in the first months of 1990 were equally critical. Many underscored that the Roundtable agreements required the government to consult

6. Barbara Błaszczyk, *Pierwsze lata prywatyzacji w Polsce (1989–1991): Dylematy, koncepcje i rywalizacja*, Studia Ekonomiczne, no. 30 (Warsaw: Polska Akademia Nauk, Instytut Nauk Ekonomicznych, 1993), 104–5. As Balcerowicz later conceded, this lack of attention to building political support for privatization was a miscalculation. Leszek Balcerowicz, *800 Dni: Szok kontrolowany* (Warsaw: Polska Oficyna Wydawnicza, "BGW," 1992), 91.

7. *Tygodnik Solidarność*, April 4, 1990.

8. *Stenogram Sejmowy*, April 5, 1990, 30.

with enterprise-level institutions, including unions and workers' councils, when making important decisions concerning socioeconomic policies.[9]

When the government's proposal arrived at the parliament for debate, almost simultaneously, a group of twenty-three deputies submitted a rival proposal, heavily influenced by the ideas of the worker self-management movement. In the course of the following few months, the parliament witnessed an acrimonious debate concerning the privatization program. The approved project that emerged from the Sejm differed markedly from the one originally envisioned by the government and included numerous provisions that the trade union and worker self-management movement saw as indispensable to the program. The debate over the design of the privatization program revealed the importance of the legal prerogatives that workers had acquired in the years prior to the 1989 transition as well as organized labor's experience at successfully confronting the state.

## Labor and the Design Process of the Privatization Program

In the late 1980s the powers of the workers' councils significantly increased and were enshrined in the Roundtable agreement. Thus, the legal prerogatives acquired before the Mazowiecki government launched economic reforms allowed the councils to play a significant role during the design and implementation process of privatization. The councils were independent from trade unions, although following the 1989 transition Solidarity frequently controlled them. The councils in turn controlled the management. The control that the councils and trade unions held over enterprises solidified the opinion among workers that the enterprises belonged to the employees. Hence, workers assumed that privatization meant that formal ownership rights would be transferred directly to them or that at the very least they should have a decisive say in the design and implementation of restructuring.[10] These perceptions of workers were not unreasonable in view of the very ambiguous structure of ownership of state firms and were further reinforced by the treatment of the issue of privatization during the Roundtable talks in 1989. Although this was not a central

---

9. See, for example, the transcript of the meeting of the Budget and Finance Committee, January 4–5, 1990, when a number of labor representatives testified concerning their views of the economic reform program. *Kancelaria Sejmu, Biuletyn, BPS/212, X Kadencja.*

10. Maria Jarosz, "Spółki pracownicze w procesie transformacji własności," in *Transformacja gospodarki: Spojrzenie retrospektywne,* ed. Witold Jakóbik (Warsaw: Instytut Studiów Politycznych Polskiej Akademii Nauk i Fundacja im. Friedricha Eberta, 1997), 179–81.

theme of the negotiations, when the issue did come up it was mostly within the context of strengthening worker self-management of enterprises.[11]

These perceptions of workers came into direct conflict with the privatization program as proposed by the Balcerowicz team, which felt that the most dangerous strategy for Poland to pursue was to choose a "third way"—developing a model that would chart a new course between capitalism and socialism. The team was particularly suspicious of workers' ownership, which it saw as inferior to alternative methods of privatization. As Balcerowicz argued during his confirmation hearings in 1989, "Our plan is to introduce a western-style market economy. All research and analysis indicates that in such a system there is no place for worker self-management in enterprises, that self-management solutions cannot be effective. In a Western-style market economy there simply is no place for self-management."[12]

These differing views were reflected in the parliamentary debate over the design of the privatization program. The government side argued that the public enterprise sector was state property and hence the state, as the legal owner, had the right to privatize these companies as it saw fit. The worker self-management side argued that within the existing legal framework, the state's ownership of the public sector was far from clear and indisputable and that, in fact, workers' councils could make an equally strong claim to having property rights within these enterprises. Furthermore, this latter group argued that it was only through preferential treatment of workers in the context of privatization that a broader social support for public sector reform could be secured. The project anticipated the existence of a greater variety of privatization methods, put bigger emphasis on the employee buyout schemes, accepted the possibility of collective ownership, and more broadly argued for greater social control of the process.[13]

The parliamentary proposal reflected these labor views and was highly critical of the top-down nature of the government project. The lack of social participation in the process, argued the deputies who were putting forth the alternative public sector restructuring program, would have detrimental consequences for the successful implementation of privatization. In their view,

11. *Życie Gospodarcze*, no. 8, 1989.

12. Balcerowicz's statement before Sejm committee during his confirmation hearings. *Biuletyn nr. 41/X Kadencja, Komisja Polityki Gospodarczej, Budżetu i Finansów, Kancelaria Sejmu*, September 8, 1989, 5–6.

13. Maciej Bałtowski, *Prywatyzacja przedsiębiorstw państwowych: Przebieg i ocena* (Warsaw: PWN, SA, 1998), 155.

privatization was an inherently political process with profound social as well as economic consequences. Its goal was not just the creation of more efficient enterprises but also encouraging citizen participation in the economy. Such participation, in turn, was essential if public support for the reforms was to be maintained.[14]

Both projects ended up in the Special Committee of the Sejm, which was charged with reconciling the two proposals. During the ensuing sessions the main points of contention were who would have the overall responsibility for the program's implementation, who would have the right to initiate privatization procedures, how workers were to be compensated within the overall framework of privatization, and how workers would be represented both during and following the sale of their companies.

The final version of the privatization program represented a major victory for the worker self-management activists, who were the driving force behind the parliamentary proposal, and was the first clear indication of how the resources that organized labor had acquired prior to the transition would continue to shape state-labor interactions during the implementation of market reforms. Initiative for commencing privatization procedures would not be the sole prerogative of state agencies, as the government wanted. Rather, enterprise-level institutions, and specifically the directors and workers' councils, would be able to initiate restructuring and privatization procedures and to decide on the privatization path for their enterprise. In cases in which the company itself initiated privatization, this had to be a joint decision between the management and the councils. Only with the transformation of the firm into a joint-stock company would the workers' council cease functioning and workers would instead have representation on the board of supervisors, electing one-third of its membership. In cases in which the privatization initiative came from the state, the workers' council and the management of the company had to agree to begin restructuring procedures. Without the approval of the council, the sale of the company could not move forward.[15] Finally, workers were eligible to purchase 20 percent of company stock on a preferential basis. On the issue of oversight over the privatization process, a compromise was reached. A ministry of privatization was to be established and charged with the privatization program's implementation. The government was required to present, on an annual basis,

14. Błaszczyk, *Pierwsze lata prywatyzacji w Polsce*, 49–52.

15. For a useful diagram of the steps required for the completion of privatization procedures at a company, see Stanislawa Gomulka and Piotr Jasinski, *Privatization in Poland: 1989–1993: Policies,*

a privatization plan that would then be reviewed, modified, and approved by the parliament.

The legislation adopted by the parliament envisioned privatization proceeding along a variety of paths. The two main methods were capital privatization and privatization through liquidation. These two methods were to apply to medium-size and large companies. There were also special provisions for a quick sell-off of small firms and workshops. Although different privatization methods could be employed, the Privatization Act clearly designated capital privatization as the preferred method of divestiture.

The issue of mass privatization, which was also under discussion, was left unresolved. The opinions on the program were deeply divided. The government was skeptical about the wisdom of distributing privatization coupons free of charge. Many deputies, however, argued that to ensure a socially just and politically sustainable privatization program, citizens should have the right to acquire shares at no cost. The act stipulated only that the Sejm was to eventually adopt legislation that would clarify how coupons were to be distributed and managed. The final version of the privatization legislation was adopted by the Sejm on July 13, 1990, and went into effect on August 1, 1990.[16] Within little more than a month the first seven public enterprises were commercialized under the new law. The Ministry of Privatization was created in July as well and was charged with designing and facilitating the privatization process. It was not until April 1993, however, that the mass privatization program was adopted as the National Investment Funds Privatization Law. The funds themselves were created in December 1994 but the distribution of coupons did not begin until November 1995.

## Labor and Implementation of the Privatization Program: The First Years of Reform

Critics of the privatization plan were worried that the sales process would quickly run into problems. Many were especially concerned that the so-called

---

*Methods, and Results* (Warsaw: Polska Akademia Nauk, Instytut Nauk Ekonomicznych, 1994), 25, 28. As one privatization ministry official commented, "Privatization did not so much entail getting the state out of enterprises but rather getting worker self-management out of them." Author interview with Tomasz Stankiewicz, deputy minister of privatization in the Olszewski government and former Solidarity advisor, Warsaw, April 27, 1999.

16. The law envisioned three methods of privatization: capital privatization, mass privatization, and employee buyouts. The first of these was designated the preferred way.

Bermuda Triangle, the alliance of unions, workers' councils, and directors of state companies, would block any attempts to restructure and privatize their firms.[17] However, these fears proved largely unfounded during the first couple of years of reform. Both trade unions and workers' councils did little to block restructuring of the enterprises and in many cases were active promoters of these changes. During the first phase of reforms, Solidarity extended what has often been referred to as a "protective umbrella" over the reforms.[18] In addition to containing strike activities, the union became one of the more active promoters of enterprise restructuring. The OPZZ also expressed support for reforms. Workers' councils, by contrast, although they seldom initiated restructuring procedures on their own, rarely opposed them and most often worked with management to promote enterprise restructuring.[19] In many cases they also began dismissing management, not because they were proceeding with privatization, but because they were not undertaking the restructuring of firms energetically enough.[20] In fact, where restructuring was being blocked, it was as likely to be blocked by management as by the workers.

Thus, far from the image in the popular media of unions putting roadblocks in the path of privatization, in many enterprises during the first year of reforms, the opposite was the case.[21] Thanks to their legal prerogatives, workers' councils in public sector enterprises had the power to shape the process of enterprise restructuring. The councils could, for example, vote against privatization and thereby drag the process out. This is indeed what took place in some firms where workers' councils refused to give approval to privatization proposals.[22]

17. See Wojciech Bienkowski, "The Bermuda Triangle: Why Self-Governed Firms Work for Their Own Destruction," *Journal of Comparative Economics* 16, no. 4 (1992): 750–62; David Lipton, Jeffrey Sachs, and Lawrence H. Summers, "Privatization in Eastern Europe: The Case of Poland," *Brookings Papers on Economic Activity* 21, no. 2 (1990): 293–341.

18. It is important to underscore that not all agreed with this union position. Ewa Tomaszewska, a onetime Solidarity MP points out that there were profound disagreements within the union about extending such an umbrella over the government, since many within the union were concerned about the social impact of the policies proposed by Balcerowicz. Author interview with Ewa Tomaszewska, Warsaw, June 28, 1999.

19. See Jerzy Wratny, *Prawne i ekonomiczne aspekty reprezentacji interesów pracowniczych w przesiębiorstwach prywatyzowanych: Raport z badań* (Warsaw: Instytut Pracy i Spraw Społecznych / Fundacja Friedricha Eberta, 1995), especially 18–20.

20. Janusz Dąbrowski, *Przedsiębiorstwa państwowe w roku 1990—wyniki badan* (Warsaw: Instytut Badań nad Gospodarką Rynkową i Prawami Własnościowymi, 1991).

21. Włodzimierz Pańkow, "Funkcje związków zawodowych w Polsce" (conference paper, Łódź, February 1999).

22. Mario Nuti, "Privatization of Socialist Economies: General Issues and the Polish Case," in *Transformation of Planned Economies: Property Rights Reform and Macroeconomic Stability*, ed. Hans Blomnen-Stein and Michael Marrese (Paris: OECD, 1991), 51–68.

However, during the first years of reform approval of such proposals was a more common outcome.[23] For example, at the Szczecin shipyard the management, unions, and workers' council came up with a rescue package for the firm that involved selling off unproductive assets, making new capital investments, streamlining the production process, and aggressively pursing new contracts. In exchange for 20 percent of the firms' shares the unions agreed to the reorganization of the production process, changes in pay schedules, and some initial layoffs. The workers' council voted to approve the restructuring package. In 1993 the shipyard was privatized and became a successful firm, now looking to further expand its production and searching for new investment opportunities.[24] By comparison, at the FSO car factory in Warsaw, the Solidarity trade union took an active role in looking for a foreign buyer and in convincing the workers' council to abandon its plans to adopt an employee buyout scheme.[25]

One of the consequences of the modifications that were made to the original government privatization proposal and one that was neither anticipated nor desired by the government was the large number of employee buyouts that took place. In fact, in the first few years of the economic reform program, this was the most popular mode of privatization. In most cases, employees felt that the firm's takeover by "insiders" was the best way to guarantee stability and security within the enterprise. An additional incentive for change was that once a company no longer was a state-owned entity, the much despised excess wage tax (*popiwek*) would no longer be levied on its workers. Here again, far from blocking restructuring, the workers' councils and unions were actively engaged in the process of privatization. In a study of twelve enterprises, for example, Kamiński found that in eight of them management and workers joined forces to take over the firm.[26] While some studies of this particular method of privatization indicate that managers have benefited from such restructuring to a much greater extent than have workers, nonetheless, employees were eager to

23. As the enthusiasm for privatization cooled, the councils did indeed begin to use their legal prerogatives to block sales of their companies.

24. For a discussion of the Szczecin shipyard privatization, see *Życie Gospodarcze,* March 12, 1995.

25. Author interviews with Jerzy Woźniak, head of FSO Solidarity, Warsaw, Spring 1999, and Alfred Konowrocki, director of the National Solidarity Union of Automobile Industries, Warsaw, April 22, 1999. For more information about the position taken by the unions at FSO during the first discussions about privatization of their company, see *Gazeta Samorządowa,* June 17, 1990; *Tygodnik Solidarność,* June 29, 1990; *Gazeta Wyborcza,* November 19, 1990.

26. Tytus Kamiński, "Zaniechanie prywatyzacji: Bariery i konsekwencje," *Transformacja Gospodarki* 86 (1997).

Table 4    Methods of privatization in Poland

| Privatization method | 1990 (number of companies) | 1991 | 1992 |
|---|---|---|---|
| Capital | 6 | 24 | 22 |
| Liquidation | 44 | 372 | 249 |

SOURCE: Data from Michał Federowicz, "Geneza i formy prywatyzacji," in *Stosunki przemysłowe w Polsce: Studium czterech przypadków,* ed. Michał Federowicz, Wiesława Kozek, and Witold Morawski (Warsaw: Instytut Socjologii Uniwersytetu Warszawskiego, 1995), 26.

support this form of sales.[27] Enterprise-level labor organizations, drawing on resources acquired prior to the transition and especially the legal prerogatives of workers' councils and the extensive historical experience of successfully confronting the state, thus significantly shaped privatization strategies. Their preference for employee buyout schemes meant that the original vision set out by the government, which anticipated capital privatization and direct acquisition of companies by strategic investors, was substantially modified.

## Labor and the Implementation of the Privatization Program: Support Dissipates

Initially, relations between management and trade unions were mostly harmonious. Industrial conflicts did, of course, occur, but these were overwhelmingly concerned with wage issues and were not aimed at derailing privatization efforts.[28] The number of strikes fell. While there were 900 strikes in 1989, there were only 250 in 1990 and 305 in 1991.[29] Nonetheless, the initiation of the reform

27. For more detailed studies of the Polish experience with employee buyouts, see Leszek Gilejko, ed., *Własność pracownicza w Polsce,* Monografie i Opracowania 436 (Warsaw: Szkoła Główna Handlowa, 1998); Leszek Gilejko, ed., *Partycypacja i akcjonariat pracowniczy w Polsce* (Warsaw: Zakład Badań Przekształceń Własnościowych, Instytut Studiów Politycznych PAN, 1995); Leszek Gilejko, Czesława Kliszko, and Rafał Towalski, *Akcjonariat pracowniczy a zbiorowe stosunki pracy* (Warsaw: Szkoła Główna Handlowa, 1997); Maria Jarosz, ed., *Blaski i cienie spółek pracowniczych, 1991–1994* (Warsaw: Instytut Studiów Politycznych Polskiej Akademii Nauk, 1995); Maria Jarosz, ed., *Spółki pracownicze '95* (Warsaw: Instytut Studiów Politycznych Polskiej Akademii Nauk, 1996).

28. For an analysis of the issues that led to industrial conflicts during the first years of reform, see Kazimierz Kloc, "Konflikty przemysłowe: Dynamika zjawiska, 1990–1992," *Przegląd Społeczny,* no. 2 (1997); Kazimierz Kloc and Władysław Rychłowski, "Spory zbiorowe i strajki w przemyśle," *Przegląd Społeczny,* no. 18–19, 1993, 5–42.

29. Główny Urząd Statystyczny, *Rocznik Statystyczny 1994* (Warsaw: GUS, 1994).

program created a dilemma for trade union organizations. On the one hand, there was widespread realization among union leaders and the rank and file that major restructuring of the economy was inevitable to curtail hyper-inflation and resume growth. Indeed, most surveys conducted at the time indicated that support for market reforms was widespread not just among the union leadership but among workers in general.[30] Although few workers embraced privatization without reservations, the majority did not oppose it. Studies conducted in the early 1990s show that only about 22 percent of workers believed that all public enterprises should remain state property.[31]

Nonetheless, even at the beginning of the reforms workers expressed concerns about the potential consequences of restructuring measures. They were especially worried about unemployment. Already in the first months of 1991, 38 percent of workers in industrial enterprises expressed fears about finding themselves out of work, 78.2 percent admitted that they did not have enough savings in case of unemployment, and 55 percent were worried that their standard of living was plummeting.[32] These concerns were reflected in the gradual decline of their support for the privatization program. As one survey of workers' attitudes noted, the increasing support for maintaining state ownership in some sectors could be attributed to the fact that "privatization causes employees to become more anxious about potential shutting down of companies and their decreasing influence on managing enterprises. Within state companies the prospect of losing a sense of self is seen as the greatest threat. . . . Also in firms that have been privatized employees are worried about the prospect of being treated as property of the new owners."[33] With support for the reforms plummeting, enterprise-level unions and workers' councils were no longer as willing to approve privatization plans for their companies. The problem became especially acute at large industrial firms.

The changing attitudes among workers presented a problem for Solidarity. Although it was still willing to support the government despite the growing disillusionment with market reforms among its rank and file, differences began emerging between the union and the government concerning the length of time that economic recovery would take. Balcerowicz anticipated that the

30. See Juliusz Gardawski, *Poland's Industrial Workers on the Return to Democracy and Market Economy* (Warsaw: Friedrich Ebert Stiftung, 1996), 39–71.

31. Juliusz Gardawski and Tomasz Żukowski, *Robotnicy 1993—wybory ekonomiczne i polityczne* (Warsaw: Fundacja im. Friedricha Eberta w Polsce, 1994), 25.

32. Witold Wiadera, *Robotnicy i liderzy związkowi* (Warsaw: Szkoła Główna Handlowa, 1992), 14.

33. Maria Jarosz, *Spòłki pracownicze* (Warsaw: Instytut Studiów Politycznyck PAN, 1994), 8.

drop in production and wages would be reversed by March 1990. Although many observers of the Polish reform program thought that this target date was unrealistic, nonetheless Solidarity viewed this as an important government commitment and expected noticeable improvement in the economic and social situation. When the date came and went and the deterioration in economic indicators continued, Solidarity's initial support of the government began to weaken and the union decided to adopt a more confrontational stance.[34]

The decision to move away from supporting government policies was also a reflection of growing tensions and rifts within the Solidarity union. In many sectors, workers, concerned with their deteriorating living standards and precarious job security, broke away from the national union federations and began seeking separate deals with the government. In particular, miners, steelworkers, and railroad employees began direct discussions with the government to ensure wage and pension benefits. Solidarity, increasingly identified with unpopular government policies, started to lose members, who sought better representation within the OPZZ or broke away to form new unions, such as Solidarity 80.[35] In other words, the continuing economic recession and the resulting changes in workers' attitudes gradually led to a shift in the strategies of union federations concerning their response to public sector restructuring measures. The willingness of the trade union leadership, at both the national and the enterprise level, to support enterprise restructuring meant that the goals they pursued began to be at variance with the interests of the workers they represented. As the number of strikes grew to 6,351 in 1992 and 7,443 in 1993, enterprise-level union leadership increasingly found itself unable to mediate between the often contradictory goals of pushing for firm restructuring and privatization and satisfying the rank and file's desire for better wages and job security. In order not to lose its support the union could no longer afford to give a blanket approval to the government reform program.[36]

With worker support for privatization dissipating, the pace of sales of state firms slowed noticeably. The problem was particularly acute among the two hundred industrial giants that formed the core of the Sieć network. Most of

34. Kazimierz Kloc, "Trade Unions and Economic Transformation in Poland," *Journal of Communist Studies* 9, no. 4 (1993): 125–32.

35. Members of Solidarity 80 argue that Solidarity has abandoned its heritage of the 1980–81 struggle and that, having become essentially a political party, it is no longer capable of representing workers as a trade union. Author interview with Andrzej Basista, member of Solidarity 80 Steering Committee, Warsaw, May 27, 1999.

36. See Maria Hirszowicz and Andre Mailer, "Trade Unions as an Active Factor in Economic Transformation," *Polish Sociological Review* 13, no. 115 (1996): 221–24.

these remained largely untouched by privatization. In a growing number of firms, differences began to emerge between management and labor organizations. At some, management whose job security was dependent on workers' councils were reluctant to push through far-reaching restructuring programs that would inevitably entail layoffs.[37] At others, management and unions clashed over issues of control and wages, pushing discussions concerning restructuring and privatization onto the back burner.[38] In more firms, workers' councils began using their prerogatives to decelerate the pace of sales. Furthermore, the perception of workers that either initiating or accepting privatization proposals for their companies would result in improved wage levels, both because *popiwek* would no longer be levied and because private companies were thought to remunerate their employees more generously, began changing. Contrary to expectations, wages in commercialized firms were not higher than in public companies, nor were working conditions perceived as better.[39] Workers, having demonstrated their capacity to modify the privatization program's design and their ability to support privatization in the early years, soon demonstrated their power to block public sector restructuring as promised benefits failed to materialize. The legal prerogatives and experience labor had acquired prior to the 1989 transition once again shaped its capacity to influence economic restructuring policies. Within a couple of years, therefore, the government's privatization program ran into problems at the implementation level.[40]

## Second Round of Government Privatization Proposals

Workers' changing attitudes toward reforms in general and privatization in particular pushed the government to rethink its public sector restructuring strategies. Most important, the government recognized that since abrogating

37. For a case study of such company dynamics, see Wiesława Kozek, "Przedsiębiorstwo państwowe S—stosunki przemysłowe w okresie wyprowadzania koncepcji prywatyzacyjnych," in Michał Federowicz, Wiesława Kozek, and Witold Morawski, *Stosunki przemysłowe w Polsce: Stadium czterech przypadków* (Warsaw: Instytut Socjologii Uniwersytetu Warszawskiego, 1995), 98–126.

38. For case studies of such company dynamics, see Michał Federowicz, "Przedsiębiorstwo państwowe B—stosunki przemysłowe w warunkach kontraktu menagerskiego," in Federowicz, Kozek, and Morawski, *Stosunki przemysłowe*, 127–50; Paweł Gieorgica, "Polska Miedź: Holding pod związkową presją," in *Społeczni aktorzy restrukturyzacji* (Warsaw: Centrum Partnerstwa Społecznego "Dialog," 1997), 98–121.

39. Mark Kramer, "Polish Workers and the Post-communist Transition, 1989–93," *Europe-Asia Studies* 47, no. 4 (1995): 89.

40. Witold Gadomski, *Instytucjonalne bariery rozwoju gospodarczego* (Warsaw: Centrum im. Adama Smitha, 1996), 23–25.

the legal prerogatives of the workers' council would be too difficult and politically costly, new incentives would have to be put in place to convince workers to resume their support for the program and not heed the increasingly vitriolic antiprivatization language emanating from some political quarters.[41]

In July 1992, minister of labor Jacek Kuroń initiated negotiations between the government and labor unions. The negotiations were to culminate with the signing of the State Enterprise Pact. The government sought to achieve a number of goals. Among the most important were accelerating the pace of restructuring and privatization, finding means for resolving the precarious financial condition of state-owned firms, guaranteeing broader participation of the employees in the process of choosing the restructuring methods, and creating modern mechanisms for providing social insurance for dislocated workers.[42] As Minister Kuroń put it, underscoring the social goals of the pact, "I want to end with bureaucratic mode of privatization. It is workers who should decide how the enterprise is to be restructured."[43]

The government approached the negotiations with a clear bargaining offer. Workers would be given shares in privatized companies free of charge in exchange for agreeing to a faster pace of state enterprise sales. The government also promised to place primary responsibility for drawing up plans for privatization in the hands of workers' councils and company management. However, since the goal was to quicken the pace of sales, the enterprise-level institutions had six months to finalize such plans. If the councils and management could not agree on a plan, the state would take over control of the firm. To further encourage worker support, the government also extended guarantees that workers would be allowed to place more representatives on the boards of supervisors and agreed to ease the financial requirements for company leasing. The government also proposed revising the system of collective bargaining and to set up a special fund to finance employee benefits in cases in which employers were unable to meet such financial obligations.[44]

---

41. For example, Jan Olszewski, the former prime minister, argued that "the invisible hand of the market turned out to be a hand of the crook" and warned that levels of malnutrition among Polish children were comparable to those during Hitler's occupation. *Wprost*, May 15, 1994.

42. For a discussion of these goals, see the text by Andrzej Baczkowski (deputy minister of labor and one of the main pact negotiators), "Pakt o przedsiębiorstwie i partycypacja i akcjonariat pracowniczy," in *Partycypacja i akcjonariat pracowniczy w Polsce,* ed. Leszek Gilejko (Warsaw: Zakład Badań Przekształceń Własnościowych Instytut Studiów Politycznych PAN/Instytut Gospodarstwa Społecznego i Katedra Socjologii, SGH, 1995), 131–44.

43. Jacek Kuroń and Jacek Żakowski, *Siedmiolatka czyli kto ukradł Polskę?* (Wrocław, Poland: Wydawnictwo Dolnośląskie, 1997), 89.

44. Baczkowski, "Pakt o przedsiębiorstwie," 190.

Ironically, the negotiations over the pact led to not the speeding up but a slowdown in the pace of privatizations as employees, hoping that a better deal could be negotiated in the end, took a wait-and-see attitude and refused to adopt restructuring plans for their companies. The negotiations themselves soon stalled. Before the final version of the pact could be signed, the government collapsed after a Solidarity-orchestrated vote of no confidence in the parliament. New parliamentary elections were called and in the fall of 1993 the Solidarity-affiliated parties were defeated by the reformed Communists, the SLD.

Negotiations over a new privatization framework did not resume until spring 1994, when minister of finance Grzegorz Kołodko proposed a new plan, called Strategy for Poland, which envisioned an extensive program of commercialization of four thousand state-owned enterprises.[45] While this particular project never went beyond the drawing board, it signaled the beginning of a new effort to rethink methods and strategies of the privatization program. As the government was considering a new privatization strategy, unions were pushing for the inclusion in any new law of the privileges they had won during the negotiations over the Enterprise Pact. Trade union deputies in the parliament were equally busy preparing legislation proposals.[46] The new government measures clearly resembled many of those first suggested by the previous government during the initial round of talks over the content of the Enterprise Pact. Nonetheless, a number of modifications were made in terms of incentives offered to workers to support enterprise restructuring, modifications that some within the opposition thought were excessive. As one commentator observed, "The proposed legislation, while substantially increasing workers' privileges, deepens the inequitable and unfair treatment of different groups of Polish citizens."[47]

The new legislative framework for privatization was finally adopted by the parliament on August 30, 1996, as the Commercialization and Privatization Act; because significant administrative changes were simultaneously taking place, the new legislation did not go into effect until the end of October 1996. In the final version, after some modifications were made in April 1997, the process of privatization and worker participation changed significantly and expanded the historically acquired legal prerogatives. The new law substantially increased the ability of enterprise-level institutions, among them workers' councils, to initiate commercialization and privatization procedures. In particular,

45. Bałtowski, *Prywatyzacja przedsiębiorstw państwowych*, 192–93.
46. For OPZZ's activities in the parliament, see *Zespół posłów i senatorów związkowych w parlamencie RP, 1993–1997* (Warsaw: SLD/OPZZ, 1997), 5–10.
47. *Rzeczpospolita*, June 20, 1995.

the appropriate ministries no longer could reject privatization and restructuring plans proposed by the enterprise. Only in cases in which the plan involved commercialization whose goal was other than privatization could the Council of Ministers reject a proposal.[48] The new law also expanded workers' ability to acquire company shares. According to previous legislation, they could purchase up to 20 percent of shares on a preferential basis. Workers were now entitled to 15 percent of stock at no cost. The law also expanded workers' representation on the supervisory boards of companies from one-third to two-fifths. At the same time, the Tripartite Commission was created as a permanent forum for negotiations on wage increases between the government, trade unions, and representatives of employers. Although the commission was not always successful in fashioning a consensus between the parties, the next couple of years witnessed a decline in the number of industrial disputes. In 1995 the number of strikes dropped to forty-two. In 1996, there were only twenty-one, and in 1997, thirty-five.[49] Contrary to the government's expectations, the new law did not accelerate the pace of sales. Neither did the new law make the process of public sector restructuring any less contentious. The problem was especially acute in heavy industry, where not only had few privatizations taken place but even the restructuring process was moving more slowly than the government expected.

## Labor and Privatization: Contesting Implementation

The ability of labor organizations to influence the implementation of privatization is well illustrated by how this process unfolded in heavy industry. The sector, pampered under the pre-transition regime, was dominated by large enterprises, each employing thousands of workers. In this sector, not only were workers able to use the legal prerogative acquired prior to 1989 that gave them the ability to shape restructuring at the enterprise level but they also drew on the long experience of successfully challenging the state and state policies in the past. Because the highly unionized workforce in these sectors and their high concentration in particular regions, especially Silesia, formed the electoral base of both major political blocks, they were that much more effective in their use of the available resources. Neither the Solidarity-affiliated nor post-Communist

48. Tomasz Stankiewicz, *Akcjonariat pracowniczy w polskiej prywatyzacji kapitałowej* (Warsaw: Centrum Prywatyzacji Biznes i Finanse, 1997), 34.

49. Główny Urząd Statystyczny, *Rocznik Statystyczny, 1998* (CD-ROM).

governments were willing to pay the political price of not being responsive to workers' demands in these sectors. These challenges were particularly intense in the coal-mining and steel industries.

In 1989 there were seventy-two coal mines in Poland, employing six hundred thousand people. Restructuring of the industry began in 1990. In the first phase, coal mines became financially and organizationally autonomous from the state. This move, however, did little to induce the sector to begin adjusting to market conditions and the financial hemorrhaging continued. While the management of coal mines was now given a freer hand in running the companies, they were still constrained by the legal prerogatives of the workers' councils. Concerned about maintaining their positions, managers were not eager to confront the councils and streamline mine operations. Unions within the sector were equally uninterested in belt-tightening measures and, unlike in some other sectors, did little to promote enterprise restructuring.

By fall 1992 the tensions between the government and unions in the mining sector had grown. The government of Hanna Suchocka, increasingly concerned about the slow pace of sales, wanted to see a new agreement reached between unions and the government. As the negotiations over the Enterprise Pact were in progress, however, coal-mining unions made new demands for wage increases and a slowdown in implementation of the mine restructuring program. In December 1992, they staged a three-week strike, with sixty-five mines participating. A compromise agreement reached between the two sides included some financial incentives but no changes in the restructuring plan. Although union leadership had signed the agreement, it met with opposition among the rank and file, concerned about the prospect of mass layoffs. A new wave of strikes swept the sector, and when the government stood its ground and refused to consider new demands, Solidarity made good on its threat of a no confidence vote in the parliament, bringing down Prime Minister's Suchocka's cabinet.[50]

Over the following seven years, successive governments proposed four more restructuring plans. Despite these proposals, little restructuring took place and the financial condition of the mining sector deteriorated. Although by 1997 thirty thousand workers left the sector, thanks to an early retirement package negotiated between the government and trade unions, wages in the sector continued to increase while productivity remained stagnant. Moreover, a report by the High Controller's Office found that the money allocated from the budget and earmarked for preparing mine closings in 1995–96 were in fact used to

50. Kramer, "Polish Workers," 20.

increase production.[51] In January 1999, ten years after the reform program began, twelve coal mining unions still had not accepted the new restructuring program. Others accepted it but with conditions.

Successive governments found it difficult to resist the demands of the coal-mining unions. Furthermore, over time the various restructuring plans proposed by the government contributed to the radicalization of coal-mining unions and relations between organized labor and governments became increasingly contentious. One reason for this radicalization was the proliferation of unions within the industry, with twenty-six independent labor organizations registered and six hundred people employed full time as union officials. While some unions, like Solidarity, remained relatively moderate, the competition from new organizations that presented bigger demands created pressure on the more established unions to also up the ante to maintain support among the workforce and avoid losing members.[52] Criticism leveled at the government program by trade unionists not opposed to changes within the sector revolved around the lack of any coherent industrial development plan for the coal-mining region.

The government recognized that without approval from the unions, there was little hope of pushing through restructuring. As deputy minister of economy Jan Szlązak remarked, "In coal mining it will be impossible to do anything without social permission."[53] That such permission was not forthcoming was illustrated in a comment made by Daniel Podrzycki, leader of Solidarity 80, during a demonstration in Katowice protesting the new program: "The government restructuring program is coming apart. There is not enough money for social support packages. The proposal to close down mines is absurd. In other words, this program needs to be changed."[54]

Ten coal-mining unions decided to take the restructuring program to the Constitutional Tribunal, arguing that the provision that wages would be frozen

51. *Rzeczpospolita*, March 5, 1997.
52. Author interviews with Adrian Cybula, sociologist at the University of Silesia who studies coal-mining unions, Warsaw, February 4 and April 22, 1999. See also *Polityka*, January 2, 1999. In fact, many Solidarity activists were criticized for being supportive of the government program. As a Solidarity leader in one mine complained, "We Solidarity are often criticized by other unions for being so permissive towards the government. People from the left-wing unions argue that once again we are extending a protective umbrella over the government. But it's necessary to underscore that reform needs to be implemented . . . of course in such a way that workers do not get hurt. The left-wing unions were in power and didn't do anything. And now all they know how to do is to demonstrate." Interview with Mirosław Malinowski, head of Solidarity at the Makoszowy coal mine, *Nowe Państwo*, January 8, 1999, 19.
53. *Polityka*, January 23, 1999.
54. *Trybuna Śląska*, February 11, 1999.

for four years, during which restructuring would proceed, violated the constitution's nondiscrimination provisions. At the same time, unions initiated occupational strikes in a number of mines and organized demonstrations, primarily in Katowice. The striking workers demanded that the plans for closing down coal mines be scrapped, wages be increased, and special pension benefits be maintained.[55] In response, the government signed an agreement with the strikers that included a provision for setting up a steering committee to coordinate the processes of restructuring and stating that every three months government officials and representatives of unions would meet in Warsaw to discuss any issues arising from the program's implementation. The government also agreed to allocate an additional Zł400 million to help maintain the special pension provisions. The government hoped that the social support packages offered to workers who were willing to leave would eventually generate support among them for the restructuring plan. However, while in 1998, twenty-five thousand workers took the package and left the industry, the 1999 budget allocated funds that covered such packages for only seven thousand workers. Once again, the restructuring plan proved unworkable and the state treasury began designing yet another privatization program for the sector in 2000.[56] Thus, during the first decade of reforms, the progress in restructuring and privatizing the coal-mining sector was slow and the government did not meet its programmatic targets. Although organized labor was not the sole reason for this lackluster experience, its opposition to the program made implementation all the more difficult and protracted.

Like coal mining, the steel industry was one of the most important sectors of the Polish economy prior to the 1989 transition. And like coal mining, this sector proved difficult to restructure. In 1990 the sector encompassed forty-seven firms and employed 136,000 people, with 65.3 percent employed in the eight largest steel mills, located primarily in the Silesia region.[57] During the first years of reform little attention was paid to steel sector restructuring, but by the end of 1991, with domestic demand down and a lack of profitable export possibilities,

---

55. Rumors that as many as thirty mines would shortly be closed down were rampant. Many unionists demanded that no mine should be shut down unless it could be demonstrated that it would never be able to become a profitable enterprise. See, for example, *Dziennik Zachodni*, January 6, 1999.

56. *Ocena przebiegu prywatyzacji majątku Skarbu Państwa w 2000 roku* (Warsaw: Ministerstwo Skarbu Państwa, April 2001), 13.

57. Jan Macieja, "Restrukturyzacja hutnictwa żelaza i stali," in *Studia nad restrukturyzacją sektorów przemysłowych w Polsce: Elementy teorii i analiza empiryczna*, ed. Adam Lipowski with Jan Macieja (Warsaw: PAN INE, 1998), 59.

production dropped dramatically and most mills were working at only half their capacity. As economic conditions in the sector worsened, unions became less willing to tolerate the situation and demanded that the sector's restructuring be placed more firmly on the government's agenda. The government, however, postponed making any definite plans until an evaluation of the sector by a Canadian consulting firm was completed. This report was finalized in August of 1992. Among its more significant conclusions was that production would have to decline and that some mill closings were unavoidable.[58] To make the sector profitable, the report estimated, by 2002 no more than forty-three thousand workers should be employed by steel mills. By the end of the month the Ministry of Industry and Trade had prepared a working version of the restructuring plan. The plan expected that by 1997 the most significant part of restructuring would be completed, including privatization and some mill closings accompanied by significant worker layoffs.

In mid-November 1992 a restructuring plan was finally presented by the Ministry of Industry and Trade and accepted by the Economic Committee of the Council of Ministers. The plan anticipated that at least eighty thousand workers, or two-thirds of all those employed in the sector, would have to be laid off. The program was expected to cost about $4.5 billion. A special agency was set up to provide assistance to the laid-off workers and early retirement and increased severance packages were made available. The plan also eased leasing requirements of firm's assets to employee-owned companies and streamlined privatization procedures. Workers were to choose their method of privatization, following more simplified and abbreviated procedures than those that generally governed the commercialization process. Given these incentives, the government anticipated that by the first quarter of the following year most enterprises would have decided to privatize.[59]

Despite this, over the following few years, little restructuring actually took place. Industry insiders complained that the government provided insufficient financial support and inadequate overall direction.[60] Because of the high capital requirements, without such support even those mills where managers, unions, and workers' councils drew up restructuring plans had little hope of successfully completing the process.[61] The proposed mill closings also concerned the sector's employees. Although the union federations were willing to, and did,

58. *PAP*, August 6, 1992.
59. *Rzeczpospolita*, November 17, 1992.
60. *Rzeczpospolita*, March 8, 1994.
61. *Życie Gospodarcze*, October 18, 1992.

negotiate with the government over the terms of restructuring, enterprise-level unions and rank-and-file members were less willing to contemplate mass layoffs. As a result, protests became common. In turn, among directors of steel companies, who were dependent on workers' council approval, such pressure from workers caused a reluctance to contemplate reducing employment rolls.

The Council of Ministers approved a new reform program in June 1998 in preparation for accession talks with the European Union (EU). According to this plan, steel output was to significantly decease and the workforce was to be reduced by forty thousand by 2003. A special social support package was to be put in place to provide financial assistance to laid-off workers and was to be financed through the budget, strategic investors, the steel mills themselves, and other support funds. These additional funds included those provided by PHARE (Poland and Hungary: Assistance for Restructuring Their Economies), one of three programs established and financed by the European Union to facilitate Central and Eastern European countries' preparation for accession to the EU. The plan also called for quick privatization of the industry to be completed within the following few years.[62]

The adoption of a new plan, however, did little to accelerate the pace of restructuring. In 1999 no mills had been closed and only one, Huta Warszawa, now known as Huta Luccini, had been privatized. Even more troubling for the program, steel mills continued to extract more subsidies from successive governments, take on more debt, and invest the funds in often dubious projects. Companies in this sector remained among the most financially troubled. Huta Katowice, for example, consistently ranked among the top money-losing firms in the country each year between 1992 and 1997 and achieved the dubious status of the top money loser in 1997. Although the government acknowledged that among the sector's most pressing problems was excess labor, employment levels at Huta Katowice remained essentially what they had been since 1990. Here, as in other steel mills, the trade unions and management often joined forces to block restructuring efforts and in 1994, after a long strike, forced the reform-minded director of the company to resign.[63] At many mills threatened with bankruptcy and closure, workers protested, often going on hunger strikes. Inevitably government ministers traveled to hold discussions and seek a compromise. The compromise usually entailed finding additional funds for the enterprise in state coffers, which allowed company to stay afloat.

62. *Gazeta Śląska,* March 1999.
63. *Rzeczpospolita,* May 1994.

The issue of how to deal with excess labor in the steel industry became a major stumbling block. Both the opzz and Solidarity trade union federations negotiated with the government concerning social package provisions.[64] The package was to include financing for retraining departing workers, generous severance pay, provision of credits to encourage workers to start their own business, and the creation of new employment possibilities. Nonetheless, through much of the 1990s, both unions remained frustrated with the lack of government follow-through on the agreements that had already been reached. Like unions in the coal-mining sector, steel industry unions were particularly unhappy with the absence of a broader industrial development strategy that would ensure alternative employment for displaced workers. Dissatisfied with the financial incentives package the government was willing to offer, the unions refused to support mass layoffs.

It was only the quickly worsening condition of the mills and the approaching deadline for lifting final import controls on steel from Western Europe in 2000 that prompted the government to initiate a new round of negotiations with union federations over a new restructuring program for the steel industry. In January 1999, an agreement was finally signed between the government, employers, and trade unions on a new social package. In exchange for more generous financial incentives, the unions agreed to layoffs as well as eventual plant closings.[65] Despite this new agreement, relations between the two sides remained tense. With financial losses mounting and more enterprises on the verge of bankruptcy, unions felt that the government was not holding up its end of the bargain and once again moved to remind it of the power of labor in the steel sector by organizing a new round of protest marches. As always, the government was quick to respond, promising that no mills would be allowed to go into bankruptcy, and assured unions that the social package, which was due to expire, would be extended.[66]

In spite of the continuously deteriorating financial situation in the steel and coal-mining sectors, during the first decade of reforms successive governments remained unwilling to confront the unions and workers' councils over the issue

64. Not all unions within the steel sector were as willing to cooperate with the government restructuring plan. Sierpień 80, a Solidarity breakaway group, for example, argued that the program's aim was to destroy the Polish steel industry for the benefit of EU steel producers. For their position, see their Web site, http://www.wzz.org.

65. See Ministerstwo Gospodarki, *Program restrukturyzacji hutnictwa żelaza i stali przyjęty przez Radę Ministrów 5 czerwca 2001* (Warsaw: Ministerstwo Gospodarki, 2001).

66. *Rzeczpospolita,* March 19, 2001.

of employment restructuring. It made little difference which coalition was in power, the post-Communist or Solidarity-affiliated parties, since both relied heavily on the support of industrial unions during electoral contests. The backing of steel workers and coal miners was particularly crucial not only because of their numbers but also because of regional concentration in southern Poland. The experience of the Suchocka government, which fell after a clash with coal-mining unions, was not lost on its successors. Thus, organized labor drew on the legal prerogatives acquired prior to the 1989 transition as well as on its long experience of successfully challenging the state to resist restructuring policies it found objectionable and effectively employed strategies afforded it by the new democratic political environment.

## Labor Activism in Electoral Politics

Using historically acquired resources, labor organizations sought to influence the process of privatization design and implementation through a variety of strategies. Trade unions, through their affiliations with political parties, lobbied the government and parliamentary deputies for modifications in the privatization law that would more closely reflect their preferences. Similarly, the worker self-management movement helped formulate an alternative privatization plan that was then presented to the parliament by sympathetic MPs. Furthermore, the two largest trade union federations, the OPZZ and Solidarity, had their own parliamentary representatives who could and did push for changes in legislation that affected their membership.

In addition to these strategies, which sought to shape the process of privatization design, labor organizations were also active during the implementation phase. Here, workers' councils had extensive prerogatives in terms of choosing privatization methods to be adopted by their companies as well as in terms of blocking any ownership changes they did not wish to see. At the same time, trade unions engaged in other forms of actions that sought to bring their demands to the government's attention. These included demonstrations, protests, and hunger and occupational strikes, as well as more traditional forms of industrial conflicts.

Although the OPZZ regularly fielded candidates in parliamentary elections and became a junior partner in the SLD-PSL government, it chose not to become more directly involved in governing, fearing that a direct association with the economic reform program could pose a challenge to it as a trade union organization. Rather, the organization defined its goals in terms of promoting and defending workers' interests through more traditional union activities.[67] In mid-1995 the Solidarity trade union, however, made a very different decision. No longer satisfied with influencing policies through lobbying parliamentary deputies and government officials or with using workers' councils, it decided to shift tactics and become more directly involved in setting the policy agenda, drawing on its experience of political mobilization. The 1993 parliamentary contest was a watershed for the organization. Recognizing that the defeat at the polls was affected by the fragmentation of the political Right and the ability of the Left to construct a broad electoral alliance, Solidarity moved to create a similar unified front on the right. Among the most important factors that tilted the balance in favor of direct involvement was the unhappiness of many within the Solidarity trade union with the program pursued by the SLD-PSL coalition, which they saw as essentially halting the progress of reforms and reasserting the nomenklatura's economic and political power. Furthermore, by becoming directly engaged in politics and presenting a concrete reform program, Solidarity could more effectively challenge the SLD's accusations that the lack of progress in pushing economic restructuring was a consequence of Solidarity's antireform opposition.

Over the summer of 1996 the debate within the union concerned two strategies. The first involved the union's direct participation in electoral contests. The second entailed more passive participation, limited to support for groups and parties with programs close to Solidarity's positions. Solidarity's chairman, Marian Krzaklewski, cautioned that the second strategy could lead to the union's repeating its mistake from the early 1990s. In other words, by closely associating itself with a particular political party while not having direct control over government decisions, Solidarity would be blamed for policies it could not fully influence. Despite these concerns, the union leadership decided to form their own political alliance, Solidarity Electoral Action (AWS), and stand in the next parliamentary elections. Solidarity argued that it had a comprehensive reform program and that in particular its proposals concerning popular enfranchisement, the method through which large public enterprises would be privatized, and the development of capital retirement funds would ensure a deepening of market reforms.[68]

---

67. See their program, as described in *Nasz program: Wybory parlamentarne 1997* (Warsaw: OPZZ, 1997).

68. *Tygodnik Solidarność*, October 1996.

The strategy initially proved very successful and following the 1997 parliamentary elections, AWS became the senior partner in a coalition government with the Freedom Union party (UW). Jerzy Buzek from AWS, a relative political unknown was named prime minister with Leszek Balcerowicz (leader of the UW) returning to the post of finance minister. Krzaklewski, leader of Solidarity and AWS chose to remain outside of the government and to head the alliance's parliamentary caucus. In the long term, however, Solidarity paid a heavy price for taking on governing responsibilities. Its stint in power exposed the difficulties of maintaining a dual identity of a political party and a trade union. Four years later, not only was AWS voted out of office, it did not manage to place even one deputy in the parliament. At the same time, its credibility as a trade union also plummeted in the public's mind.

For a time, however, Solidarity, through its political wing, could set the agenda. Some of its first tasks were to accelerate the industrial restructuring program; to initiate territorial-administrative reform; and to push forward reform of the health care, pension, and education systems. The design and implementation process of these various reforms, however, precipitated numerous crises both within the governing coalition and in AWS itself, frequently pitting unionists against politicians from the smaller liberal-conservative and nationalist parties that constituted the alliance. Furthermore, the process of implementing these reforms frequently sparked public protests, with demonstrations in Warsaw and other major cities becoming commonplace. The protests and demonstrations in turn further exacerbated tensions within the coalition government.

The first proposal of major reforms focused on the pension system. Announced shortly after the new coalition took over, its reception became a harbinger of both the persistent conflicts within the government and the challenge for Solidarity as it attempted to simultaneously function as a political party and as a trade union. As the pension system reform program was being drawn up, the government realized that additional funds would be required for its implementation and that the only source of that financing could be privatization. In addition to pension reform, initiating long-postponed reprivatization became more urgent and was expected to absorb large amounts of budget funds as well. The renewed interest in privatization, however, posed a problem for AWS. The electoral platform of the alliance placed emphasis on citizen enfranchisement.[69] As the electoral campaign progressed, these proposals became the main

69. *Tygodnik Solidarność*, September 27, 1996, October 25, 1996.

organizing principle around which all other AWS proposals were formulated. The cooling of the government's enthusiasm for enfranchisement, which went hand in hand with its renewed interest in capital privatization, precipitated a major rift with its supporters, who were unwilling to see it become financially impossible to implement.

In the summer of 1998, the government, dissatisfied with the legal framework that governed privatization, proposed a new amendment to the law on the privatization and commercialization of enterprises. It justified this move by arguing that "as a result of the excessive distribution of shares, we are losing funds that could be used to implement important social reforms that would benefit the whole society."[70] The proposal sparked criticism from various quarters. Labor organizations protested that the new legislation would in effect mean that the number of free shares to be distributed to workers in privatized companies would be limited. Both Janusz Lewandowski and Wiesław Kaczmarek, two former ministers of privatization, argued as well that the free distribution of shares to workers of privatized companies could not be rescinded, since this would likely slow down privatization even further. The reason that these privileges were granted to workers in the first place, Lewandowski pointed out, was precisely to get them to accept privatization.[71] Labor support of privatization was essential in light of workers' council legal prerogatives.

With the government trying to accelerate privatization, AWS deputies in the parliament, who supported enfranchisement, began flooding the Sejm with proposals. The government, in turn, objected to all of them. The major point of contention throughout 1998 was the Office of Prosecutor General (Prokuratoria Generalna). The idea of a prosecutor general had its roots in the electoral platform of AWS. The proposal, introduced in the Sejm by the AWS MPs, envisioned the creation of an independent office that would have oversight over privatization. In particular, the prosecutor general's office would have the power to oppose (ex ante) any large privatizations. The MPs argued that privatization had been characterized by too many shady deals and frequently amounted to little more than giving away state assets at prices well below their market value. The conflict over the prosecutor general's office finally came to a head during the 1999 budget debate, leading to widespread speculation about the possible fall of the government. To gain support for the budget of the enfranchisement

70. Jacek Ambroziak, deputy secretary in the Ministry of State Treasury, in *Nowe Życie Gospodarcze*, August 1998, 35.

71. *Rzeczpospolita*, January 14, 1999.

camp, the Sejm agreed to pass legislation giving substantial powers to the prosecutor general.[72]

In response to the Sejm passing the legislation on January 8, the UW brought the matter to the Constitutional Tribunal, arguing that establishing the Office of Prosecutor General would slow down privatization even further and violate the constitutional division of powers between the president, the government, and the Sejm. President Aleksander Kwaśniewski refused to sign legislation creating the Office of Prosecutor General and Sejm's attempt to override the veto failed.

Although the prosecutor general proposal was defeated, the issue of privatization and in particular attempts to restructure and eventually sell-off heavy industry sparked numerous clashes between the government and the unions. The challenge of pushing through restructuring over union objections was well illustrated by the fate of minister of transport Eugeniusz Morawski, who resigned in 1998. The resignation was the direct result of the confrontation between Morawski and the railway company unions, which objected to the restructuring scheme the minister proposed. In his letter of resignation he cited as the primary reason behind his decision the "insufferable levels" of union influence in the government. His views were shared by others as well. As Marek Goliszewski, the head of the Business Centre Club (one of the main organizations of private entrepreneurs) argued, "If the situation where the real center of power lies outside the government continues, then nothing will come of the wonderful plans of the governing coalition. Poland is not ruled by the government but by the Solidarity trade union."[73] These perceptions of union influence on policy intensified throughout 1998 and 1999 as the number of protests and demonstrations challenging various government restructuring proposals increased. The policy of minister of labor Longin Komołowski, a former Solidarity representative to the Trilateral Commission, of holding informal discussions with protesting trade unionists further created the impression that unions were directly involved in government decision making. At the same time both Solidarity and the reenergized OPZZ MPs in the Sejm clashed with the government over the unions' right to be consulted during the designing of the state budget and joined forces in voting for excluding union funds from taxation.[74]

As the number of labor protests and demonstrations grew, the impossibility of Solidarity's continuing to simultaneously function as the governing party and

72. *Rzeczpospolita,* January 9, 1999.
73. *Polityka,* May 1, 1999, 12.
74. At the time, Solidarity had sixty MPs and six senators. There were also four senators from the farmers' Solidarity and one from Solidarity 80. OPZZ had forty-two MPs and four senators. In

as a trade union increasingly challenging its own government in the Sejm and on the street became clear. The conflicts within the governing coalition were often related to the dual role that Solidarity was playing of a governing political party and a trade union. Although AWS was the senior partner in the coalition, Solidarity MPs in the Sejm frequently broke with party discipline and voted against government proposals. The many demonstrations that moved through Warsaw, moreover, were often led by Solidarity and frequently personally by Marian Krzaklewski, leading to the peculiar spectacle of the chairman of the senior partner in the coalition government, AWS, protesting, in his role as the chairman of the Solidarity trade union, in front of the Sejm against policies pursued by the government. Solidarity defended such action. Jacek Rybicki, AWS deputy chairman in the Sejm, for example, argued that "Solidarity never promised this government a protective umbrella."[75]

Despite these protest activities by the Solidarity leadership, the organization was encountering a similar dilemma to the one it faced almost a decade earlier when the rank and file began deserting it in response to the union's support for reforms. As the senior party in government, and then, after the UW left the coalition government in the fall of 2000, the sole party, it could not escape the responsibility for the policies it pursued. Hence, ironically, while Solidarity increased its influence over the course of state policies, including the privatization program, it began to weaken and fragment internally.

One reason for this turn of events was the very different preferences of the union federation's leadership and of its rank and file. As Gardawski points out, Solidarity leaders "tended to idealize institutions of the market economy and tended to treat opinions that pointed to the difficult social consequences of market economy as a sign of defeatism and even hostile Communist propaganda."[76] In surveys, Solidarity leaders consistently declared themselves to be on the right of the political spectrum and were more supportive of capitalism than was society in general.[77] Later surveys among leaders and rank-and-file members found continuing differences in preferences, although by 1998 they

---

other words, at least 22 percent of the Sejm were union activists. Although the two union federations were often at loggerheads politically, when it came to union issues, MPs from both unions tended to vote together.

75. *Wprost*, June 14, 1998, 20.

76. Juliusz Gardawski, *Poland's Industrial Workers on the Return to Democracy and Market Economy* (Warsaw: Friedrich Ebert Stiftung, 1996), 38.

77. For a discussion of Solidarity leadership's ideology, see Marc Weinstein, "Solidarity's Abandonment of Workers' Councils: Redefining Post-socialist Poland," *British Journal of Industrial Relations* 38, no. 1 (2000): 49–73.

Table 5    Union activists' views on the economy

| Support for | Leaders | Members |
|---|---|---|
| Central planning | 6.5% | 27.9% |
| State ownership of enterprises | 7.5% | 21.2% |
| Striving toward equality of incomes | 8.6% | 34.7% |
| Upper ceiling on highest incomes | 16.1% | 41% |
| Unemployment | 26.9% | 9.6% |
| Laying off unneeded workers | 68.8% | 38.6% |

SOURCE: Data from a 1993 survey in Juliusz Gardawski, *Przyzwolenie ograniczone: Robotnicy wobec rynku i demokracji* (Warsaw: DWN, 1996), 50.

were beginning to narrow, with a growing number of union leaders cooling in their enthusiasm for unfettered functioning of the market economy.[78]

These differences are of more than anecdotal interest. The Solidarity leadership did not just express promarket sentiments. It worked to ensure that these ideas became a reality. The largely Solidarity-designed AWS electoral platform, while containing such populist proposals as enfranchisement, was to a large extent a blueprint for further reduction of the state's role in the economy. In other words, the economic program of Solidarity's leadership was far removed from the preferences of its support base. Furthermore, it was precisely the dissatisfaction of the rank and file with the program that pushed Solidarity in the early 1990s to withdraw its support for the government. It was therefore not all that surprising that AWS saw its political support crumble and that it proved no more successful than its nonunion predecessors in government to make workers at state enterprises enthusiastic about the privatization program.

## Conclusion

Organized labor and especially the Solidarity trade union and workers' councils emerged as influential actors following the 1989 transition. They were particularly successful in shaping the process designing and implementing the privatization program. Drawing on the resources they had acquired in the pre-transition period, relying most heavily on the legal prerogatives and long historical experience

78.  See Juliusz Gardawski, "Członkowie i zakładowi liderzy związków zawodowych," in *Rozpad bastionu? Związki zawodowe w gospodarce prywatyzowanej* (Warsaw: Instytut Spraw Publicznych, 1999).

of successfully challenging state policies, organized labor significantly modified the design of the program, affected the types of privatization methods employed once the program was approved by the parliament, and influenced the pace at which sales of state firms took place. Initially, the support of the trade unions and workers' councils facilitated the initiation of public sector restructuring. Later, once political support for the reforms began to dissipate, their opposition to privatization made quick sales more difficult.

As we will see in the two chapters that follow, the strategies used by organized labor as it sought to shape the design and implementation of privatization varied depending on the nature of the political regime. These strategies were therefore very different in Poland and the Czech Republic, where market reforms were accompanied by the introduction of democracy, and in Egypt and Mexico, where authoritarian rule persisted. As we will also see, however, the effectiveness of these strategies depended on the historically acquired resources rather than the political regime type.

# 5 LABOR AND PRIVATIZATION IN EGYPT

In 1991, unable to resolve the persistent economic crisis and with the patience of its international creditors waning, Egypt began reforming its economy. The first phase of the program focused on stabilization, including unifying the exchange rate, liberalizing the banking system and the financial sector, bringing the budget deficit under control, and lowering inflation. The second phase of reforms focused on more structural issues and included plans to privatize public sector companies.

As in Poland, organized labor was able to significantly shape the process of privatization program design and then its implementation, thanks to the resources it had acquired in the decades prior to the initiation of structural adjustment policies. The ETUC extracted a number of procedural concessions from the state that enabled it to play a direct role in policy making. Over time, the ETUC also became less financially dependent on the state. Alongside the legal prerogatives and significant financial autonomy, Egyptian organized labor could draw upon the years of experience of successfully confronting the state.

During the 1990s, as the government was implementing reforms, the militancy of enterprise-level unions and of rank and file members grew. As in previous decades, workers took to the streets in protest when their economic interests were threatened. The high concentration of industrial workers in Cairo and its immediate vicinity meant that labor protests over wages and job security could easily be transformed into collective action with political overtones. The Egyptian regime, concerned about maintaining political stability and mindful of past explosions of workers' anger, during the first decade of reforms was reluctant to suppress labor protests without meeting workers' demands. At the same time, the ETUC leadership, although not accountable to the rank and file, nonetheless could not simply ignore the demands of its members. The hostility of public sector workers toward privatization put pressure on the ETUC not to cave in to regime demands.[1]

Egyptian labor employed various strategies in resisting economic restructuring policies. Because, unlike Poland, Egypt did not experience a political transition when market reforms were initiated, the strategies that organized labor used differed from those of its Polish counterpart. Labor activism proceeded along two distinct, albeit interrelated, paths. The ETUC was actively engaged in direct discussions with the regime concerning changes in the organization of the public sector, making use of the legal provisions that guaranteed it a voice in government decisions that affected its rank and file, while lower levels of trade union organization engaged in direct protest actions over issues related to job security, wage payments, and benefits. Although these collective expressions of worker anger were generally mounted without ETUC support, and often directly against ETUC directives, they nonetheless bolstered the ETUC's negotiating position, since its leadership could play on the regime's fear of widespread social unrest.[2]

## Organized Labor and the Early Privatization Proposals

By 1964, following a mass nationalization program, the Egyptian private sector was essentially wiped out and public sector enterprises came to dominate the economy. In 1974 President Anwar al-Sadat sought to reorient economic policies and initiated a process of liberalization (*infitah*) aimed at reviving the private sector and attracting foreign investment. The open-door policy, however, proved no panacea for Egypt's economic woes and revitalization of the public sector remained as elusive as ever. Despite this lackluster performance, President Hosni Mubarak initially did little to reorient his predecessors' policies.

Although the regime had contemplated public sector restructuring since the mid-1970s, until 1991 the various proposals floated by the government met with a quick demise because of the opposition of organized labor. Unions opposed

1. Asef Bayat, "Activism and Social Development in the Middle East," *International Journal of Middle East Studies* 34, no. 1 (2002): 1–28.
2. Author interview with USAID consultant, Cairo, August 10, 1998.

privatization for a number of reasons. First, the socioeconomic policies initiated by Nasser provided workers with many benefits. They guaranteed employment security and access to health, pension, and retirement benefits, which substantially raised living standards as compared with the prerevolution days. Second, as the public sector expanded, so did other labor privileges. Most important, workers acquired guarantees to a share in the profits of state enterprises and gained representation on the boards of directors of public companies.[3] Finally, unions were mainly based among public sector employees. All these factors combined to create hostility within organized labor toward any privatization proposals. Throughout the 1970s and 1980s the ETUC rejected all plans that included provisions for the sale of state firms and was very effective in ensuring that none of these proposals went beyond the drawing board.

The first public sector restructuring attempt came in December 1973 when the government recommended setting up joint ventures between Arab investors and state companies. The ETUC did not agree with the proposal's assessment that such joint ventures would be beneficial to workers and in February 1974 rejected it. In a formal statement the ETUC argued that "workers will not allow any decisions that would threaten the socialist gains achieved by the July Revolution."[4] Although in the initial years of *infitah*, public sector managers began establishing such partnerships with private sector firms, as Waterbury points out, "due primarily to the objections of organized labor, the initial surge in the formation of joint ventures petered out by 1980."[5]

The next restructuring attempt came in 1980 when the minister of public enterprise, Taki Zaki, floated the idea of selling up to 51 percent of shares in state firms. Again, the ETUC denounced the proposal. Shortly thereafter, in a public statement, the ETUC rejected it in "form and content" and came out against any trend toward selling the public sector or allowing private sector participation. The minister's proposal was shelved.[6] Over the following couple of years the government presented various proposals, one in the spring of 1981, another in November that year, and a third in October 1982. All three met with opposition from the union leadership, which, thanks to the procedural

3. Salah El-Sayed, *Workers' Participation in Management* (Cairo: American University in Cairo Press, 1978), 15–16.

4. Muhammad Khalid, *Al-haraka al-niqabiya bayna al madi wa al-mustaqbal* (Cairo: Cooperative Institute for Printing and Publishing, 1975), 95.

5. John Waterbury, *Exposed to Innumerable Delusions: Public Enterprise and State Power in Egypt, India, Mexico, and Turkey* (New York: Cambridge University Press, 1993), 140.

6. *Rose al-Youssef,* October 6, 1980, October 13, 1980; *Al-Ahram al-Iqtisady,* October 17, 1980.

concessions granted by Sadat, had the right to participate in government decisions that affected its rank and file. The proposals were not pursued further.[7]

The issue of privatization was put aside for a number of years by Mubarak, who shortly after taking office proclaimed his full support for the public sector and assured workers that no sales would be contemplated. By the mid-1980s, however, economic crisis flared up again. Oil revenues plummeted from twenty-eight dollars to nine dollars a barrel in 1986. Worker remittances, affected by a recession in the Gulf, fell from an estimated $6 to $10 billion annually to between $1.5 and $3 billion.[8] Finally, a series of attacks on tourists decimated the industry, with tourist receipts contracting by 90 percent.[9] At the same time, external debt rose from $21 billion to $50 billion.[10] By 1986 the situation was so dire that Egypt was forced to open negotiations with the International Monetary Fund (IMF) to gain access to additional financial assistance.[11]

The IMF made this assistance conditional on Egypt's implementing structural reforms, including bringing the budget deficit under control, devaluing the currency, rationalizing exchange and interest rates, restructuring the public sector, and cutting subsidies. Although by signing the agreement the Egyptian government had formally committed itself to economic restructuring, nonetheless it remained reluctant to implement the promised changes. In particular, the regime viewed cuts in subsidies as politically dangerous and destabilizing.[12] The reductions that were made occurred at the margins and by stealth.[13]

At the same time, at the insistence of the IMF, privatization reemerged on the government's policy agenda. This time, the ETUC did not wait for a government proposal and in a preemptive move came out against public sector sell-off.[14] Although by the late 1980s the ETUC conceded that state firms would have to be restructured, it remained opposed to outright privatization, arguing that the

7. Marsha Pripstein Posusney, *Labor and the State in Egypt: Workers, Unions, and Economic Restructuring* (New York: Columbia University Press, 1997), 186–87. For more details about the ETUC's opposition to joint ventures, see Mustafa Kamel al-Sayyid, *Al-mujtama' wa al-siyasa fi misr: Dur jama'at al-masalih fi al-nizam al-siyasi misri, 1952–1981* (Cairo: House of the Arab Future, 1983).
8. For a further discussion of the importance of worker remittances, see Abd el-Basit Abd al-Muti, "L'émigration et l'avenir de la question sociale en Égypte," *Maghreb-Mashrek*, no. 112 (April/May/June 1986): 43–55.
9. Yahya Sadowski, "The Sphinx's New Riddle: Why Does Egypt Delay Economic Reform," *Arab-American Affairs* 22 (Fall 1987): 29–30.
10. Stanley Reed, "The Battle of Egypt," *Foreign Affairs*, September/October 1993, 95.
11. *Middle East Economic Digest*, August 29, 1987, 46.
12. *Washington Post*, June 26, 1986.
13. For example, by shrinking the loaf of bread and using inferior flour while keeping prices constant. *Financial Times*, June 5, 1985.
14. *Al-Taqrir al-Istiratiji, 1986,* 384–85.

economy would be better served by foreign capital's setting up new ventures rather than trying to take over public sector firms.[15] During this period, in addition to using its legal prerogatives to participate in governmental deliberations on issues affecting its members, trade unions began turning to the courts to challenge sales of individual enterprises.[16]

## The Privatization Program in the 1990s

In the early 1990s the combined influence of persistent economic malaise; the changing international intellectual climate concerning the state's role in the economy; and the growing impatience of Egypt's main financial backer, the United States, persuaded many within the policy-making community in Egypt that the status quo was unsustainable. But it was the Gulf crisis of 1990–91 that finally pushed structural adjustment to the forefront of the government's agenda. Egyptians working in Iraq and Kuwait were forced to return home, thereby dramatically reducing remittances, one of the main sources of foreign exchange earnings. Traffic through the Suez Canal, another important source of state revenue, was also affected. The Mubarak regime's support for the U.S.-led coalition, though, translated into additional assistance. Shortly after the hostilities came to an end, the Paris Club, along with IMF and World Bank, came to an understanding with the Egyptian government that in three tranches, 50 percent of Egypt's foreign debt would be forgiven. In exchange for debt forgiveness, Egypt agreed to implement an ambitious structural adjustment program.[17]

The Economic Reform and Structural Adjustment Program was signed by Egypt, the IMF, and the World Bank in June 1991. The eighteen-month standby agreement with the IMF provided support for macroeconomic stabilization and the World Bank earmarked $300 million for a structural adjustment loan.[18] The

15. *Al-Ahram al-Iqtisadiy,* August 21, 1989.

16. For a discussion of a number of such successful court challenges before 1990, see, for example, Marsha Pripstein Posusney, "Labor as an Obstacle to Privatization: The Case of Egypt," in *Privatization and Liberalization in the Middle East,* ed. Iliya Harik and Denis J. Sullivan (Bloomington: Indiana University Press, 1992), 85–87.

17. See Arvind Subramanian, "The Egyptian Stabilization Experience: An Analytical Retrospective" (IMF working paper, International Monetary Fund, Washington, D.C., September 1997); Ahmad Zabit, "Ta'ir tabi'a wa dur al-dawla al-misriya fi dua al- namu al-tabi'a siyasat sunduk naqd al-dawli," in *Mujtama'a wa dawla fi al-watan al-arabiy fi zil al-siyasat al-rasmaliya al-jadida—Misr,* ed. Samir Amin (Cairo: Maktabat Matbuli, 1996), 113–38.

18. This represented 34.6 percent of Egypt's quota. See Dieter Weiss and Ulrich Wurzel, *The Economics and Politics of Transition to an Open Market Economy: Egypt* (Paris: OECD, 1998), 23.

World Bank, in association with the United States Agency for International Development (USAID), the European Union, and other bilateral donors, also established the Social Fund for Development, which was to provide financial assistance to people affected by the reform process.[19]

The first phase of the program focused on stabilization measures. These included unifying the exchange rate, liberalizing the banking system and the financial sector, bringing the budget deficit under control, and lowering inflation.[20] Within a few years of the program's initiation, the IMF and the World Bank pronounced themselves satisfied with Egypt's performance and went ahead with all three tranches of loan forgiveness, thereby reducing Egypt's foreign debt to $27.5 million.[21]

With the agreement with the IMF in place, the government began formulating a privatization plan. Former minister of defense 'Abd al-Halim Abu Ghazala was charged with preparing the program, which would emphasize first shedding financially weak entities. Given previous union opposition to privatization proposals and the history of labor unrest during the 1980s the government attempted to make divestiture more appealing to workers. It instructed the National Investment Bank to begin working on a plan that would allow workers to purchase shares in privatized companies, thus giving them a stake in the success of the program. Simultaneously, with the assistance of USAID, the government embarked on designing a program of employee buyouts based on American ESOPS (employee stock ownership programs).[22] It also initiated a media relations campaign promoting the benefits of privatization. The clearest indication of the changing government strategy came during President Mubarak's May 1, 1990 speech to trade unionists. Although the president took care to assure labor representatives that strategic industrial sectors would remain under state control, he also emphasized that the government would initiate the process of shedding publicly owned companies.[23] However, before the privatization proposal was presented to the People's Assembly for approval a dispute

19. For a more detailed overview of the activities of the Social Fund, see their annual reports and the annual reports of the Delegation of the European Commission in the Arab Republic of Egypt.

20. For a discussion of other aspects of the economic reform program, see, for example, Mona Qasim, *Islah al-iqtisadiy fi Misr: Dur al-bunuk fi khaskhasa wa aham al-taqarib al-dawla* (Cairo: Maktabat al-Usra, 1998); various issues of *Awraq al-Iqtisadiya,* published by Markaz al-Buhuth wa al-Dirasat al-Iqtisadiya wa Maliya.

21. "Economic Profile," American Chamber of Commerce in Egypt, Cairo, June 1991, 5.

22. Initially, however, unions were not sure if ESOPS would benefit workers and were reluctant to support the program. Author interview with Abdel-Ghani Hassan, managing director, Agriculture and Development Holding Company, Cairo, October 14, 1998.

23. *Middle East Economic Digest,* June 8, 1990.

erupted between the government and the ETUC over the legislation. Because the ETUC had the legal right to participate in deliberations over policies likely to affect workers, the government found it politically costly to ignore the ETUC's opinion. Before the law could be adopted these differences between the two sides had to be resolved.

## Labor and Privatization Program Design

The fact that Egypt, unlike Poland, did not undergo a simultaneous transition to democracy as it embarked on its economic restructuring program meant that the channels available to trade unions as they sought to influence the process of policy design differed markedly. Polish labor activists employed a number of strategies as the government privatization program was being formulated and presented to the parliament for approval. Various labor groups, and in particular workers' self-management activists, designed their own privatization plan as an alternative to the government's blueprint. Trade unions also worked through their own deputies in the parliament to push for legislation that reflected union preferences and lobbied political parties and their representatives. Similarly, during electoral campaigns the unions used their political clout and the votes they could deliver to candidates to extract additional concessions from governments.

Similar strategies, however, were of limited utility in the Egyptian context. Although parliamentary elections were held on a regular basis, they were hardly the political contests that take place in democracies. The opposition parties usually garnered a small minority of seats, while the ruling National Democratic Party's (NDP) overwhelming majority was never threatened. The NDP landslides were guaranteed by the uneven playing field among the various political organizations. Not only did the ruling party dominate media outlets and have at its disposal the vast resources of the state apparatus, but also the opposition parties were constrained by restrictions on public gatherings and campaigning. In addition, open harassment of opposition candidates and vote rigging were common. Furthermore, while the Egyptian parliament was constitutionally empowered to propose legislation, debate proposals presented by the government, and question cabinet ministers, it was rarely an arena of vigorous discussion and it tended to approve government proposals with little input from the deputies. In other words, interest groups seeking to influence and modify policy decisions had little reason to spend resources lobbying political parties or parliamentarians.[24] The ETUC did establish a special office to maintain contacts with the parliament and a number of its leaders were deputies in both Majlis al-Sha'b and the Shura Council. However, the more effective strategy was lobbying and negotiating with government officials, making alliances with bureaucrats with similar preferences and interests, and using clientelist networks. Such strategies were all the more effective because of the presence of multiple factions within the ruling NDP, which represented very different policy preferences.

By early 1990, the ETUC leadership recognized that the continuing economic crisis and increasing international pressure for reforms meant that its outright opposition to any and all public sector reform proposals was likely to be futile. However, although the ETUC was willing to consider public sector restructuring, the government's initial proposals were not received positively by the unionists. The ETUC flatly refused to accept the possibility of a quick state sector sell-off, arguing that it was "a social bomb threatening social peace and stability which will lead to social explosion."[25]

The first confrontation between the ETUC and the government erupted during parliamentary debate in the summer of 1991 over the adoption of Law 203, which was to provide the legal framework for privatization. The draft of the law was greeted with hostility by the unionists within both the ETUC and the People's Assembly. The ETUC, arguing that the law threatened workers' interests, refused to endorse it. The government, though, was not prepared to pay the political price of ignoring the legal guarantees that gave the ETUC the right to be consulted on any policy matter likely to affect union membership. Discussions were held between union representatives and government officials, with the various ministers trying to convince labor leaders that the law was a necessary component of the reform program.[26] Before the People's Assembly voted on the law, a final meeting was held between the ETUC leadership and government representatives, during which the government agreed to several significant concessions. Most important among them were guarantees against mass layoffs of workers; additional protections of health and pension insurance coverage; retention of a profit-sharing scheme for workers; and a guarantee that, as the laws passed in the 1970s required, only the adoption of a new labor

24. For a discussion of the growing restrictions on political competition during the 1990s, see Keinle, *A Grand Delusion: Democracy and Economic Reform in Egypt* (London: I. B. Tauris, 2001). Most of these restrictions remained in place in the following decade.
25. Weiss and Wurzel, *Economics and Politics of Transition*, 45.
26. *Al-Ahram al-Iqtisadiy,* July 29, 1990.

code could override these provisions.[27] The unionists also received assurances that, as the existing laws guaranteed, they would be consulted on any future decisions that could affect the situation within the public sector and that adequate compensation would be provided to any worker who was harmed by public sector restructuring.[28]

The passing of Law 203 in June 1991 signaled the beginning of the privatization program. Known as the Public Enterprise Law, Law 203 sought to level the playing field of the private and public sectors. To ensure greater autonomy for state firms, the law contained provisions for minimizing direct ministerial interference in enterprise affairs. From now on the main goal of public firms would be profit maximization, and therefore direct and indirect subsidies to loss-making companies would end. Three hundred and fourteen public sector companies were covered by the new law and were organized into seventeen newly formed holding companies, which were to have overall responsibility for managing their affiliates and preparing them for restructuring and eventual privatization.[29]

The government established a new independent entity, the Public Enterprise Office, and charged it with supervision of the privatization process.[30] In 1993 the office published *General Procedures and Guidelines for the Government's Program of Privatization, Restructuring and Reform System,* outlining the plan for public sector reform. The program was to be based on a number of principles: it was to ensure that a variety of assets would be offered to the private sector and that the responsibility of initiating sales would be decentralized; it was to be transparent; and it aimed at broadening the ownership base while at the same time seeking to transfer assets to private firms that had the necessary expertise and financial means to ensure successful restructuring. Privatization was to proceed along a number of tracks that included sale of shares through public auction or tender, public stock offerings on the stock exchange, employee buyouts, and lease or management contracts.[31]

Despite the passage of Law 203, the process of privatization implementation over the following decade was highly contentious. The government consistently

27. *Al-Ahali,* November 13, 1991, November 27, 1991.
28. *Rose al-Youssef,* April 15, 1991.
29. *Business Today,* July 1996.
30. Ahmed Muhammad Makrar, *Al-khaskhasa: Nitham qanuniy lil-tanwil al-qita' al-'am ila qita' al-khas* (Cairo: Economic al-Ahram Books, 1996), 22–25.
31. Mahmoud Mohieldin and Sahar Nasr, "On Privatization in Egypt: With Reference to the Experience of the Czech Republic and Mexico," in *Privatization in People's Assembly, Cairo,* ed. Badran Wadouda and Azza Wahby (Cairo: Cairo University Center for Political Research and Studies), 44.

fell behind its sales timetables and this lack of progress contributed to tensions between the Egyptian government and the IMF. The international financial institutions remained concerned about the government's insistence that workers would not lose jobs as a consequence of the public sector restructuring program, which they regarded as highly unrealistic, given the estimates of excess labor in the state sector.[32] In July 1994, citing a lack of progress in structural reforms, the IMF suspended its approval of the reform program.

In 1995, after successful negotiations with the IMF, the government announced that within a year, a third of public sector companies would be privatized. However, loss-making companies would remain in state hands and sold only after undergoing significant restructuring. This represented a significant shift in the government's privatization plans. Initially, loss-making enterprises were to be the first to be sold, to reduce their drain on the budget. However, loss-making enterprises tended to also struggle with excess labor problems. Selling these firms first implied mass layoffs and was therefore too politically costly. The government formed a consulting committee, which brought together officials from the Capital Markets Authority and the Ministry of Public Enterprise to coordinate the process of company valuation, share floatation, and designation of share prices. It also formed another committee that together with the Social Development Fund was charged with examining overstaffing problems in the public sector and reviewing restructuring proposals. Using the results of this committee's work, the ETUC would prepare a plan of action for individual enterprises.[33] The government, however, dismissed layoffs as unacceptable. As the director of the Social Fund, Omar al-Faruq Amin Ugumar, commented, "If we dismiss 500,000 people, the rate of unemployment will reach 20% and the social situation will become explosive. This means revolution. Besides, the state would have to pay $1.8 billion in compensation which it cannot finance."[34] Over the course of the decade, it was this confrontation with the public sector workforce that proved to be one of the most difficult challenges in implementing the privatization program.

## Labor and the Implementation of Privatization

The ETUC succeeded in modifying original government proposals concerning the legislative framework that was to govern the privatization process. These

32. *Al-Ahram,* September 12, 1992.
33. *Business Today,* January 1996.
34. *Égypt/Monde Arabe,* 22, 1995.

modifications of Law 203 meant that as the privatization program moved forward, the trade unions continued to have a substantial say in how the process of state divestitures was implemented. During the implementation phase, past experience of successfully confronting the state also proved invaluable, not least because the ETUC could use the regime's fears of social unrest to extract concessions. The issue of changes in the laws governing labor relations as well as the problem of excess labor within the public sector became a source of tension between the government and organized labor. The difficulty of pushing both debates forward meant that privatization implementation proceeded much more slowly than the government initially anticipated. At the same time, as the pain of the economic reforms became more perceptible to the public, labor protests began to rise at the enterprise level, thus making the government ever more cautious about pushing privatization over union objections.

## The New Labor Law

The adoption of a new labor law became one of the main points of contention during the implementation of the privatization program. When structural adjustment policies were initiated, the laws regulating the labor market were seen by private business as excessively favoring employees and severely constraining their ability to effectively manage their companies. The labor code that was in force when the program began was adopted in 1976 and amended several times, most recently in 1981. The law stipulated that workers, once hired, could be fired only under certain very restrictive conditions, specifically if "the worker had been finally sentenced for crime or misdemeanor involving dishonesty and immorality." At the same time, strikes were illegal and participation in a strike was a crime punishable by imprisonment.[35]

The government was concerned that the lack of flexibility of labor regulations was discouraging foreign investors from entering the Egyptian market. Without generating the interest of both domestic and foreign investors, the progress of the privatization program was in serious jeopardy. Furthermore, changing laws governing labor relations was crucial if other components of the structural adjustment package were to succeed. In particular, the changes

35. While the old labor law prohibited strikes, this did not prevent workers from staging them. Although the government often responded to these actions by sending in security forces to quell protests, generally only individual strike leaders faced arrest. Furthermore, during the 1990s, when the regime's response to the Islamist opposition became increasingly brutal, harassment of labor activists appeared to decline.

in the trade regime and consequently the growing openness of the Egyptian economy to the international flow of goods and services meant that the Egyptian business environment had to be improved if the country was to become internationally competitive.

To attract these investors, the labor law needed to be rewritten. Large domestic investors saw the existing regulations as severely constraining their ability to effectively run their companies. Surveys conducted by the World Bank in 1992 and 1994 among company managers revealed that the business community saw the existing labor regulations as among the most significant constraints on the development of the private sector.[36] Another survey found that according to managers, the larger the firm, the more the labor law constrained business activities.[37] As Fathi Nemattah, National Democratic Party MP, pointed out, "Businessmen need to be confident in the investment atmosphere to commit funds. The current law makes many of them reluctant, which hurts the economy. The [new] law simply adds a measure of balance to employer-employee relationship."[38] In other words, the labor legislation, proponents of changes argued, placed too many restrictions on employers' freedom of action, discouraging private, and especially foreign, investors and thereby stifling economic growth.

Critics of the labor code were careful to frame the need for restructuring labor market regulations in terms of benefits that would also accrue to the average worker as a result of changes. In particular, they pointed out that the difficulty of dismissing workers had resulted in several problems in the labor market. Most notably it had led to the unwillingness of the private sector to hire. Rather than taking on additional employees, the private sector had preferred to invest in capital-intensive production.

Unions and workers, however, opposed changing the labor code and were particularly concerned about proposals that would undermine job security provisions. The lack of an adequate safety net for the unemployed as well as workers' experiences with private sector employers added to these anxieties. For example, one favored method within the private sector of getting around the labor law had been to hire workers only on temporary three-month contracts, dismissing them before the three-month period elapsed and therefore

36. International Business and Technical Consultants, *Quarterly Review for Period October 1, 1997 to December 31, 1997*, 109.

37. Ahmed Galal, "Which Institutions Constrain Economic Growth the Most in Egypt?" (working paper 001, Egyptian Center for Economic Studies, Cairo, n.d.), 12–13.

38. Interview with Fathi Nematallah, *Cairo Times*, January 13–19, 2000.

before the worker automatically became a permanent employee. Alternatively, workers were forced to sign an undated letter of resignation when signing the employment contract. This provided the employers with the flexibility to dismiss workers at will by simply placing a date on the already signed letter of resignation. Another common practice was moving workers to another plant belonging to the same company, often located hundreds of kilometers away. Given the severe housing shortage in Egypt, moving one's family to a new location was not a viable alternative in most cases, thus often forcing workers to resign.[39]

Moreover, the lack of employment security within the private sector meant that employees were actively discouraged from voicing dissatisfaction with working conditions or wages, since the threat of dismissal was very real and frequently carried out. Such abuses, in addition to the much less attractive benefits and pension packages in the private sector, made unionized public sector workers unenthusiastic about the prospect of leaving their current jobs, which, while not well paid, had always been secure and ensured a pension as well as access to health and other benefits.[40] Thus, although the government was eager to see labor market regulations reformed, and large segments of the Egyptian labor force may well have benefited from such changes, the attempt to change the labor law came up against organized labor's opposition.

The law was first proposed in 1993 and the government anticipated that the legislation would pass quickly through the People's Assembly. But it took a full decade for the parliament to actually vote on the new code. During that time union officials, the business community, and the government, with representatives from the International Labor Organization participating as observers, sought to hammer out the details of changes in the labor code.[41]

Although the new law also anticipated changes in the collective bargaining process and procedures for management-labor dispute resolution, the two issues that generated the most controversy were the right to strike and the issue of worker dismissal. While the positions taken by business and labor

39.  For a discussion of the differing experiences of employees in the public and the private sector, see, for example, Ragui Assaad, "Do Workers Pay for Social Protection? An Analysis of Wage Differentials in the Egyptian Private Sector" (working paper 9610, Economic Research Forum for the Arab Countries, Iran and Turkey, Cairo, 1995); on abuses of the current labor law by private employers, see Nader Fargany, "Impact of the Proposed Labour Law on Labour Market Flexibility and Social Conditions in Egypt: A Preliminary Assessment," June 1998; Al-Ahrar, May 13, 1997.

40.  The American Chamber of Commerce in Egypt, The Egyptian Labor Force (Cairo: American Chamber of Commerce in Egypt, 1996), 2–6.

41.  'Abd al-Khaliq Farouq, Al-niqabat wa at tataur al-dusturiy fi Misr, 1923–1995 (Cairo: Center for Legal Assistance and Legal Rights, 1997), 59.

groups were far apart from the beginning, as unemployment climbed and living conditions became more precarious, union representatives became more vocal in their demands that any changes in the labor law must restrict business prerogatives to dismiss employees without cause and guarantee the right to strike.[42]

The right to strike was an especially contentious issue during the negotiations. Because this right was among the most important demands of opposition union activists, the ETUC leadership was under pressure not to cave in to government pressure on this issue. These activists were also directly challenging the ETUC's legitimacy and monopoly status and demanding the right to form union organizations independent from the ETUC. Labor activists pointed out that the High Constitutional Court twice ruled that workers had the constitutional right to form such independent unions.[43] Significantly, these calls were emanating not just from the enterprise-level union activists who were personally involved in work stoppages but also from presidents of various federations. Especially vocal were the leaders of the Mining Federation and the Chemical Workers Federation.[44] In light of this growing opposition within its ranks, the ETUC had little choice but to continue insisting that the right to strike be guaranteed by the new law, although it sought to ensure that the ETUC leadership controlled when and how strikes could be staged.

The business community, for its part, rejected the idea of a guaranteed right to strike, and the government was willing to entertain it only if it was highly restricted. Moreover, as the negotiations progressed, it became clear that other disagreements divided the three parties. The ETUC argued that the proposed law favored the employer at the expense of workers, objecting in particular to the removal of provisions in the existing labor law that protected workers from arbitrary dismissals and to the lack of minimum wage provisions in the new law. The business community, conversely, argued that the law did not go far enough in creating a level playing field for employers and employees and that too many vestiges of Nasserism remained, hindering the establishment of a flexible labor market.[45] The deep differences between the three sides meant that the draft law could not be put to a vote in the parliament.

---

42. *Al-Sha'b*, December 4, 1992.

43. *Al-Sha'b*, December 4, 1992; *Al-Ahrar*, June 18, 1995. The court also noted that the international treaties Egypt had signed obligated it to allow workers the right to strike.

44. *Al-Ahrar*, September 18, 1996.

45. Kamel al-Manufi, ed., *Tahlil nataij al-intihabat al-'ummaliya* (Cairo: Friedrich Ebert Stiftung and Jama'at al-Qahira, Kulia al-Iqtisad wa al-'Ulum Siyasiya, 1997), 23–24.

The government, concerned about the potential backlash from workers, conceded to labor demands and announced that the new law would include provisions guaranteeing protection of workers' rights in their relationship with employers, maintain their rights to a share of company profits, and pledged to increase wage levels.[46] In the eyes of business groups, these proposals appeared to tilt the negotiations too far in labor's favor. Consequently, business refused to entertain them, arguing that the government had pledged that the new labor law would give owners the ability to dismiss workers and set wage levels. The business community also continued to resist granting the right to strike. The negotiations also revealed the deep divisions within the business community. Although large business was interested in pushing through changes in the labor code, others saw little reason to support any changes in the existing labor legislation if the right to strike was included in the new provisions. In particular small and medium-size businesses had little difficulty in circumventing the existing labor law and, therefore, saw only marginal benefits in codifying flexibility in hiring and dismissal policies if such flexibility was at the expense of creating a potentially more militant labor force.[47]

With negotiations deadlocked by late 1996, the government again sought to jump-start the talks by introducing modifications to the draft labor law. This only made matters worse. The government proposal included provisions for mandatory compensation for workers in case of dismissal, aimed at bringing labor back to the negotiating table. However, because the proposal was presented without prior consultation with either business or the ETUC, it did little to overcome differences between the two sides.[48] The unionists continued to point out that the institutional framework necessary to manage the increase in unemployment that was anticipated following the enactment of the law simply did not exist. As Abdel Hamid al-Sheikh, head of the Tagammu' Party's labor committee, noted, "We have a crisis in Egypt . . . unemployment compensation is very difficult to secure. Theoretically, workers have six weeks of compensation, but getting it is so fraught with red tape that in effect it is nonexistent."[49]

46. *Al-Taqrir al-Istiratiji, 1996,* 285.

47. *Al-Ahram Weekly,* January 6–12, 2000.

48. *Al-Ahrar,* January 25, 1997.

49. Interview with al-Sheikh, *Cairo Times,* January 13–19, 2000. He argued that unless an unemployment insurance plan was in place, the new law would only contribute to the already difficult economic situation of the workers. He further pointed out that "there is unemployment everywhere. That's normal. But when you look at European countries they all have unemployment insurance so even if you do not have a job at the moment you can still survive. This, however, is not the case in Egypt." Author interview with 'Abdel Hamid al-Sheikh, Cairo, September 23, 1998.

By late October 1998, negotiations over the labor law were still at an impasse. While the government was assuring business and labor groups that the new law did not seek to undermine anyone's rights but rather sought to bring the existing legislation in line with the changing economic conditions, the two groups disagreed. Business continued to complain that the proposed changes were insufficient and maintained too many employee protections while adding few new rights for the business sector. Labor took the opposite view, arguing that the law threatened basic rights of the workers by giving business the right to dismiss them and close down factories.[50]

The government seemed increasingly frustrated by the deadlock, placing the blame primarily on the union delegation to the negotiations. As one legal advisor in the Ministry of Public Enterprise commented, "The Confederation is creating obstacles. It is the negotiations that are going on with the Confederation that are delaying the presentation of the law to the parliament for debate and approval."[51] However, circumventing the ETUC would have been politically costly in light of its legal right to participate in government deliberation on policy changes affecting its membership.

The stalemate continued through 2000. In January that year once again there were expectations that the law, in its seventeenth version, would be passed by the parliament. But this did not happen.[52] The stalemate in negotiations came just as wildcat protest actions were on the rise. Also in direct response to the government campaign to restructure labor market regulations, a coalition of five opposition parties and three workers' rights groups formed the National Committee in Defense of Workers Rights. The committee argued that the draft law needed more input from labor groups before a parliamentary vote.[53] The government decided that, given this increasingly vocal labor opposition to the legislation and with the negotiations with the ETUC and business groups at a stalemate, it would wait until after the November 2000 parliamentary elections

---

50. *Al-Ahali,* October 21, 1998.

51. Author interview with a legal advisor in the Public Enterprise Office, Cairo, September 28, 1998.

52. The revised version of the law included provisions that were generating much opposition. Among them was the extension of the daily working hours from seven to eight in industrial enterprises without any concomitant pay increases, a reduction in the number of nonholiday vacation days to seven a year, a reduction from three to two months of allowed maternity leave, an increase in the percentage that could be withheld from a worker's paycheck for payment of loans from 25 percent to 50 percent, and the termination of employer-provided health insurance.

53. Among the group's goals was to campaign during the November 2000 elections against all the parliamentarians who supported the legislation. The threat was never carried out, since the government did not present draft legislation for a vote.

before considering any changes.[54] As the first decade of reforms drew to a close the legislation remained on the drawing board.[55]

### The Early Retirement Program

The lack of progress in negotiations over the new labor law made tackling the problem of excess labor all the more urgent because labor redundancy within the public sector was estimated at anywhere between 30 and 50 percent of the workforce. Without a new labor law that would permit the dismissal of workers, such high rates of redundancy were discouraging potential investors from purchasing state firms. Because the first wave of sales involved viable companies, the debate about how to deal with labor redundancy could be pushed to the back burner.[56] The problem became more acute once profitable companies were sold. The remaining companies needed significant restructuring and infusions of capital. In some firms the losses were so great that it was more profitable to stop production altogether and pay workers to do nothing.[57] Such firms, therefore, were not good candidates for stock offerings. Rather, they needed the technical and managerial expertise, and capital, that a strategic investor could offer. However, finding anchor investors for these enterprises, which one Public Enterprise official dubbed "the white elephants," was difficult and convinced the government that the problem of excess labor would have to be tackled for privatization to move forward.[58]

The government decided that excess labor would have to be dealt with prior to sales of firms because the possibility of new private owners attempting to fire redundant workers was likely to be detrimental to the program's sustainability.

54. Statement of a World Bank representative to the author, September 15, 2000, Washington, D.C.

55. Eventually a compromise was reached and the Unified Labor Law was finally adopted in 2003. Neither business groups nor organized labor received all the concessions they had sought. Workers were granted the right to strike but under only very restrictive conditions and wildcat strikes continued to be illegal. Employers were granted flexibility in dismissing workers for economic reasons but could do so only after negotiations with the trade unions.

56. The decision was a political, not an economic, one. Author interview with Fouad Abd al-Wahab, director of the Public Enterprise Office, Cairo, September 23, 1998. See also Muhammad Salih al-Hanani and Ahmed Mahir, *Al-khaskhasa: Bain al-nathariya wa al-tatbiq al-misriy* (Cairo: Al-Dar al-Jamma'iya, 1995), 59–63.

57. Author interview with Mokhtar Khattab, advisor in the Public Enterprise Office (later minister of public enterprise), Cairo, September 23, 1998. For a similar assessment, see International Business and Technical Consultants, Inc., *Privatization Case Study,* special study for the Privatization Program in Egypt: Privatization Case Study, Final Report (Cairo, n.d.), 65–66.

58. Author interview with Mohamed S. Hassouna, acting specialist, Valuation and Financial Analysis, Public Enterprise Office, Cairo, September 21, 1998.

Table 6   Egyptian public sector firm losses and employees
Data for 1996–97

| Company | Losses (in LE) | Employees |
|---|---|---|
| ESCo | 119,687,000 | 5,000 |
| Misr for Rayonne | 125,979,000 | 9,173 |
| Misr Helwan Spinning | 149,942,000 | 10,191 |
| Misr Fine Spinning and Weaving in Kafr Dawar | 214,159,000 | 21,420 |

SOURCE: Data provided by the Public Enterprise Office.

A more politically viable strategy was to reduce the labor force in advance of privatization and sell companies once the problem of excess labor was resolved.[59] Because the labor law made dismissals difficult and because the government, fearing social unrest, wanted to avoid mass layoffs, it focused on providing incentives for workers to leave their jobs voluntarily.

Various government attempts to deal with excess workers quickly ran into opposition from the ETUC. As in the case of changes in the labor code, the ETUC had a historically acquired legal right to participate in government deliberations over the early retirement package. Organized labor insisted that no workers should lose their jobs as a result of privatization and extracted from the government a pledge that a provision against the dismissal of employees be included in all sale contracts. In the first companies that were sold, ensuring security of employment was feasible, since these firms were profitable and did not have to restructure their workforce. In fact, some privatized firms, such as Pepsi, hired more employees to expand production following privatization.

Although early retirement schemes were on the drawing board from the early 1990s, it was only in January 1997 that the government decided to form a committee, composed of chairmen of the holding companies, the minister of labor, and representatives of the ETUC, to work out program details.[60] The government did not expect the negotiations to last long and anticipated that

59. Author interview with Mokhtar Khattab, Cairo, September 23, 1998. See also Mokhtar Khattab, "Constraints of Privatization in the Egyptian Experience" (paper prepared for the Public-Private Partnership in the MENA Region Workshop of the Mediterranean Development Forum, Marrakech, Morocco, September 3–6, 1998). Despite the fact that the labor code did not allow for mass dismissals, given the private sector's history of circumventing the law's provisions, the possibility of private owners devising creative ways of dealing with the excess labor problem could not be discounted.

60. *Al-Ahrar*, January 27, 1997.

the program would go into effect by mid-February 1997, first targeting workers in loss-making enterprises.[61]

But the negotiations quickly hit a snag. Two issues, the level of compensation and whether the program should be voluntary, became especially difficult to resolve. Union representatives rejected the initial government proposal, arguing that the financial benefits package was insufficient. The ETUC also rejected the minister of labor's suggestion that the compensation package had to take into account the financial condition of state firms. Additionally, the ETUC demanded modifications in the social insurance law in light of changing economic realities.[62] Finally, the ETUC wanted the early retirement program to be strictly voluntary.[63]

The government scrambled to come up with an alternate proposal that would be more acceptable to the unions. But when they did, the new one also met with a cool reception from the ETUC leadership. A flurry of meetings between the minister of public enterprise, Atef Ebeid; the minister of labor, Ahmad al-Amawi; and the ETUC president, Sayyed Rashid, failed to resolve the impasse.[64] Furthermore, now the ETUC was also demanding that the scheme be accompanied by clear enforcement mechanisms that could ensure that the retirement package offered to workers was in line with initial government promises.[65] The ETUC continued to insist that the maximum benefits package be thirty-five thousand pounds rather than the twenty-five thousand pounds that the government had offered and was adamant that the program be completely voluntary.[66] The compensation package the unions were demanding sparked opposition from the holding company chairmen, who refused to discuss this larger amount, arguing that the first order of business was paying down the outstanding debts of the companies.[67] By March 1997, none of these issues was resolved and the prime minister suspended the project's implementation.

A new round of negotiations between the government, labor, and company officials revealed differences over even such basic issues as the exact number of excess workers and the number of workers who would be eligible to participate in the program.[68] By now the impasse in negotiations was affecting the pace of

61. *Al-Ahram*, January 27, 1997; *Al-Wafd*, February 3, 1997.
62. *Al-Wafd*, February 5, 1997.
63. *Al-Ahram*, October 23, 1997.
64. *Al-Ahali*, February 12, 1997; *Al-Ahram*, February 14, 1997.
65. *Al-Wafd*, February 15, 1997.
66. *Al-Alam al-Youm*, February 18, 1997.
67. *Al-Ahrar*, February 17, 1997.
68. *Al-Ahrar*, March 9, 1997.

divestitures. In mid-March 1997 the government concluded that the privatization program had effectively collapsed when none of the twelve companies slated for sale in the first quarter of the year were sold. It pointed to the lack of progress in negotiations with the ETUC over the early retirement scheme as the primary cause of this failure.[69] It was only in May that a compromise was reached. It set the highest retirement package at thirty thousand pounds and the lowest at fifteen thousand pounds, depending on the years of service, and guaranteed that participation in the program would be strictly voluntary. The ETUC, drawing on its historically acquired right to participate in government deliberations, thus succeeded in modifying the early retirement package.

The compromise between the government and the ETUC did not translate into its smooth implementation. Although the inability of government to secure adequate financing also significantly contributed to the delay in program implementation, the willingness of workers to participate in the program was an important constraint. The financing of the early retirement scheme remained a contentious issue. The government estimated that the program would cost about 11 billion pounds. However, the money was simply not available. Although the government had assumed that proceeds from privatization would be used to finance the program, because of the slow pace of sales, privatization had generated only 3 billion pounds. Furthermore, the Social Fund for Development refused to contribute more than seven thousand pounds per worker.[70] The government was also forced to admit that its estimate of 18 percent labor redundancy was inaccurate and that the rate was closer to 35–40 percent, suggesting that program's costs were likely to be much higher.[71] As the Public Enterprise Office pointed out, the persistent problems with financing early retirement required additional government monies "if the remaining public sector companies are to find their way onto privatization list."[72] For example, at the Egypt-Helwan Spinning and Weaving factory, only two hundred out of eighteen hundred workers who applied for early retirement were actually paid. Funds were lacking for the remaining workers.[73]

Implementation of the early retirement program faced other challenges as well. The government had anticipated that although it conceded to labor

69. *Al-Ahrar*, March 15, 1997.

70. *Al-Ahrar*, May 1, 1997.

71. *Business Today*, May 1997; *Al-Ahram al-Iqtisadiy*, June 7, 1998.

72. *Al-Ahram Weekly*, July 8–14, 1998.

73. As a spokesman for the ETUC pointed out, the confederation was aware of many other cases in which there were problems with workers receiving promised compensation in full. *Al-Sha'b*, September 15, 1998.

demands and made participation in the program voluntary, many workers would apply. In particular the government expected that workers in loss-making enterprises, most of whom, various studies estimated, worked little in their primary place of employment and had second jobs in the informal sector, would be especially interested in early retirement.[74] And indeed initially it seemed that the government's assumption was correct. Many workers expressed interest in participating in the program. Many applied to be considered and many went into business for themselves using money they received as part of the early retirement package.[75] But quickly, a number of problems emerged. Many observers were highly critical of the Social Fund for Development for not adequately assisting workers who were taking early retirement. Those workers who established their own private business ventures often supplemented their retirement benefits with additional loans. However, as some new businesses failed, many former public sector employees were unable to meet their loan-repayment obligations. As one consultant observed, "Thousands of former public sector employees are doing time in what has been coined 'the Lada Prison.' They get conned into purchasing overpriced 20-year-old Lada taxis, can't make their debt payments and end up in jail."[76]

These problems did not come as a surprise to critics of the program, who had long argued that the early retirement program was not a long-term solution to labor redundancy and unemployment. Further souring the program's popularity were reports that in some companies, management pressured workers into taking the early retirement package, through, for example, forced transfers to other jobs, in retaliation for their refusal to participate in the program.[77] By summer 1998 the number of workers applying for early retirement began declining and in some factories the whole workforce refused to even consider the offer.[78] With problems mounting, some union federations began pressing for an increase in the compensation package, arguing that the thirty-thousand-pound maximum provided under the plan was insufficient, given the deteriorating economic conditions. 'Abdel Monem al-Azaly, president of the Union of

74. These employment patterns among public sector workers were not a new phenomenon and were already apparent a decade earlier. See, for example, John S. Henly and Mohamed M. Ereisha, "State Control and Labor Productivity Crisis: The Egyptian Textile Industry at Work," *Economic Development and Social Change* 35, no. 3 (1987): especially 512–14.

75. In some years, government officials claimed, more applied than could be accommodated financially.

76. *Business Today,* May 1998; *Al-Ahram al-Iqtisadiy,* June 7, 1998.

77. *Al-Ahram Weekly,* November 4–10, 1999.

78. *Ayam al-'Ammal,* August 1998.

Metallurgical Workers, for example, argued that forty-five thousand pounds was a more appropriate sum.[79] Never popular, the privatization program was now generating vocal opposition among industrial workers. In the summer and fall of 1998 the number of large-scale protest actions by workers in large, loss-making enterprises rose significantly.[80] As in the past, when workers' employment security and living standards were threatened, they were willing to confront the state. They knew from past experience that although the regime might initially respond with repression to quell protests, it was also likely to grant the substantive concessions workers demanded.

One of the largest protest actions over the early retirement program took place in Helwan. Although this particular protest attracted much media attention, by the late 1990s such confrontations between workers and management were taking place in a growing number of firms. In mid-July 1998 in Helwan, a sprawling, industrial suburb that had long been the site of labor activism, a leaflet was distributed among workers of the Helwan Iron and Steel factory by labor activists. The leaflet warned workers that if they decided to take the offer of early retirement, the decision would be financially costly for them and result in overall lower pension benefits than if they chose to retire at the usual age. Workers at the Helwan Iron and Steel factory decided that they would reject the government offer of early retirement. The mounting anger at the factory, located only a short metro ride from downtown Cairo, prompted minister of labor al-Amawi to address the issue publicly in a speech at the opening of a health clinic in Helwan, on July 20. His argument that those willing to take the early retirement package would be helping to preserve the jobs of those who would continue working at the factory did little to persuade workers to change their minds.[81] As one of them explained his unwillingness to take the offer, "I am 45 years old. I don't get a good package when I leave now and I won't get another job either because I am too old; even younger men are not finding jobs. So why should I take it?"[82]

Helwan Iron and Steel was one of the biggest public sector companies. It was also one of the most inefficient. The government knew that the only hope for finding an anchor investor for the firm was to undertake massive restructuring

79. *Business Today,* April 1998, 45.
80. *Al-Ahram Weekly,* August 13–19, 1998.
81. Author interview with an Egyptian journalist who covered the protests in Helwan, Cairo, August 20, 1998.
82. *Al-Ahram Weekly,* August 13–19, 1998.

before the company was offered for sale. The reasons for this were twofold. First of all, it was clear that making the company more appealing to potential buyers would be difficult, given its poor financial condition and its bloated payroll. By restructuring the enterprise, the company was likely to become a more attractive candidate for privatization. The second reason was political. It was clear that one of the primary goals of company restructuring would be the reduction of its workforce. The government did not want this to be undertaken by the new private investor. It worried that the specter of a private business, potentially foreign in origin, laying off hundreds, if not thousands, of workers, presumably in extralegal ways, given that the labor code had not been modified, would undermine the public's support of the privatization program. Hence, the government felt that it would be more politically viable if such reduction of the workforce occurred while the state was still the owner.[83]

The lack of progress in the negotiations over the new labor laws and the decreasing enthusiasm of workers for the early retirement scheme contributed to the slow implementation of the privatization program. Organized labor's opposition to the proposed changes presented the government with a dilemma. Although it preferred anchor investor sales, it was willing to sell public enterprises only with strict provisions that there would be no labor layoffs once the company was turned over to private owners. Because anchor investors were uninterested in investing in companies that were in poor financial condition and where their hands were tied with respect to the kinds of restructuring program they could implement, the government was forced to rely much more heavily on public share offerings. The predominance of this method meant that during the first decade, companies did not have access to the same amount of new capital and technical expertise that would have been provided by anchor investor sales.[84] The government recognized this problem and announcements of each next phase of the program anticipated that the majority of companies would be sold to strategic investors. During the first ten years of reforms, however, with a few exceptions, these proposals remained on the drawing board.

83. The American Chamber of Commerce in Egypt, *Privatization in Egypt: An Update* American Chamber of Commerce in Egypt, (Cairo: 1997), 22–31. One study found that there was a strong perception among those charged with overseeing privatization about the inevitable trade-off between anchor sales and labor peace, even though the fear of turmoil was greater than the actual risks of such turmoil taking place. International Business and Technical Consultants, *Privatization Case Study*, 70–71.

84. Author interview with International Business and Technical Consultants consultant, Cairo, August 31, 1998.

Table 7   Methods of privatization in Egypt

| Year | Method | | | |
|---|---|---|---|---|
| | AI | ESA | IPO | Other |
| 1994 | 2 | 4 | 0 | 0 |
| 1995 | 1 | 4 | 5 | 2 |
| 1995 | 3 | 0 | 17 | 4 |
| 1997 | 2 | 0 | 13 | 5 |
| 1998 | 2 | 7 | 8 | 5 |
| 1999 | 9 | 3 | 0 | 27 |
| 2000 (January–August) | 7 | 0 | 0 | 0 |

NOTE: AI—anchor investor; ESA—employee share association; IPO—public offering.
SOURCE: Data from the Ministry of Economy.

*Labor Opposition at the Enterprise Level*

The negotiations over changes in the labor code and the process of implementing the early retirement program came at a time when opposition to privatization was growing among industrial workers and the public in general, becoming a hot-button issue during parliamentary and union elections. The threats to job security that public sector restructuring and labor law reform posed contributed to the growth in labor activism at the enterprise level. Studies of changing levels of poverty suggested that Egyptians had good reason to be concerned about employment. Unemployment remained high and GNP growth during the 1990s did little to resolve the problem of job creation. Five hundred thousand people were entering the workforce annually, making employment expansion an urgent task. The purchasing power of Egyptians declined in the course of the decade and the number of people living below the poverty line rose steadily. Furthermore, while the majority of poor households were in the countryside, the rise in relative poverty was primarily an urban phenomenon, hitting the unionized industrial workforce hard.[85]

During the years preceding the implementation of economic reforms, the public sector provided employment to 35 percent of the nonagricultural workforce. During the 1990s, when public sector downsizing began, the private formal sector did not expand sufficiently to absorb the growing labor force.[86] Although

85. Nader Fergany, "The Growth of Poverty in Egypt" (working paper, Al-Mishkat Research Notes, As-Mishkat Centre for Research, Cairo, January 1998).
86. Jackie Wahba, "Labour Mobility in Egypt: Are the 1990s Any Different from the 80s?" Egypt Labor Market Project (working paper, Economic Research Forum for the Arab Countries, Iran and Turkey, Cairo, 2000).

government employment outside state-owned enterprises continued to increase, a major change in the structure of employment during the 1990s was the growth of the informal sector.[87] By the end of the decade half of employees worked with no contract or social security coverage. During the same period, incomes eroded, with real wages declining in almost all sectors of the economy. Consequently, by 1994 the average wage was only two-thirds of that in 1985–86.[88] By 2000, half the population was living below the poverty line and income disparities grew.[89]

Although in the first years of reforms there were relatively few industrial disputes, over the decade the number of labor protests and strikes rose steadily. In the 1991 trade union elections, candidates of the opposition Tagammu' and Socialist Labor parties made substantial inroads. At the same time, labor activists, dissatisfied with the ETUC, renewed efforts to organize workers in opposition to public sector reform. In November 1993 these activists formed the National Committee to Combat Privatization, and groups such as the Center for Trade Union Services became active in disseminating information to workers about government reform proposals. A long stand-off between workers and management at the textile plant in Kafr al-Dawwar in November 1994 proved to be a harbinger of the clashes that would occur later in the decade.

A survey of six thousand public sector workers, conducted by the *Al-Arabi* newspaper in 1996, suggested that government attempts to push forward with privatization were likely to encounter strong labor opposition at the enterprise level. The survey found that 91.2 percent of workers were opposed to privatization. Of the 8.8 percent who supported the program, 80.6 percent were against the sale of public sector companies to foreigners and only 35.5 percent were willing to accept the sale of their own enterprise.[90] This fear and opposition that public sector restructuring generated among workers translated into an increase in protest actions and work stoppages and growing calls that the right to strike was absolutely essential. The summer of 1998 witnessed an unprecedented wave of labor protests and by the winter of 1998 it was evident that Egypt was experiencing the largest wave of labor unrest since the 1952 revolution.[91] The Land

87. Ragui Assaad, "The Transformation of the Egyptian Labor Market: 1988–1998," Egypt Labor Market Project (Cairo: Economic Research Forum for the Arab Countries, Iran and Turkey, 2000).

88. Samir Radwan, "Employment and Unemployment in Egypt: Conventional Problems, Unconventional Remedies" (working paper 70, Egyptian Center for Economic Studies, Cairo, August 2002).

89. *Business Monthly*, February 2002.

90. *Business Today*, August 1996.

91. For a discussion of protest actions at the end of the 1990s, see *Al-Ahali*, July 29, 1998; *Al-Ahram Weekly*, August 13–19, 1998; *Al-Ahrar*, August 12, 15, 24, 28, 1998; *Ayam al-'Ammal*,

Center for Human Rights estimated that in 1998 alone there were approximately eighty labor protests, and this trend continued in 1999.[92] As Kamel Abbas, director of the Helwan Center for Worker and Trade Union Services, commented, "The only way to understand the wave of strikes that have taken place . . . is that they have one thing in common: they are targeting—at least in part—the measures taken within the framework of privatization."[93] The government's program of earmarking 10 percent of shares in privatized companies at a discount to workers did little to assuage labor concerns.

Even more troubling for the government, the protests began spreading beyond the industrial areas. For the first time, they were staged not just by blue-collar workers but also by EgyptAir pilots and civil servants. In February 1999, for example, employees of the Central Bank Misr Insurance and the High Council of Youth and Sports staged sit-ins.[94] Between January 1998 and June 1999, 176 protests, including 52 strikes, took place.[95] By comparison, a decade earlier, during the same period in 1988 and 1989, only 37 occurred.[96] Furthermore, most of these protest actions in the 1980s took the form of sit-ins, demonstrations, or court petitions rather than strikes.[97] In the 1990s workers were clearly becoming more militant.

As in past decades, such labor militancy was a source of concern to the government. The events of 1977 made clear that industrial unrest could quickly spread to broader sectors of urban society. The pattern of the government's response to labor protests and strikes during this period in many ways mirrored its reaction to similar waves of labor mobilization in previous decades, with one significant difference. As in the past, the government tended to yield to workers' demands, but over time the level of repression employed to quell the protests declined, a particularly striking change, given the increasingly brutal

August 1998; *Al-Wafd,* February 20, 1999; author interviews with labor activists, Cairo, Summer and Fall 1998.

92. Land Center for Human Rights, *Ahwal al-'umal fi bir Misr 'am 1998* (Cairo: Land Center for Human Rights, 1998).

93. *Al-Ahram Weekly,* August 13–19, 1998.

94. *Al-Wafd,* February 20, 1999.

95. Land Center for Human Rights, *Ahwal al-'umal fi bir Misr 'am 1998*; Land Center for Human Rights, *Conditions in Egypt, First Half of 1999* (Cairo: Land Center for Human Rights, 1999). For a discussion of labor protests during this period, see also Nicola Pratt, "Maintaining the Moral Economy: Egyptian State-Labor Relations in an Era of Economic Liberalization," *Arab Studies Journal* 8/9, nos. 2/1 (Fall 2000/Spring 2001): 111–29.

96. Huwaida 'Adli, *Al-haraka al-'ummaliya wa aliyat muqawamat al-ifqar, 1987–1993* (Cairo: Center for Trade Union and Workers' Services, 1997), 4–5.

97. Al-Ahram Center for Strategic and Political Studies, *Taqrir al-Istiratiji, 1994* (Cairo: Al-Ahram Center for Strategic and Political Studies, 1995), 432.

campaign the regime launched against radical Islamic groups during the 1990s. Its unwillingness to push public sector restructuring and sales over labor objections is all the more notable in comparison with how the other authoritarian regime examined in this study, Mexico, reacted to similar outbursts of labor opposition.

## Conclusion

As the government began to design and implement an ambitious structural adjustment program in the 1990s, Egyptian organized labor was able to ensure that its preferences would be taken into account. In particular, the ETUC was able to significantly shape the privatization program and other legislation that formed the basis for public sector restructuring plans. During the 1980s, the ETUC's opposition to public sector reforms meant that various government proposals did not go beyond the drawing board. Although by the 1990s, the ETUC reluctantly accepted that some kind of restructuring of state firms would have to be undertaken, it was not willing to remain on the sidelines of the ensuing debates. It managed to modify the original government privatization design and was involved in the discussions concerning changes in the labor code and the early retirement scheme, both of which were indispensable to the implementation of the privatization program. At the same time, workers at the enterprise level made their opposition to the reform known through staging strikes and protests, with the number of these actions growing as the decade wore on.

Organized labor was able to significantly shape the process of privatization design and implementation because it could draw on resources it had acquired prior to the initiation of the structural adjustment program. Legal prerogatives gave the ETUC the right to be consulted before the government adopted measures likely to affect the unions' rank and file. The growth in the ETUC's financial resources not controlled by the state also made the organization more resistant to government pressure. Finally, the long history of successful confrontations of state policies made the regime acutely aware of the potential consequences of labor unrest for the country's political stability. Despite the regime's vast security apparatus, its growing reliance on the military to prop up its authority, and the halting of the political liberalization experiment, the regime was unwilling to pay the political price of ignoring organized labor's demands.

# 6 LABOR AND PRIVATIZATION IN THE CZECH REPUBLIC AND MEXICO

Like Poland and Egypt, Mexico and the Czech Republic embarked on a fundamental restructuring of their economies. Mexico initiated reforms in 1982 in response to a profound economic crisis. The Czech Republic began its transition to a market economy in the 1990s following the fall of the Communist government. In both, the restructuring and privatization of the public sector was a central component of economic reform programs. Both Czech and Mexican administrations viewed the shedding of state enterprises as indispensable to the establishment of an efficient and internationally competitive economy.

What distinguishes the Mexican and the Czech case from Poland and Egypt is the very different ability of trade unions to influence the processes of designing and implementing privatization. In the Czech Republic organized labor was largely invisible when the government and parliament were considering public sector restructuring. And although the Tripartite Council, which brought together the unions, government, and employers, was designed to facilitate dialogue and ensure social peace as the government implemented reforms, it did not become a forum where union voices substantially contributed to policy design. Despite the dissatisfaction of unions with many of the reforms and with their lack of influence on the reform process, during the first decade of reforms they were unable to translate their disappointment into a more effective voice in policy making.

Similarly, during the first decade of reforms Mexican trade unions were unable to shape the process of public sector sell-offs. Official organized labor initially supported the government's stabilization policies that were implemented after the 1982 crisis, since it too saw inflation as one of the most significant problems affecting workers. As the reforms went on, however, it took a more critical stance toward the economic restructuring policies pursued by successive governments. In particular, the official labor organizations viewed with concern plans for privatizing the public sector, which historically had been its power base. However, they were never prepared to fully break with the government. Nor were they willing or able to actively oppose privatization policies or push for public sector reform strategies that would have been more acceptable to their rank and file. Some enterprise-level official unions as well as independent labor organizations did engage in strikes and demonstrations to protest government privatization policies, but Mexican governments remained unmoved by this opposition and were prepared, if necessary, to suppress dissenting voices, not hesitating to send in the military to quell the protests. The inability of unions in both countries to shape privatization policies was a consequence of their dependence on the state, which had deepened during the decades proceeding reform initiation. They confronted the changing economic environment with a dearth of financial, legal, and experiential resources.

## The Czech Experience

### Economic Reforms Following the Political Transition

The economic crisis in Czechoslovakia in the later part of the 1980s was less severe than in other Eastern and Central European countries. Nonetheless it was clear that the policies the Communist Party had pursued for the previous decades were no longer sustainable. In particular, the dominance of an internationally uncompetitive heavy industrial sector, the underdevelopment of light industry and services, and very high energy consumption necessitated a shift in policies.

Although the pre-transition Czechoslovak leadership was much less inclined than its counterparts elsewhere in Eastern Europe to take its cue from the changes initiated by Gorbachev, by the late 1980s the regime did attempt to restructure the economy. While this tinkering did little to improve economic performance, it did provide the opportunity for a broader debate about policy changes. In the mid-1980s the government established the Institute for Prognosis and became the main forum for discussions about future economic policies.[1]

1. As Adam, for example, argued, the establishment of the institute "was really a signal from the political leadership about its determination to ease control over intellectuals. Several top economists from the Prague Spring again found jobs in the field in the Institute." Jan Adam, *Planning and Market in Soviet and East European Economic Thought* (London: Macmillan, 1993), 262; Zdenka

Unlike in Poland, the transition from Communism in Czechoslovakia was not a negotiated agreement between the outgoing party and the opposition movement. Rather, the regime in effect collapsed from within.[2] The particular nature of the transition reflected the very different post–World War II history of Czechoslovakia. Unlike what occurred in Poland, the κsč stifled internal elite dissent and established effective control over interest groups, including labor unions. This meant that as political changes were sweeping the rest of Eastern Europe and the Soviet Union, there were few organized opposition groups within Czech society that could effectively push for political liberalization. The few dissident groups that did emerge during the 1970s, in particular, Charter 77 and the Committee for the Defense of the Unjustly Prosecuted, did not extend their membership beyond the small circle of the Prague intelligentsia. The κsč itself was unable to effectively confront the changing international political circumstances. Ironically, its very success at creating a cohesive party organization meant that there were no groups within the party elite who could offer strategies for reform. When the pressure for change became unmanageable the party simply withdrew from the scene in what became known as the Velvet Revolution.[3] The new government that came to power following the June 1990 elections thus did not confront organized groups with the resources or experience to significantly shape policy making.[4]

Although debates about economic reforms receded into the background during the Velvet Revolution, with the fall of the Communist government, they quickly came to dominate the new government's agenda. Immediately following the June 1990 elections, the parliament began debating economic restructuring policies, placing particular emphasis on privatization of the public sector. In July the parliament instructed the government to present a plan for economic reforms by the first of September. Although there was an agreement within the Civic Forum, the broad political coalition that came to

---

Mansfeldova, "Professional and Political Strategies in Economic Discourse" (paper prepared for the "Symbolic Politics and the Processes of Democratization in Eastern Europe" conference, Berlin, August 21–28, 1994).

2. As Adam argues, the transition was more the result of the domino effect. The opposition within Czechoslovakia was not strong enough to force a change of the regime. As he puts it, "If not for the Hungarians and the Polish events and, what is more important, Gorbachev's glasnost and perestroika, Czechoslovakia would have continued to be a socialist country." Adam, *Planning and Market*, 193.

3. Zdenek Kavan and Bernard Wheaton, *The Velvet Revolution: Czechoslovakia, 1988–1991* (Boulder, Colo.: Westview Press, 1992), 23–30.

4. Carol Skalnik Leff, *The Czech and Slovak Republics: Nation Versus State* (Boulder, Colo.: Westview Press, 1997), 80.

power with the KSČ's downfall, about the need and desirability of market reforms, there was no consensus about how fast the reforms should proceed. Supporters of Vaclav Klaus, the first minister of finance, argued for a radical break with the past. A larger group led by Valtr Komarek, the deputy prime minister, was more inclined to proceed more gradually.[5] The gradualist approach was initially favored by a majority within the Civic Forum, many of them Prague Spring veterans still leaning toward reforming socialism rather than completely abandoning it. Eventually, however, the government adopted Klaus's more radical plan, although it retained many of the social provisions favored by the gradualists.

The government presented the economic reform program on September 1, 1990. By mid-September the parliament had approved the proposals, and the reforms went into effect in January 1991. The reform package included a plan for a mass privatization program, liberalization of the trade regime, including the scrapping of trade licenses and quantitative restrictions on imports; price liberalization; cuts in subsidies; and restrictive fiscal, monetary, and wage policies. The reforms were supported by a standby agreement with the IMF.[6]

Despite the immediate and negative impact of the restructuring measures on real wage levels, the speed of reform, Klaus argued, was vital to their success: "We know that we have to act rapidly, because gradual reform provides a convenient excuse to the vested interests, to monopolists of all kinds, to all beneficiaries of paternalistic socialism to change nothing at all. We are well aware of the fact that losing time means losing everything, losing time means falling into the 'reform trap' of high inflation and economic, social and political disintegration we see in some other countries."[7]

The economic reform program received another boost when Klaus was elected to lead the Civic Forum, thereby fully consolidating the dominance of radical reform supporters. Furthermore, against the objections of other Forum members, most notably President Havel, Klaus pushed for transforming the Forum from an umbrella organization into a more tightly organized political party that could mobilize popular support for market reforms. By early 1991, as the impact of the first phase of economic reforms began to be felt, tensions

5. Previously, Komarek was the director of the reform-oriented Forecasting Institute of the Czechoslovak Academy of Sciences, where Vaclav Klaus also worked.

6. Gerard Belanger, *Czech Republic: IMF Economic Review* (Washington, D.C.: International Monetary Fund, 1995), 1.

7. Vaclav Klaus, "Policy Dilemmas of Eastern European Reform: Notes of an Insider" (paper presented at the "Central Banking in Emerging Market-Oriented Economies" symposium, organized by the Federal Reserve Bank of Kansas City, Jackson Hole, Wyoming, August 1990).

within the Civic Forum intensified and disputes between the Czech and Slovak republics became more acrimonious. When such internal reorganization proved impossible, at the Forum convention in mid-January 1991 it broke apart into two factions: Klaus's Civic Democratic Party grouped those supporting a liberal-capitalist program, while the Civic Movement advocated a social-market approach. Klaus immediately launched an attack on the Civic Movement's proposals, arguing that they amounted to squaring the circle and retained too many features of the old socialist system.

The Civic Democratic Party won the June 1992 parliamentary elections, allowing Klaus to readily push necessary legislation through the parliament. The other consequence of the elections was the split of Czechoslovakia into two independent republics, which left Klaus with even more freedom to maneuver, since he no longer had to contend with Slovak leader Vladimír Mečiar's social democratic policy preferences.[8]

A central component of the economic reform package was a plan for mass privatization. Klaus's program differed markedly from the one advocated by the gradualists. Komarek, the first posttransition deputy prime minister, had insisted that before privatization could begin, enterprises needed to be restructured and made profitable. In his view, privatization would be a long process, with the enterprises first financially restructured, which would enable a realistic valuation of shares. He also favored "a program of employee ownership to balance the employees' desire to acquire shares cheaply with the interests of the state as share owners to sell its shares at the highest price."[9] He was not alone in arguing that employee stock ownership ownership programs (ESOPS) should be considered within the overall privatization strategy. The Communist Party, the religious-based Czechoslovak People's Party, and labor activists also advocated ESOPS.[10] Klaus, by contrast, argued that rapid privatization would be preferable and wanted to accomplish it through the sale of share vouchers. Furthermore, he and others within the Civic Forum rejected the preferential

8. In the remainder of this chapter I focus on the relationship between the Czech government and organized labor only. I do not discuss the first decade of reforms in the Slovak republic because the Mečiar government took a very different approach to the post transition challenges and did not initiate any meaningful economic restructuring measures.

9. Constance Squires Meaney, "Foreign Experts, Capitalists, and Competing Agendas: Privatization in Poland, the Czech Republic, and Hungary," *Comparative Political Studies* 28, no. 2 (1995): 292.

10. Karel Dyba and Jan Svenjar, "An Overview of Recent Economic Development in the Czech Republic" (working paper series 61, Center for Economic Research and Graduate Education, Charles University, and Economic Institute of the Academy of Sciences of the Czech Republic, Prague, April 1994), 31–33.

treatment of public sector employees as both economically inefficient and socially unjust.[11] Klaus contended that "it became clear that in this situation it is absolutely necessary to launch a critical mass of reform measures which will rapidly bring about an essential systematic change: to create in the shortest period of time, and at the very beginning, elementary conditions and then let the market function. In short, we must liberalize, deregulate and privatize, even if by doing that we are confronted with rather weak and therefore not fully efficient markets."[12]

The privatization program had six major components that were to be pursued simultaneously: restitution of expropriated property to former owners, transfer of state property to municipalities, transformation of cooperatives, auction of small businesses, conventional sales of large enterprises to domestic and foreign investors, and transfer of shares in large enterprises to citizens through the voucher scheme. Large-scale privatization, which included most of the state-owned assets in industry, agriculture, and trade, was implemented in two stages, with the first, involving 2,404 enterprises, completed in May 1993, and the second, involving 2,406 enterprises, in 1994.[13] The emphasis was on a quick sell-off of state assets without any restructuring prior to the sale. Rather, the restructuring of enterprises would be undertaken by their new owners.

In the first years following the reforms, there was a flurry of acts and decrees, often supplemented by amendments, that governed ownership transformation. Between 1990 and 1994, close to seventy new privatization acts and decrees were adopted.[14] In August 1990 the Ministry of Privatization was established and charged with the conceptual and implementation oversight of the process. In addition, District Privatization Committees, organized in all twenty-seven local districts, were responsible for preparing auctions through which small privatization would proceed. The Privatization Ministry in each republic was responsible for the final approval of each sale in the small privatization program. The Ministry of Privatization was also responsible for determining how

11. Jan Mladek, "Privatizing the Czech Republic," *World Policy Journal* 12, no. 3 (1995): 125; Martin Kupka, "Transformation of Ownership in Czechoslovakia," *Soviet Studies* 44, no. 2 (1992): 309.

12. Qtd. in Mario I. Blejer and Fabrizio Coricelli, *The Making of Economic Reform in Eastern Europe: Conversations with Leading Reformers in Poland, Hungary, and the Czech Republic* (Aldershot, U.K.: Edward Elgar, 1995), 79.

13. Belanger, *Czech Republic*, 10.

14. Alena Buchtikova, "Privatization in the Czech Republic," in *Privatization in Post-Communist Countries*, vol. 1, ed. Barbara Błaszczyk and Richard Woodward (Warsaw: Center for Social and Economic Research, 1996), 76.

claims to property within the framework of small privatization should be resolved. In cases in which previous owners lay claims to large industrial enterprises, the Ministry of Finance was responsible for the resolution of these claims.[15] Finally, the Ministry of Privatization had overall responsibility for the implementation of large-scale privatization and prepared binding schedules for privatization projects.

The first step in the privatization process, begun with the adoption of the Act on State Enterprises in April 1990, was the "commercialization" of public enterprises, which clarified property rights through transfer of 100 percent ownership to the state. An executive board appointed by shareholders, initially the state, and a supervisory board appointed by the shareholders and employees controlled commercialized companies. Privatization of each enterprise was based on a privatization project submitted by the management of each state company. Third parties could also submit their own projects. These outside proposals came primarily from lower-level management, local government, consulting firms, and restitution claimants. If the firm was included within the voucher privatization scheme, the management had to submit a proposal that transferred the bulk of the firm into a joint-stock company. If the company was not included in the scheme, management had wide latitude in designating the sale method. Although outsiders could and did propose privatization schemes, the most successful players were the managers of public sector enterprises.[16]

The actual privatization could proceed according to one of five eligible methods: (1) transformation into a joint-stock company and further transfer of the shares (voucher privatization); (2) direct sale to a predetermined buyer; (3) public auction; (4) public tender; or (5) transfer to municipal property, social security, health insurance, and other publicly beneficial institutions.[17] In June 1991 the government published a list of companies to be included in the privatization program and later designated the firms that would be included in the voucher scheme. The number of shares allotted per voucher in individual companies was determined through negotiations between the Ministry of Privatization, founding ministries, enterprise managers, and the Center for Voucher Privatization. Once the privatization project was approved, the firm was transferred as a joint-stock company to the Fund for National Property.

15. Stanisława Teresa Surdykowska, *Prywatyzacja* (Warsaw: Wydawnictwo Naukowe PWN, 1997), 160–61.

16. Josef Kotrba, "Czech Privatization: Players and Winners" (working paper series 58, CERGE-EI, Prague, April 1994), 17.

17. Kotrba, *Czech Privatization,* 6.

Privatization was considered complete once the fund sold a company's shares according to the privatization project. Although the process of divestiture was rather complex, unlike in Poland the final decision about sales was left to the Ministry of Finance, Ministry of Privatization, and other government agencies, with no oversight role for the parliament. Thus the debates surrounding the implementation of privatization became administrative rather than political.[18]

Initially, privatization proceeded more slowly than anticipated in large measure because of the variety of ways through which companies could choose to privatize themselves. Similarly, voucher privatization, contrary to the government's hopes, at first generated little interest among the public, with only a few hundred thousand eligible citizens registering during the first couple of months of the registration period preceding the first wave of privatization (November–December 1991). However, in January 1992 the newly established Investment Privatization Funds launched an aggressive advertising campaign that promised investors a 1,000 percent return on their initial investment. Thanks to this campaign, 82 percent of adults registered to purchase their voucher booklets.[19] By the end of 1994 the ministry had approved a form of transformation for about 94 percent of the property submitted in the first and second wave of large privatization with a nominal value of čzk896 billion, or about 90 percent of the former state sector property.[20]

## Organized Labor's Reactions to Reforms

Czechoslovak trade unions emerged out of the Communist period with few resources and with little experience in successfully challenging the state. Prior to the transition they were fully subordinated to the ksč, and their primary function, as defined by law, was to increase worker productivity. Aside from promoting shop floor innovations, the unions concentrated on providing their members with cultural and recreational facilities and assisting them financially in times of need. After their brief experiment with autonomy during the Prague Spring they lost legal prerogatives that had given them a significant voice in company management and employee representation. In contrast to Polish labor,

18. Michael Mejstrik and James Burger, "Vouchers, Buy-Outs, Auctions: The Battle for Privatization in the Czech and Slovak Republics," in *Privatization in the Transition Process*, 187–222.

19. Pavel Mertlik, "Czech Privatization: From Public Ownership to Private Ownership in Five Years?" in *Privatization in Post-Communist Countries*, ed. Barbara Błaszczyk and Richard Woodward, vol. 1 (Warsaw: Center for Social and Economic Research, 1996), 108–9.

20. Buchtikova, "Privatization in the Czech Republic," 84.

Table 8    Change in ČMKOS membership

| Year | 1990 | 1993 | 1997 |
|---|---|---|---|
| ČSKOS membership | 7 million | 3.5 million | 1.7 million |

SOURCE: Martin Myant and Simon Smith, "Czech Trade Unions in Comparative Perspective," *European Journal of Industrial Relations* 5, no. 3 (1999): 268.

which could claim ownership rights to public sector firms by means of workers' councils' within companies, Czechoslovak labor could not make such a claim.

As the Communist regime crumbled, some workers began grassroots organizing, setting up the National Association of Strike Committees in 1990. At the March 2, 1990, All-Union Congress, delegates of the fifty new unions formally dismantled the seventeen industrial unions of the old Revolutionary Trade Union Movement and established the Czechoslovak Confederation of Trade Unions (ČSKOS) with the actual management of trade union activity to be coordinated separately in the Chambers of Trade Unions in the Czech and Slovak republics.[21] The newly established ČMKOS (later renamed ČSKOS) had about 7 million members (or about 80 percent of the active labor force) at the end of 1990. Unlike the RUH, the ČSKOS was much less centralized, with individual union organizations that made up the confederation having substantial autonomy in decision making and control over revenue. In addition to ČSKOS, the only other union federation is the Confederation of Arts and Culture (KUK), established on February 27, 1990. With twenty-two organizations, the KUK had about two hundred thousand members.[22] Despite these changes, what was striking about Czech and Slovak unions was a great deal of organizational and personnel continuity. Close to 40 percent of the leadership and 60 percent of the apparatus remained the same. And despite some new amendments the 1966 labor law remained in force. Within a few years union membership began declining, although union density remained high by West European standards.

What differentiates the Czech from Polish and Egyptian reform is the lack of trade union leadership participation in policy debates. Although unions were generally supportive of the economic reforms and believed that only a move toward a market economy would ensure long-term prosperity, the government did not seek to include the unions in designing the reforms. When the

21. David Stark and Laszlo Bruszt, *Postsocialist Pathways: Transforming Politics and Property in East Central Europe* (New York: Cambridge University Press, 1998), 184.
22. Martin Myant, "Czech and Slovak Trade Unions," in *Parties, Trade Unions, and Society in East-Central Europe,* ed. Michael Waller and Martin Myant (Portland, Ore.: Frank Cass, 1994), 62–63.

program was being debated in the fall of 1990, the unions were not consulted. They were unable to force the government to bring them into the policy-making process and had difficulty in formulating coherent ideas and proposals aside from vague warnings that the society was not prepared for the hardships that lay ahead and that the exclusion of trade unions from the process could result in social disturbances.

The inability of unions to insert themselves into the policy-making process was particularly striking during debates about the privatization program.[23] Although the unions were not opposed to privatization in principle, they were concerned about the potential impact of public sector sell-offs on employment and job security. The ČMKOS drafted a number of proposals concerning the restructuring of the state sector and submitted them to the parliament. In particular, the proposals emphasized that a significant percentage of shares within the voucher privatization scheme should be reserved for workers. However, there was little support within the parliament for the union position, with only Communist Party members coming out in support of the proposals. As Appel notes, "Following the Velvet Revolution, many parliamentarians believed trade unions to be a remnant of the political past and refused to support labor's proposed legislation. In essence, they considered any appearance to support labor groups in the post–velvet revolutionary environment to be politically risky."[24] Communists' support only weakened the unions' position, because the party was viewed with suspicion by others in the parliament. Neither did ČSKOS want such an alliance, given that it was attempting to reinvent itself as a new organization with no links to the Communist past.

Unlike in Poland, where organized labor could point to its past history of successfully challenging the PZPR, the Czech unions lacked these experiential and reputational resources. Unions had little support among the public, which, despite the political transition, viewed them with suspicion. In 1992 about one-third of the public continued to identify unions with the Communist regime.[25] They also lacked the legal prerogatives that allowed Polish workers' councils to claim ownership of public sector enterprises. Although in the original draft of the voucher privatization law the government included a provision that 10 percent of the shares would be reserved for employees, in the final legislation this

23. Myant, "Czech and Slovak Trade Unions," 65.

24. Hilary Appel, "The Ideological Determinants of Liberal Economic Reform: The Case of Privatization," *World Politics* 52, no. 4 (2000): 15.

25. Aleš Kroupa, Renáta Vašková, and Jaroslav Hála, "Public Views of Trade Unions," European Industrial Observatory On-line, November 29, 2004, 1.

declined to 5 percent. During the actual implementation of the program, the percentage allotted was even lower. As one of the main architects of the voucher privatization scheme and a deputy of Prime Minister Klaus, Dušan Tříska, commented, "In all of the post-Socialist countries except Czech Republic, the employees got some preferences, such as if the company is privatized 50% had to go to employees. We were very much against that, it was totally economically insane and socially unfair, and pragmatically speaking . . . if I were to bribe someone to get my program to go ahead, it is definitely not the employees, it is the government bureaucrats."[26]

The failure of the unions to influence the privatization program was symptomatic of the their inability to have much impact on other reforms that directly affected its rank-and-file members. While the government was not very receptive to union demands, the unions themselves were unable to mount effective action and pressure the government to be more attentive to their positions.

Although the posttransition government elected in June 1990 proclaimed that it welcomed the establishment of strong trade unions that could function as an effective social partner for the government, relations between the government and organized labor quickly turned tense. Already in 1990, the government tried to push through the parliament a bill governing strike activity that met with strong opposition from the unions, which were angered by the lukewarm response of the federal minister of labor and social affairs to their demands that the right to strike be unambiguously guaranteed by law. Both the čskos and the kuk criticized the government proposal, arguing that if adopted it would in effect abolish the right of unions to protect workers from being laid off. Furthermore, the unions were upset that the government failed to include in the amended labor code an article that gave workers the right to participate in the management of enterprises in which they worked.[27] The leader of the Trade Union Federation, Roman Kováč, was also angered by the government's refusal to hold direct talks with the unions on the various legislative proposals that dealt with socioeconomic issues.[28] Unable to shape legislation on their own, the čskos sought new allies. Hoping to increase its influence on policy making, it turned to the International Labor Organization (ilo) for assistance in preparing drafts of labor legislation that the unions could present to the parliament. The involvement of the ilo, however, did not significantly boost union influence.

---

26. Tříska, interview by Hilary Appel. I want to thank Hilary Appel for making this interview available to me.

27. *čtk National News Wire* (hencheforth *čtk*), December 4, 1990.

28. *čtk*, September 27, 1990.

On October 10, 1990, the Coordinating Council, representing the confederation of business associations, the Czechoslovak Confederation of Labor, and the government agreed to establish the Tripartite Council of Economic and Social Affairs. In 1991 the Act on Wages was passed, as was the Act on Collective Bargaining. These two pieces of legislation gave unions and workers strong legal protections. For example, employers were now prohibited from hiring replacement workers during a strike, the right to strike and collective bargaining was protected, and dismissed workers were eligible to receive substantial severance packages.[29] However, the labor code maintained a number of original government proposals that had angered unions. Although the law legalized strikes, it also contained requirements that had to be met before a strike could be called, thereby effectively limiting the use of work stoppages. Among its many restrictions, the new law stipulated that at least half the workforce had to agree to a strike before it could be staged and that once a collective agreement was signed, workers were not allowed to challenge its provisions through strike action.

Although the legislation seemed to provide organized labor with some mechanisms for augmenting its influence on policy making, in reality its ability to do so remained limited. This became clear following the adoption of the Scenario for Social Reforms in October 1990. These reforms focused on social and economic policies designed to soften the reforms' impact and to shore up political support for the reform effort. At the center of social consensus-building was the Tripartite Council, created as a forum for discussions between the government, labor, and business representatives. Each year, the council was to negotiate the General Agreement, which set the policy agenda and wage regulations for the year. The Tripartite Council was to serve as a forum for discussions of all important legislation affecting unions and employees prior to the government's submitting the proposals to the parliament. The goal of these discussions was to arrive at a consensus among the three partners. However, an agreement by all parties was not required and even in the absence of such an agreement the government was not precluded from moving ahead with presenting the legislation to the parliament. The only stipulation was that if the Tripartite discussions did not result in a consensus, the government had to inform the parliament of business and labor group positions. Despite these limitations, according to one deputy minister involved in its establishment, the Tripartite Council "quickly proved to be extremely effective and timely measures, because they gave parties

29. Stark and Bruszt, *Postsocialist Pathways,* 184.

time to organize, pass through the necessary initial period of confrontation and learn how to negotiate and cooperate in finding solutions to social problems in the interest of all parties concerned."[30] Organized labor, however, did not share this positive assessment. In fact, unions quickly became disillusioned with the functioning of the council.[31]

During the first years of reform, the Klaus government did not hesitate to push through reforms that were opposed by the trade unions within the Tripartite discussions. In particular, Klaus was able, over strong protests from labor, to implement restrictive wage policies, including an excess wage tax. As Orenstein points out, "While willing to discuss its plans in the tripartite forum, the government has not compromised on core elements of its policy. . . . The trade unions have failed to make a significant impact on vital areas of social policy reform."[32]

Soon after the Tripartite Council was established, the unions accused the government of ignoring the compromises and agreements reached during Tripartite discussions. The first conflict erupted during the negotiations over the new labor code. The ČMKOS argued that the government had agreed to include a clause guaranteeing union participation in enterprise management, which did not appear in the final government proposal of the amended labor law. On November 28 the unions announced a strike alert. However, within days they agreed to call it off. On December 6 the alert was again announced, following the parliament's passing of the government's amendment to the labor code.[33] Igor Plesnot, the chairman of the biggest union within ČMKOS, the Metal Workers Union, declared that "the curtailing of trade union rights

30. Mitchell Orenstein, "The Czech Tripartite Council and Its Contribution to Social Peace," in *Evolution of Interest Representation and Development of the Labour Market in Post-Socialist Countries,* ed. Jerzy Hausner, Ove K. Pedersen, and Karsten Ronit (Cracow: Cracow Academy of Economics, 1995), 340.

31. Frydman et al. argue that the establishment of the Tripartite Council contributed to the curtailing of the newly found independent role of the trade unions following the transition since "the nation-wide employer-employee bargaining brokered by the national government restores the right of Prague bureaucrats to review wage deals and thus influence how labor is allocated. This may stop the cutting of cozy bargains between old state bosses and their union cronies, but it begs to stifle the independence and initiative that privatization is meant to encourage," in *Capitalism with a Comrade's Face,* 87.

32. Orenstein, "Czech Tripartite," 348. Despite this, he maintains that the Council has played an important role in providing for social peace in the Czech Republic.

33. According to the amended labor code, employees have the right to be informed about the work of the enterprises and raise questions concerning its economy and development through the trade union bodies. However, they do not have the right to participate in management of the enterprise.

pushes us [trade unions] to confrontation which we do not want."[34] Despite these tense relations with the government and labor's growing dissatisfaction with Klaus's policies, unions lacking the legal and experiential resources that had made Polish labor a central player in reform design and implementation found it difficult to shape policies.

On January 28, 1991, a General Agreement signed between the trade unions, the government, and employers resulted in an easing of tensions. But by April tensions were rising again, with the unions insisting on an increase in the minimum wage.[35] The reforms had depressed real income levels and most Czechs believed they were living at barely subsistence levels.[36] The government was also interested in renegotiating some articles of the General Agreement that dealt with wage cost of living adjustment. However, concerns about inflation made it unwilling to contemplate raising the minimum wage.[37] Despite trade union objections, the minimum wage was maintained, prompting trade union leaders to suspend participation in the Tripartite Council. The government was not persuaded by this move on the part of labor. Rather, the minister of labor and social affairs, Petr Miller, reminded the unions that the Tripartite discussions were meant as a preliminary consultation of materials concerning working and social conditions prior to their submission to the parliament, but were in no way binding on the government.[38]

Tensions flared again when the government presented its 1992 budget proposal. The ČMKOS criticized the proposal, arguing that rather than taking a "systemic approach toward resolving employment issues and creating labor force market the government takes global administrative steps."[39] In particular, the unions were critical of the wage regulations contained in the budget proposal and argued that maintaining social peace would be increasingly difficult. The ČMKOS was also angered by the lack of consultations in the Tripartite Council over budget priorities prior to its submission to the parliament. Once again, however, union objections were ineffective and the government refused to change wages regulations, prompting president of ČMKOS Richard Falbr to

34. ČTK, December 6, 1990.
35. Kupka, for example, estimates that by 1991 wages declined by 24.5 percent, private consumption by 32.9 percent, and more than 40 percent of the population's savings were lost. Martin Kupka, "Transformation of Ownership in Czechoslovakia," 630.
36. Mitchell Orenstein, "The Failures of Neo-Liberal Social Policy in Central Europe," *Transition* 2, no. 14 (1996): 17.
37. ČTK, April 2, 1991.
38. ČTK, July 21, 1991.
39. ČTK, December 15, 1991.

accuse Klaus of trying to marginalize trade unions. In October 1992, the ČMKOS presidium called on the government to restore the Tripartite Council and dismiss its chairman, deputy prime minister Miroslav Macek, who they believed was not interested in the council's activities.

The unions also failed to influence other legislation that directly affected their members. Most important, the unions were unable to push through the Tripartite Council its version of the new pension system. The unions wanted to see the adoption of an industry-based collective pension insurance scheme, which they argued was the only way to guarantee sufficient basic pensions for all employees. They also wanted mandatory employer contributions to the insurance scheme and thought that a basic pension of less than 50 percent of the average wage, which the government proposed, was unacceptable. The government disagreed and instead suggested the establishment of individual pension plans that would be partially funded by the state. These differences came to a head during Tripartite negotiations in September 1993. The unions and the government were unable to reach a compromise and the government presented to the parliament its own version of pension system reform, which the parliament accepted. Once again, organized labor failed to shape policies.

Similar clashes between the government and the unions continued throughout 1993 and 1994, invariably with the government emerging from these conflicts victorious. The lack of legal prerogatives and experiential resources once again hampered organized labor's ability to effectively shape policies it cared about. During this time Klaus and organized labor clashed on several occasions, leading to public protests. Among the most important conflicts which erupted when unionists, dissatisfied with the workings of the Tripartite Council, accused the government of breaking the 1993 General Agreement. The unions argued that the Tripartite Council was neither facilitating nor encouraging social dialogue. Although there were constant discussions within the forum, these were not real consultations, because the government would come to the negotiating table after the cabinet had already made decisions concerning issues that were to be discussed with the unions in the Tripartite Council. Furthermore, according to the union leadership, "materials submitted by unions are treated as informal statements and not as debating points."[40] Despite these protests, the unions quickly agreed to come back to the negotiating table after a strong, negative reaction from Klaus.

By 1995, the Czech voucher privatization program was largely completed. The unions, despite increasingly vocal protests, had been unable to influence

40. Orenstein, "Czech Tripartite," 352–53.

the process of public sector reform. Neither were they able to turn the Tripartite Council into a forum where they could effectively pursue their demands concerning such issues as wage levels and pension and social security reforms. Even in the few instances when they were able to mobilize mass demonstrations, the Klaus government remained unmoved by their demands and unwilling to change the course of policies Klaus was pursuing.

The lack of labor mobilization in the Czech Republic has often been attributed to the country's low unemployment levels. Since unemployment remained low, in particular when compared with rates in other countries undergoing structural reforms, this argument suggests, workers had no reason to protest government policies. Yet, as discussed here, unions were far from satisfied with the economic reforms. Furthermore, while in the first year following the transition, the Czech public was supportive of the transition to a market economy, concerns about the social impact of the reforms started to emerge as restructuring progressed. Although unemployment remained low, anxiety about the potential impact of job losses began to mount.[41] Despite unions' opposition to various reforms, they were hampered by a lack of resources that could have made their objections more effective. Unlike Polish workers, Czech labor could not draw upon legal prerogatives or on a historical experience of effectively confronting the state. Consequently, during the first decade of reforms it was unable to force the government to respond to union demands.

## The Mexican Experience

### Prelude to the Crisis

In August 1982, after decades of impressive growth, Mexico faced a deep economic crisis. For decades the country had followed import-substitution policies, developing local industry and protecting it from external competition by high trade barriers. Until the 1960s this strategy produced high rates of growth and

41. As Przeworski argues, the fear of unemployment has a profound and negative impact on public perceptions of reforms. Furthermore, the fear of becoming unemployed increases faster than the actual unemployment rate. See Adam Przeworski, "Economic Reforms, Public Opinion, and Political Institutions: Poland and the Eastern European Perspective," in Luiz Carlos Bresser Pereira, Jose Maria Maravall, and Adam Przeworski, *Economic Reforms in New Democracies: A Social-Democratic Approach* (New York: Cambridge University Press, 1993), 132–98; Jiri Burianek, Ivana Mazalkova, and Pavel Kuchar, "The Czech Republic," in *Labour Relations in Transition*, ed. Hans Moerel (Nijmegen, Netherlands: Institute for Applied Social Sciences, 1994).

low inflation. Then, in the late 1960s, critics began demanding that the state focus more on reducing profound income-distribution inequalities and alleviating rural poverty. At the same time, the government became increasingly concerned about growing guerilla activity, labor militancy, and peasant land seizures. In 1968, student demonstrations and the accompanying riots further exposed deep tensions within the society. Echeverría, after ascending to the presidency in 1970, sought to address these problems by reorienting economic strategies. Government spending on various social programs increased, as did the number of state-owned enterprises and regulations, but because government revenue did not grow, fiscal deficits and high inflation became a problem.[42]

The business community reacted negatively to this deteriorating macroeconomic climate and growing state intervention in the economy. As investor confidence eroded and capital flight became pervasive, the government resorted to foreign borrowing to maintain growth. By late 1970s, foreign debt had ballooned and inflation rates rose into the double digits. The government's remedy of freeing the exchange rates did little to resolve economic problems.[43] Rather, shortly after the peso was allowed to float, inflation increased further and industrial output declined. For the first time, Mexico was forced to turn to the IMF for relief.

In exchange for access to the Extended Fund Facility, the government agreed to implement structural adjustment measures. With massive oil discoveries, however, the need for belt tightening no longer seemed so pressing. Rather, as President José López Portillo (1976–82) argued, the problem for Mexico now would be how to "administer the abundance."[44] Both the public and private sector went on an investment spree financed by oil revenues and foreign borrowing.

When oil prices began declining in mid-1981 the impact on the Mexican economy was therefore immediate and painful. As the price of oil fell, the Mexican government was forced to either refinance or repay nearly half of all its foreign debt within the year. To arrest the economic free fall, the Portillo administration imposed stabilization measures that included cuts in public investment and subsidies, an increase in energy prices, and a devaluation of the

---

42. For an overview of this period, see, for example, Stephan Haggard, *Pathways from the Periphery: The Politics of Growth in the Newly Industrializing Countries* (Ithaca: Cornell University Press, 1990), 184–87.

43. Freeing the exchange rate resulted in a 40 percent devaluation of the peso.

44. Merilee S. Grindle, *Challenging the State: Crisis and Innovation in Latin America and Africa* (New York: Cambridge University Press, 1996), 51.

peso. At the same time, to maintain social peace, the government increased minimum wages by 30 percent. This move sent shock waves through the business community and led to massive capital flight. In August 1982 Mexico became the first Latin American country to default on its foreign debt obligations. Then on September 1, 1982, in the final act of his presidency, Portillo nationalized the banking sector and reimposed controls on foreign exchange.

Although initially the Mexican government was reluctant to see the economic troubles as more than a short-term stabilization problem, by the mid-1980s it realized that the crisis had deeper structural roots. The stabilization package signed in 1983 by the IMF and the de la Madrid administration (1982–88) included a devaluation of the peso, bringing the budget deficit under control, reducing government investment, and taking first steps toward restructuring the public sector. In return, for these belt-tightening measures Mexico was allowed to reschedule its foreign debt.[45] As had happened earlier, though, when growth resumed in 1984 the government retreated from pursuing strict stabilization policies.

The expectation that economic growth would continue was shattered when petroleum prices once again declined in the mid-1980s. Because Mexico was unable to meet performance criteria, the IMF suspended loan disbursements. Other banks also refused to extend new credits. Over the following couple of years, negotiations with the IMF and foreign creditors continued. After a few failed attempts, an agreement was finally hammered out between the IMF and Mexico in 1989. The IMF provided assistance with debt relief and the World Bank granted three loans of $500 million each to finance reform implementation.[46] The Brady Plan provided additional debt relief.[47]

The economic reform program initiated by the de la Madrid administration and continued during the Salinas *sexenio* (1988–94) had a number of components. Along with the liberalization of the trade regime, the successive Mexican administrations committed themselves to implementing greater fiscal discipline through reducing the budget deficit, improving tax structures and incentives, cutting subsidies on various consumer goods, and privatizing the public sector. The government underscored its commitment to open trade, with Mexico's formal application to join the General Agreement on

45. Grindle, *Challenging the State*, 55.
46. Judith A. Teichman, *Privatization and Political Change in Mexico* (Pittsburgh: University of Pittsburgh Press, 1995), 91.
47. It is estimated that between 1989 and 1994 the Brady Plan reduced Mexico's net transfers abroad by $4 billion. Teichman, *Privatization and Political Change*, 90.

Tariffs and Trade (GATT) in 1986 and the signing of the North American Free Trade Agreement (NAFTA) in 1992.[48]

### The Privatization Program

Privatization of the public sector was a central component of the Mexican economic reform program. However, unlike what took place in the Czech Republic, first the de la Madrid and later the Salinas administrations argued that selling state enterprises to private owners was not enough to ensure an efficiently functioning economy. Hence, Mexican governments emphasized restructuring public sector enterprises regardless of whether they would eventually be privatized or not.

The privatization program officially began in 1983, although the government preferred to use the more neutral term *disincorporation*.[49] The promotion of public sector restructuring and privatization was closely linked to the other components of the economic reform program and, in particular, to the new emphasis the de la Madrid administration placed on making Mexican exports competitive. The administration argued that unless the public sector became more efficient, this goal could not be achieved. Public sector dominance in domestic production and its crucial role in supplying inputs to the private sector meant that inefficient state companies would inevitably affect the competitiveness of private sector exports. The government therefore set out to modernize state firms, bring in new investments, change management and administration, and renegotiate labor-management relations.

In 1983 the government established the Office of Comptroller General and charged it with the oversight of public sector finances. It also created the Intersecretarial Commission for Expenditures and Financing to ensure coordination of public sector policies, strengthen executive control over state-owned enterprises, and curtail autonomy in individual enterprises. The Finance Ministry now approved all public sector firm expenditures; cabinet secretaries responsible for particular sectors of the economy sat on the boards of state companies and the mangers of public firms needed the board's approval for all financial decisions. These policy changes were codified in the 1986 Federal Law of Public Enterprises.[50]

The program got off to a slow start. As in Egypt, in Mexico the government wanted to first sell those public sector enterprises that were in the worst financial

---

48. See, for example, *Financial Times*, September 30, 1991, 36.
49. *Financial Times*, June 13, 1988, 12.
50. Teichman, *Privatization and Political Change*, 108–10.

shape and were the greatest drain on the state budget. Private investors, however, were more interested in purchasing the most viable state firms. In addition, few Mexicans were in a position to become strategic investors in public sector companies. This meant that foreign investors were more likely to bid for state assets. As in other countries implementing privatization, the issue of selling national assets to foreigners was politically thorny.[51] Despite the challenges, as he left office President de la Madrid proclaimed that of the 1,115 public sector companies that existed at the beginning of his tenure only four hundred remained in state hands in 1987. Critics, though, pointed out that many of these "privatizations" involved small companies or projects that existed only on paper and therefore their dissolution had little discernible impact on the state budget. Moreover, many enterprises were simply transferred from the federal to state governments and thus remain publicly owned.[52]

The privatization process accelerated with the beginning of the Salinas *sexenio*. The Salinas administration expanded the program to previously untouchable sectors of the economy, including infrastructure, pensions and insurance, telecommunications, commercial banking, agriculture, television and radio, ports and airports, potable water distribution, mining, steel, fertilizers, and tobacco, among others.[53] The new president saw the sell-off of state-owned enterprises as the key to ensuring adequate funds for improvements in social services and education.[54] By 1994 only 206 companies remained in state hands, with another 48 slated for privatization as the Salinas tenure was coming to an end. According to most estimates the privatization program generated $22 billion for the government during his administration.[55]

Shortly after assuming the presidency, Salinas created the Office to Coordinate Economic Deregulation, based in the Ministry of Commerce and Industrial Development, and charged it with designing ways to limit the state's involvement in the economy. To prevent the misuse of funds and avoid charges of corruption,

---

51. Trade unions, for example, called privatization a "national give-away." See, for example, *US News and World Report*, October 16, 1989, 96.

52. Dag MacLeod, "Privatization and the Limits of State Autonomy in Mexico: Rethinking the Orthodox Paradox," *Latin American Perspectives* 32, no. 4 (2005): 47.

53. Roberto Salinas-Leon, "Between Mercantilism and Markets: An Analysis of Privatization in Mexico," in *The Privatization Process: A Worldwide Perspective*, ed. Terry L. Anderson and Peter J. Hill (Lanham, Md.: Rowman and Littlefield, 1996), 178. The zeal with which Salinas pursued these policies earned the program the name of Salinostroika, linking it to the reforms initiated by Gorbachev in the Soviet Union.

54. *Financial Times*, January 30, 1990, 6.

55. Salinas-Leon, "Between Mercantilism and Markets," 181.

he also created a trust, the Contingency Fund, into which the revenue received from sales was deposited. While privatization during the de la Madrid administration was carried out in an ad hoc manner, procedures were formalized under Salinas. A twelve-step process was designed that governed the sale of state property under the supervision of the Ministry of Finance. Once the ministry in charge of a particular company decided on a sale, it took the privatization proposal to an interministerial committee for study and discussion. The committee, in turn, decided the best means of selling the asset. With this decision made, the Budget and Planning Ministry selected one of the commercial banks to handle the actual preparation of procedures for the sale and auction of the company. Once a winning bid was picked, the Budget and Planning Ministry approved the sale.[56] About 80 percent of the revenues from privatization were earmarked for the repayment of domestic and foreign government debt. And in fact, during the Salinas administration divestiture of state assets helped to reduce the debt service ratio from 44.2 percent of GDP in 1989 to 12.5 percent in 1993.[57]

*Labor Unions and Economic Reform*

The move to privatize state firms threatened the interests of labor unions, especially since the government saw lowering labor costs as a key to the success of the public sector restructuring program. Even more important, the privatization program was a direct blow to the relationship established between the state and organized labor during the previous decades. Although initially the de la Madrid administration continued working within the framework of a state-labor alliance, as government policies expanded beyond concerns with short-term macroeconomic stabilization to the restructuring of the economy, the government began to see union organizations less as partners in policy-making dialogues than as obstacles to the implementation of the structural adjustment program. In particular, as Berins Collier points out, "the government saw its traditional relationship with labor as an obstacle to privatization. . . . Some within the government expressed the view that labor leaders not only misallocated resources and impeded economic restructuring, but also abused the privileges and concession they received. The labor movement was seen as a

---

56. For more details about this procedure, see Victor Flores, "Mexican Privatization," *Mining Magazine,* October 1992; Pedro Aspe, *Economic Transformation the Mexican Way* (Cambridge, MIT Press, 1993), 196–200.
    57. Salinas-Leon, "Between Mercantilism and Markets," 181.

Table 9  Mexican trade union membership in the early 1990s

| Unions | Membership |
| --- | --- |
| CTM | 5 million |
| FSTSE | 1.8 million |
| CROC | 600,000 |
| Other in CT | 675,000 |
| Independent | 1.5 million |

SOURCE: Data from the ILO.

source of corruption, gangsterism and featherbedding."[58] However, the close relationship between the PRI and the official unions suggested that moving against organized labor would be politically difficult for the regime.

In the initial phase of reforms, the government emphasized restoring macro-economic stability and bringing inflation under control. Initially, the CTM agreed to support the austerity measures because it too was concerned by the high inflation rate. However, it made its backing conditional on the de la Madrid administration's willingness to guarantee social programs and adequate minimum wages.[59] In December 1982, de la Madrid, in exchange for union support, agreed to introduce provisions that would allow negotiations on minimum wage adjustment to take place as the economic situation warranted, as opposed to the annual review system previously in force. He also gave assurances that price controls on consumer goods would be maintained to ensure that workers' living standards would not plummet further. This goodwill between the government and the unions lasted only five days. Already in January 1983, the government went back on its promises and relaxed price controls on numerous basic goods.

In light of the government's abandoning its pledges to the official unions and the worsening economic situation, lower-level union officials and the rank and file became increasingly critical of CTM leadership. The rank and file were especially worried about the rising unemployment rate and continuing inflation, which was eroding the purchasing power of their wages.[60] Real wages

58. Ruth Berins Collier, *The Contradictory Alliance: State-Labor Relations and Regime Change in Mexico* (Berkeley: University of California, International and Area Studies, 1992), 105–7.

59. For more details about the initial response of the unions to the economic reform program, see Kevin J. Middlebrook, "Sounds of Silence: Organized Labour's Response to Economic Crisis in Mexico," *Journal of Latin American Studies* 21, no. 2 (1989): 195–220.

60. For example, the 1980 population census found that 61 percent of the economically active population earned less than the legal minimum wage and more than half the total population suffered

declined by an estimated 41.9 percent between 1982 and 1987.[61] It seemed that both the state and organized labor were ready to discard an alliance that was so central to Mexico's postrevolutionary political and social stability. For the regime, seeking to privatize public sector firms and open the economy to international investment and competition, organized labor was no longer a valuable partner but rather an obstacle to the program's implementation. Official unions, by contrast, increasingly under pressure from the rank and file, saw their privileged position eroding and their traditional channels of communication with the political elite closing. Instead, parts of the state bureaucracy charged with preparing and implementing privatization plans established close links with program supporters within the private sector.[62]

With the government pushing forward with reforms, anger among workers intensified. The number of strike petitions filed in federal jurisdictions more than doubled in 1981–82 and the number of legal strikes increased six times in 1982 when compared with 1981.[63] To preserve the loyalty of its members the CTM and the Labor Congress (CT) decided to take a more critical stance toward the economic reform program.[64] The CTM called on the government to index wages to price increases and demanded that it negotiate a new economic recovery plan with the unions. The government rejected these proposals and promised the continuation of economic reforms. Rather than giving in to union pressure, even after the CTM threatened to call a general strike, de la Madrid announced publicly that, as president, "I pledge that the national interest is above all other considerations; my position will not be affected by old styles of negotiations or pretensions to influence."[65]

The government's lack of response pushed the CTM to look for other allies. Although previously hostile to independent labor organizations, it now turned

---

from malnutrition. Data cited in Alejandro Alvarez Bejar, "Economic Crisis and the Labor Movement in Mexico," in *Unions, Workers, and the State in Mexico,* ed. Kevin J. Middlebrook (San Diego: Center for U.S.-Mexican Studies, University of California, 1991), 33.

61. Middlebrook, "Sounds of Silence," 195.

62. MacLeod, "Privatization and the Limits of State Autonomy," 55.

63. Kevin J. Middlebrook, *The Paradox of Revolution: Labor, the State, and Authoritarianism in Mexico* (Baltimore: Johns Hopkins University Press, 1995), 260.

64. The Labor Congress was created on February 18, 1966. It joined a number of union confederations as a means of unifying the labor movement, which during the 1950s was characterized by confrontations between various unions. The CTM has been able to control most decision-making positions within the Congress since its inception. The Congress has been affiliated with the PRI from the beginning of its existence.

65. De la Madrid cited in Middlebrook, *Paradox of Revolution,* 260. See also Katrina Burgess, *Parties and Unions in the New Global Economy* (Pittsburgh: University of Pittsburgh Press, 2004), 75–76.

to them looking to join forces in the fight against the austerity program. For the first time, in 1983, the official and the independent labor organizations marched together in the May Day parade. The CT and the independent unions also agreed to mount a joint campaign against the government's wage policy and the continuing inflation. The CTM coordinated a strike action that generated about fourteen thousand strike petitions. The official unions argued publicly that after years of declining living standards and few tangible improvements in the economy, it was clear that the economic reform program was not working and should be scrapped.[66] Instead, the CTM proposed an alternative program that emphasized price-index wage increases, improved worker profit-sharing arrangements, and nationalization of the food products industry.[67]

Despite pressure from the CTM and the CT, the government, rather than giving into union demands, went on the offensive. The de la Madrid administration employed primarily two tactics. One was to create divisions within the labor movement. In particular it offered to assist the CROC and the CROM in their unionization drive in exchange for support of the austerity program.[68] The second tactic was to employ a provision in the 1931 Federal Labor Law that allowed the government to intervene in strikes. The Board of Conciliation and Arbitration could declare a strike illegal, nonexistent, or legal. In cases in which a strike was declared illegal the employer was allowed to fire workers or to call on the police or military to intervene. If the strike was declared nonexistent, workers had to resume work within forty-eight hours.[69] The ability to declare a strike nonexistent proved to be one of the most potent weapons at the government's disposal as it implemented economic reforms.[70] Furthermore, through the labor conciliation and arbitration boards, which handled most industrial issues, including contract provisions enforcement and individual and collective grievances and disputes, the government was able to push through policies that

66. Victor Manuel Durand Ponte, "The Confederation of Mexican Workers, the Labor Congress, and the Crisis of Mexico's Social Pact," in *Unions, Workers, and the State in Mexico*, ed. Kevin J. Middlebrook (San Diego: Center for U.S.-Mexican Studies, University of California, San Diego, 1991), 99–100.

67. Middlebrook, *Paradox of Revolution*, 262.

68. Durand Ponte, "Confederation of Mexican Workers," 99–100.

69. Teichman, *Privatization and Political Change*, 113–14.

70. J. Fernando Franco G.S., "Labor Law and the Labor Movement in Mexico," in *Unions, Workers, and the State in Mexico*, ed. Kevin J. Middlebrook (San Diego: Center for U.S.-Mexican Studies, University of California, San Diego, 1991), 111. The Conciliation and Arbitration Board could also choose "not to proceed" with a strike petition filed by a union that did not hold a legally recognized title to the contract governing the work site in question, or when the petition is to obtain the signing of a contract when a signed contract already exists. Franco, "Labor Law," 112.

increased employers' flexibility in handling employee matters, including enterprise restructuring and renegotiations of collective agreements. Thanks to this legal and institutional environment, during the first decade of reforms the Mexican government did not feel the need to push for a labor law.[71] Thus the laws inherited from the pre-reform period significantly limited organized labor's ability to confront the state.

Although the CTM and the CT were prepared to criticize the government's restructuring plans, and despite the regime's shift away from labor toward the private sector, official unions found it difficult to break their traditional alliance with the PRI and carve out more independence. Rather, they continued trying to preserve the coalition and press their demands through well-established channels within the party. Despite occasionally threatening a general strike, the official unions never made good on this threat, instead limiting action to filing strike petitions with the conciliation and arbitration boards.

The reasons for the reluctance of official unions to break their alliance with the PRI and their inability to shape reforms can be located in the legacies of the pre-reform period. In the decades preceding reform initiation, official unions had become increasingly dependent on the state. Breaking this relationship would have been extremely costly and possibly threatening to the very existence of these unions. As Berins Collier notes, "While the initiation of reforms generated conflict between the government and the CTM, that conflict took place only within well-defined parameters since the CTM still depended on the state for its institutional viability."[72] The official unions depended on the state for financing their activities and defending them against challenges from independent labor organizations. The regime's support for the CTM, however, was predicted on the unions' control of workers' demands and their political backing of the PRI. When the CTM wavered in performing this role, the regime was willing to back other confederations, and especially the CROC and the CROM, in exchange for their support of the austerity program. These government policies underscored the CTM's vulnerable position and convinced it to restrain its opposition to restructuring policies. Indeed, after an initial rise in the number of strikes following the initiation of reforms, they declined to 165 in 1985.[73]

This continued willingness of the CTM to cooperate with the government despite voicing criticism became clear after the severe downturn in the economy

71. Maria Lorena Cook, *The Politics of Labor Reform in Latin America: Between Flexibility and Rights* (University Park: Pennsylvania State University Press, 2007), 163; Burgess, *Parties and Unions*, 82.

72. Berins Collier, *The Contradictory Alliance*, 82.

73. Middlebrook, "Sounds of Silence," 204.

that followed the November 1987 crash on international stock markets, which unleashed a new wave of inflation, renewed capital flight, and halted the debt equity swap program. Although the government, employers, and unions negotiated the Economic Solidarity Pact in December 1987, which met the CTM and CT's demands that the government control inflation and protect workers' wage levels, the impact of these provisions was minimal. Income levels continued to decline and the regime's commitment to structural adjustment did not waver.

## Labor and Public Sector Restructuring and Privatization

Having decided to privatize the public sector, the Mexican governments were willing to implement the program, even over labor objections. The first sign that the implementation of the public sector restructuring program would set the government and unions on a collision course came in March 1984 when the de la Madrid administration announced that the government would hand back 339 out of the 483 companies that were taken over a couple of years earlier during bank nationalizations. The decision signaled that the cooperative relationship between the state and the official labor unions was coming to an end. Trade unions were very opposed to the idea of privatizing the banks' assets and giving former bank shareholders the "first bite at the cherry." They argued that there should also be no return of state holdings in "strategic" sectors such as mining, petrochemicals, and food production and processing. The government was unmoved by this union opposition and the return of nationalized banks' assets went ahead.[74]

Although the CTM did not approve of the government's privatization program and viewed public sector restructuring as directly threatening its power base, initially it responded cautiously and was unwilling to mount outright opposition to the measures.[75] Some independent union organizations as well as official union locals did on occasion resist restructuring plans. However, both the de la Madrid and Salinas administrations proved more than willing to ignore such opposition and, if necessary, crush it. The response from official unions to the suppression of local union protests against privatization varied. During a strike of AeroMéxico, when ground workers were protesting government proposals to sell the company, for example, the CTM leader Fidel Velázquez intervened with the government on behalf of the workers. By contrast, Napoleon

---

74. *Financial Times*, March 15, 1984, 24; April 19, 1984, 22.
75. Middlebrook, *Paradox of Revolution*, 256.

Gomez Sada, the head of the Miners and Metal Workers Union, affiliated with the PRI, did not intervene when the Cananea copper mine was occupied by the army and declared bankrupt.

After 1985 when negotiations involving the renewal of contracts took place in public sector firms, representatives of the government were always directly involved. Because the emphasis was now on making state-owned enterprises more efficient, the government pushed to make labor contracts more flexible. This usually meant reductions in employment levels, allowing company managers to introduce new technology without prior consultation with unions and to transfer workers between company departments and regions also without first seeking union agreement.

After 1986 the government became much less willing to alter privatization plans for specific enterprises because of union opposition. If during initial negotiations union leaders were unwilling to back government proposals, the de la Madrid government would often threaten to either close the company or declare it bankrupt. The threat was far from an idle one as the cases of the steel company Fundidora Monterrey, Cananea, and AeroMéxico indicated. Although not carried out, the threat of closure was also used at National Diesel Enterprise (DANA), Concarril, and Sicartsa to overcome union resistance to restructuring proposals.

In some cases, strikes were put down by the police and the army. This occurred, for example, at Fundidora Monterrey, when the factory was closed down in May 1986 and about fifteen thousand jobs were eliminated, and at Cananea, the biggest Mexican copper mine.[76] Cananea had a long history of labor union activism.[77] After two government privatization proposals fell through, workers demanded renegotiation of their contracts. The government, arguing that if fulfilled, the workers' demands would mean a 330 percent increase in salary and benefits, refused to hold discussions with the Industrial Union of Mines. A week before a strike was to begin, the army was sent in to occupy the mine, the company was declared bankrupt, and three thousand union mine workers were fired. As Arturo Borjorquez, union spokesman at the mine observed, the move to declare the company bankrupt was a way of making it more appealing to private investors: "I think the government wants to dress up the bride so she can get married."[78] Similar events unfolded at AeroMéxico.

76. The mine had been producing 3 percent of the world's copper and 45 percent of Mexico's production.

77. The unionists at Cananea became the leaders of the Mexican Revolution.

78. *Los Angeles Times,* October 1, 1989, 4. See also *Latin American Weekly Review,* September 7, 1989; *New York Times,* August 30, 1989.

Here, when workers resisted plans to privatize the company, the government declared the firm bankrupt in April 1988, only to immediately open it under the name of Sindiatura de Aeroméxico.[79]

De la Madrid employed various strategies to break union resistance to restructuring and privatization policies, often resorting to outright repression. The government was equally unreceptive to demands for wage and benefit increases in enterprises. When workers struck to press for these increases, the government, making use of provisions in the 1931 Federal Labor Law, would declare the strike illegal. For example, in February 1986, workers at the Dina and Renault auto plants began a strike. In response, the government sent its leaders to jail for seven days. In February–March 1987, a strike by electrical and telephone workers was dealt with in a similar fashion when the strike was ruled nonexistent.[80] The government increasingly responded to demands for wage increases or renegotiation of collective contracts not by coming to the bargaining table but with massive layoffs. Thousands lost their jobs at Aceros Esmal Fonolos, Altos Hornos de Mexico steel mills, and others. In 1986 as part of the restructuring program of the sugar industry almost eleven thousand were laid off. Similar developments were taking place in the service sector, in particular, in health care and education; sixty thousand doctors and twenty thousand nurses lost their jobs in the mid-1980s, as did thirty-five thousand elementary school teachers.[81]

The election of Salinas, whose nomination as the PRI presidential candidate the official unions strongly opposed, spelled further deterioration of official unions' ties with the ruling party. The Salinas government took an even harder line toward union resistance to privatization.[82] The first clash came shortly after Salinas began his tenure and involved taking on the most powerful of all the official unions, that at the petroleum conglomerate PEMEX. In January 1989 the government arrested Joaquín Hernández Galicia, aka La Quina, leader of the powerful Petroleum Workers Union, on charges of homicide and illegal weapons possession.[83] Along with La Quina, a number of his associates were also arrested.[84] Although the charges were criminal it was an open secret that La Quina

79. *Economist,* May 7, 1988, 65.

80. *Latin American Weekly Report,* March 12, 1987.

81. Alvarez Bejar, "Economic Crisis and the Labor Movement in Mexico," 42–44.

82. Maria Victoria Murillo, *Labor Unions, Partisan Coalitions, and Market Reforms in Latin America* (New York: Cambridge University Press, 2001), 106–10.

83. *New York Times,* January 12, 1989.

84. He, his gardener, two bodyguards, and three others are serving thirty-year sentences. The murder with which they were charged was concocted by the government, although if it chose to do

had angered the PRI during the presidential elections by openly supporting the candidacy of Cárdenas and he was reported to have threatened to withhold support from Salinas in the Electoral College.[85] The move against La Quina was also widely seen as a way of breaking the power of the union, which had blocked restructuring of PEMEX. The union was opposed to the changes in labor contracts and to opening up basic petrochemical industries to the private sector. As La Quina himself had said, "I was an obstacle to the way they wanted to run PEMEX."[86] Once again, the institutional and legal environment allowed the regime to move against organized labor. In fact, La Quina's fears that the government was looking to privatize the oil giant proved correct. Over the next couple of years, parts of PEMEX were privatized and more than one hundred thousand workers lost their jobs. Workers in the steel, electricity, mining, and automobile industries had also lost their jobs as a result of privatization and restructuring.[87]

At the same time, over union objections, Salinas pushed through Congress legislation changing the way the social security system was to be administered. The proposed changes further weakened the power of unions. Under the new system employers would pay 2 percent of a worker's wages into individual interest-bearing retirement accounts. In addition, payments to the housing fund for workers would now be also deposited directly into these individual accounts rather than disbursed to unions.[88] Previously the official unions distributed monies from the housing fund at their discretion, thus providing union leadership with an important mechanism for regulating workers' behavior.

## Conclusion

During the first decade of reforms, Czech and Mexican labor unions were unable to significantly shape the design and the implementation process of privatization programs. In both countries, governments largely accomplished their goal of selling off state enterprises even when organized labor opposed such changes. In the Czech Republic labor remained largely invisible during the debates about privatization program design. In Mexico, the official labor

---

so, Salinas could have easily charged La Quina with any number of real crimes, including homicides that the union boss had committed over the years.

85. *New York Times,* January 12, 1989.
86. *Guardian,* December 14, 1996, 11.
87. Murillo, *Labor Unions, Partisan Coalitions,* 111–14.
88. *Economist,* March 14, 1992.

unions, despite occasionally criticizing the economic reform program, were unwilling to break off their alliance with the PRI and engage in a more direct confrontation with the government. The government, even when factory-level and independent unions staged strikes and demonstrations, was willing to go through with threats of bankruptcies and closures of public enterprises and in a number of cases to send in the police or the army to occupy striking firms.

Organized labor in Mexico and the Czech Republic found it difficult to influence privatization policies because neither could draw on the kind of financial, legal, or experiential resources that allowed Polish and Egyptian unions to significantly shape these reforms. Unlike in those latter two cases, in the previous decades reforms became subordinate to and dependent on the state for financial and institutional survival. This dependence and lack of resources made official unions in Mexico reluctant to oppose government policies even when these threatened their interests. Likewise, in the Czech Republic, unions that emerged following the 1989 political transition were hampered by the legacies of the Communist unions' subordination to the state.

# CONCLUSION

Beginning in the 1980s, numerous countries across the developing and post-Communist world began the difficult process of reforming their economies, moving away from state-led development models toward a greater reliance on market mechanisms. Advocates of economic restructuring identified state intervention in the economy as the main cause of low productivity, inefficiencies, anemic growth rates, and corruption. Getting the state to retreat from such direct involvement became the main focus of these reforms. Given this objective, it is not surprising that privatization of the public sector became a central feature of such restructuring programs.

Three decades after neoliberal reforms were first introduced in many developing countries, it is clear that in many cases the reforms have not resulted in the changes that were anticipated. The tenets underlying the Washington Consensus have been much debated in the policy community and many have been significantly modified. With time, the reform programs have come to place a greater emphasis on providing sufficient safety nets to cushion the inevitable hardships associated with such profound economic transitions. Likewise, the rule of law, the reform of the state administration, and the inclusion of civil society organizations in the process of reform design have come to be seen by many within the policy community as key to long-term success. The emerging consensus sees good governance and local ownership of reforms as indispensable to long-term, sustainable growth.

It is now clear that for many social groups the costs of transition have been much higher than was initially anticipated by promoters of neoliberal reforms. In many societies undertaking reforms, social inequalities have increased and growth has not been restored. Likewise, the role that interest groups have played in the process of economic reform design and implementation has been more complex than originally anticipated in both academic and policy-making circles. Organized labor, which has been the focus of this study, has played varied roles during this process, sometimes supporting reforms, at other times opposing them. Its ability to shape reform strategies has also not been uniform across cases.

As Chapters 4, 5, and 6 have shown, in the four cases examined in this study organized labor differed significantly in its ability to influence the process of privatization design and implementation. In Poland and Egypt, organized labor became an important actor during both phases of the program, but in Mexico and the Czech Republic, it was unable to ensure that the reforming governments take its preferences into account when public sector reform programs were being debated, designed, and implemented.

In Poland, although the first posttransition government came to office with large reservoirs of popular goodwill and was staffed by highly committed technocrats, the process of privatization quickly became embroiled in controversy. The original government privatization proposal was significantly modified as a result of organized labor's lobbying of the parliament. Although initially workers were supportive of the restructuring program, once economic conditions worsened and especially once unemployment rates began to climb, their enthusiasm for privatization diminished. With labor opposition growing and more workers' councils blocking sales, the pace of divestitures slowed. To jump-start the process of selling public firms, the Polish government was forced to make concessions to organized labor, granting workers' councils additional legal prerogatives to initiate commercialization and privatization processes, and expanded workers' representation on company supervisory boards. Toward the end of the first decade of reforms, the Solidarity trade union formed its own political party, which won elections and sought to shape restructuring policies from within the government.

In Egypt, the process of public sector restructuring has been equally contentious and, overall, a disappointing process for those within the regime who envisioned a quick pace of sales. Despite ambitious goals that were set by the government, time and again these goals remained largely unfulfilled, with the number of sales consistently falling behind the government's targets. The ETUC successfully lobbied the government to modify the original privatization proposal. Once the privatization program began, the ETUC concentrated its energies on negotiating the details of the new labor code and formulating guidelines for the early retirement scheme. At the enterprise level, workers staged protests and strikes, manifesting their opposition to economic reforms and contributing to regime fears of potential social unrest.

In the Czech Republic and Mexico, organized labor was largely absent from debates concerning public sector restructuring during the first decade of reforms. Although in the Czech Republic, unions were generally supportive of the economic reform and privatization plans, they objected to a number of provisions in the government's divestiture plan. However, the government ignored those demands and the unions, despite occasional threats of strikes and demonstrations, were unable to mount an effective challenge to this decision. Government was equally unwilling to engage unions in a dialogue concerning changes in labor law provisions or on issues of wage regulation.

In Mexico, the CTM initially backed the structural adjustment program, since, like the regime, it saw the skyrocketing inflation rate as a serious threat to the well-being of its rank-and-file members. However, once the debate shifted toward considering privatization strategies, the CTM proved unable, despite its long-standing close relationship with the ruling PRI, to have much input into program design. Even when pressure from its rank-and-file membership to challenge the regime grew, the CTM, despite occasionally engaging in rhetorical criticism, was unwilling to oppose the government's plans outright. The independent trade union organizations that did mount challenges to the government's policies and staged strikes at firms slated for sale were quickly crushed by the regime. Successive Mexican governments did not hesitate to close down striking factories or to send security forces to quell the protests.

As the evidence from Poland, Egypt, Mexico, and the Czech Republic suggests, therefore, the ability of organized labor to influence the process of designing and implementing privatization during the first decade of reforms varied greatly. This study has argued that to understand these reform dynamics, we need to examine the pre-reform relationships that developed between organized labor and the state. Even dramatic breaks with the past, such as the ones that took place in Eastern Europe, do not mean that the new governments work with a blank slate. Rather, institutions formed in the past affect how future policy conflicts are resolved by shaping resources that states and social actors bring to the negotiating table as economic reforms are being considered.

Prior to the initiation of reform, Poland, Egypt, Mexico, and Czechoslovakia were dominant-party regimes that looked to labor as one of their main bases of support. All four embarked on constructing corporatist labor institutions that were to ensure workers' political mobilization in support of the regimes while providing the regimes with the means to control labor. Whether such corporatist institutions were able to accomplish these two tasks was influenced by intraregime dynamics. As scholars of social movements have long pointed out, the degree of elite cohesiveness has significant consequences for the elite's relationship with social groups.[1] Most important, the lack of elite cohesion, elite conflicts, and factionalism creates new opportunities for social groups to more effectively press their demands. In cases in which elites are engaged in factional struggles for power, social groups can expect to find elite allies willing to make common cause with them. Thus, even groups that have few resources at their disposal may have the ability to extract concessions from the regime. By contrast, when the elite maintains cohesion and disputes are effectively managed, interest groups are hard pressed to find elite allies willing to reach out to them. Hence, even if groups manage to overcome collective action problems and articulate their demands, these demands are unlikely to be backed by disgruntled elite members, and thus social groups are likely to be less successful at extracting concessions from the state. In other words, whether corporatist labor institutions will be able to perform as expected will depend on whether the regime is a cohesive one or is torn by factionalism.

The very different dynamics within the ruling parties in Poland, Egypt, Mexico, and Czechoslovakia had far-reaching consequences for the relationship that evolved between state and organized labor. While the Czechoslovak and Mexican elites succeeded in constructing mechanisms for elite conflict resolution, neither the Polish nor the Egyptian elites were able to devise such mechanisms. In the first two cases, the ruling elites built political parties that ensured constructive management of elite conflicts and facilitated communication with the public. Although the mechanisms that were created in the two cases differed, what they did have in common was an incentive structure that rewarded loyalty and punished disloyalty to the ruling party among the elite. Hence, in both cases, for those looking to advance their political careers it paid to be faithful to the party line and made little sense to look to social groups as a means of shoring up their intra-elite positions.

1. See, for example, Doug McAdam, "Conceptual Origins, Current Problems, Future Directions," in *Comparative Perspectives on Social Movements: Political Opportunities, Mobilizing Structures, and Cultural Framings*, ed. Doug McAdam, John D. McCarthy, and Mayer N. Zald (New York: Cambridge University Press, 1996), 23–40; Sidney Tarrow, *Power in Movement: Social Movements and Contentious Politics* (New York: Cambridge University Press, 1998), 71–90.

In Poland and Egypt the opposite was the case. Although, again, the mechanisms through which such elite factionalism was manifested differed, the lack of cohesion within the elite produced similar consequences. Here neither elite managed to construct political parties that could serve as a means of both institutionalizing popular support for the regime and facilitating elite conflict resolution. In Poland, the PZPR, despite its seeming omnipresence, was often immobilized by conflicts between its various factions and was often unable to establish central control over regional bosses. In Egypt, the very establishment of a political party proved problematic because of the deep distrust between various regime factions. Here, the party and the state, rather than working in tandem, were frequently at loggerheads. Furthermore, unlike in the other three cases, the military was never fully subordinated to civilian control and became yet another player in the elite power struggles. In neither Poland nor Egypt was there a set of incentives in place that promoted elite loyalty to the party-state. The sanctions for disloyalty were few and only sporadically enforced.

The persistent elite factionalism had similar outcomes in both cases, with two distinct, but interrelated, consequences. First, it made pursuit of coherent policies difficult, thus contributing to the recurrence of economic crises. The worsening economic conditions, in turn, would trigger labor mobilization. Second, once labor was mobilized, because of the favorable opportunity structure that elite factionalism provided, it was better placed than organized labor in Mexico or Czechoslovakia to successfully extract concessions.

Equally important, over time as economic conditions in Poland and Egypt worsened, both regimes, with fewer material resources at their disposal, were less able to offer only substantive concessions in the form of higher wages, benefits, and subsidies to placate protesting workers and bring them back into the regime support coalition. Increasingly they were forced to turn to procedural concessions to diffuse labor protests. Although in both cases the ruling parties attempted to abrogate these procedural concessions once the immediate crisis was over, as their material resources declined they were less able to do so. Furthermore, although procedural concessions often appeared less costly in the short run, over the long term they profoundly reshaped the relationship between the state and organized labor. For labor organizations, these concessions proved crucial to the ability of unions to insert themselves into policy-making processes once economic reforms had commenced. In both countries, organized labor gained important legal prerogatives that guaranteed them the right to participate in debates concerning policy decisions that were likely to affect workers. In Poland, workers gained additional concessions through extensive powers granted to workers' councils in terms of participation in the daily management of their companies. Equally important, organized labor extracted these concessions as a result of successfully confronting the state. Thus, in both countries organized labor gained the valuable experience of resisting the state and its policies, experience it could draw upon when economic restructuring programs began in the 1990s. Moreover, in both cases, organized labor acquired significant autonomy from the state by having access to independently controlled financial resources. In other words, in both Poland and Egypt organized labor had significant financial autonomy, legal prerogatives, and experiential resources that facilitated its ability to transform itself from an actor largely subordinated to the state into one that could effectively confront the state and shape policies. In Mexico and Czechoslovakia, by contrast, organized labor became increasingly dependent on and subordinate to the state. Over the years it was unsuccessful in challenging state policies, it relied on the state to finance its activities, and it had few meaningful legal prerogatives it could draw upon. Those legal prerogatives it did have proved of little value because they were granted by the state rather than extracted by organized labor.

## Implications for State-Interest Group Dynamics

Although this book focused only on privatization and organized labor, the conclusions that emerge from this study are broader. In the first place it suggests that analyses of interest group influence on policy reform should begin with the disaggregation of reforms into discrete components. Different reform measures, as I have suggested, are likely to draw the interest of different social groups. While labor may pay little attention to some aspects of reform, for example, changes in laws on intellectual property rights, business groups can be expected to be interested in this type of change and seek to influence the new legal framework.[2] Both organized labor and business groups are likely to attempt to shape other reforms, such as reform of the labor code, since such changes have a direct impact on the members of both communities.

Another broader conclusion that emerges from this study is that history matters because previous interactions between the state and social groups

2. In fact, in Egypt, the business community, both domestic and foreign, has been following the changes in the intellectual property rights quite closely.

influence the resources that both have at their disposal during their future encounters. By looking at the resources that both state and interest groups bring to the table when fundamental policy changes take place, we can better understand what the relative power between the two is likely to be. In the cases under investigation here, the ability of organized labor in Poland and Egypt to influence privatization strategies was the consequence of a gradual shift in the balance of power between unions and the state. Although following the establishment of Communist rule in Poland and after the Egyptian revolution it appeared that the unions would be subjugated to and dependent on the state, over time, labor organizations in both countries gradually extracted more concessions, leaving them in a much stronger position than they had been in initially. In Czechoslovakia and Mexico unions traveled the opposite trajectory, with time leaving them increasingly dependent on the state. In all four cases, therefore, the resources at the disposal of labor organizations as they confronted economic restructuring programs were the result of incremental changes in their relationship with the state during the pre-reform period.

Thus, by examining the legacies of the period preceding the reforms, we can better understand the dynamics of the state–interest group relationship once restructuring begins. In turn, by focusing on the balance of power between the state and various social groups, we will be better able to account for the variation in governments' capacities to implement economic reform measures. The resources that groups bring to the negotiating table will shape how such measures are designed and implemented.

For example, there is no question that the first posttransition Polish government was very committed to the reform effort and in particular wanted to see a quick privatization of the public sector. Despite this commitment on the part of the state, Polish labor organizations were able to significantly influence the design and implementation of the privatization program. Their support of reforms proved crucial in the first stages of public sector restructuring and once that support cooled, it made quick shedding of state firms much more difficult. The explanation for this ability of Polish organized labor can be found in the prerogatives they have acquired in the years preceding reforms. This does not mean that it would have been impossible for the government to proceed over union opposition. However, the government felt that the costs of such a course of action were too high politically. One of the main reasons why ignoring labor was difficult in the Polish case was that removing unions and workers' councils from the decision-making process required nullifying previously acquired legal privileges. As the Czech case shows, when such prerogatives do not exist and therefore do not have to be abrogated, even a democratic government can ignore labor opposition. By the same token, although reformers became more prominent in the Egyptian government during the 1990s, the Egyptian regime found it difficult to push through its privatization program without organized labor's input. As in Poland, by the time the reforms started, the labor unions had acquired important legal prerogatives, significant financial autonomy, and experience of successfully confronting the state, and ignoring their demands would have been politically costly. What allowed the Mexican regime to disregard labor as it pushed through privatization policies was not only the cohesiveness of the elite and its full commitment to the reform effort. Commitment, of course, mattered. However, trade unions were unable to shape privatization program design and implementation less because of elite commitment to the reform effort and more as a consequence of the few resources organized labor could draw upon to compel the regime to take its views into account. Those resources had dissipated over the previous decades.

This conclusion suggests that it is difficult to establish the strength of a particular interest group without reference to the other actors that the interest group encounters. In other words, strength and weakness are not absolute qualities but rather are relative and relational. The power of organized labor, business groups, or agricultural associations can be gauged only when it is clear who their interlocutors are. Similarly, the strength of the state can be established only by knowing which groups the state is interacting with. For example, in the Polish case, during the first posttransition years the strength of the state vis-à-vis private business groups and trade unions was quite different. Whereas during the first posttransition decade the Polish state had to contend with an organized labor that had extensive resources at its disposal, private business organizations were weak and ineffective and therefore unable, to their great chagrin, to lobby the government as effectively as unions have.[3] Hence, even in a single case the balance of power between the state and different interest groups can vary. An analytical framework that explores historical patterns of state–interest group interaction and how these interactions shaped relative power, therefore, can more fully account for the differing ability of governments to successfully implement one set of policies but struggle with implementing others.

3. The reasons for their weakness, of course, are their relatively short existence and the time necessary to develop a financially powerful business class in a context in which such a class had not, for all intents and purposes, existed only twelve years ago.

## Continuity and Change

Although historical legacies shape the institutional environment in which reforming governments act, the process of economic restructuring initiates incremental changes in the structure of both the state and labor organizations. In other words, the process of reform affects both the state and the interest groups it confronts. The changing economic context thus reshapes both the actors and the relationships between them. A previously cohesive state may begin to fracture. An initially weak labor organization may devise better means of pressing its demands and often because of the reforms themselves gains access to previously unavailable resources that shore up its position. Evans's observations concerning state-business relations aptly describe the evolving relationship between state and labor as well:

> When state policies succeed in reshaping the business community, they are likely to undercut the very patterns of government-business relations that made the policies effective to begin with. Government-business relations must be seen as iterative. If embedded autonomy fosters a more economically powerful business community, the state then has a very different interlocutor to deal with. Business-government relations in succeeding periods will change to reflect the new character of the business community. Previously effective state structures may be undermined.[4]

Similarly, the process of reform and the end of the bargain that previously connected state and organized labor reshapes the economic and political environment in which both the state and labor groups function. In particular, the restructuring of the public sector pushes trade unions to redefine their role in political and economic life. At the same time, the deepening economic reform affects intra-elite dynamics. The reassessment of strategies within both the state and labor organizations as well as the shifting of the resources available to both and the emergence or strengthening of other interest groups is likely to gradually usher in changes in the interaction between the two actors.

Since 2000 the NDP in Egypt has faced an increasingly restive public. Additional external shocks, including the economic fallout of the September 11, 2001

---

4. Peter Evans, "State Structures, Government-Business Relations, and Economic Transformation," in *Business and the State in Developing Countries,* ed. Sylvia Maxfield and Ben Ross Schneider (Ithaca: Cornell University Press, 1997), 67.

attacks on New York City and Washington, D.C., and the global recession further weakened the already struggling economy. By the early 2000s, half the population was living below the poverty line and income disparities grew.[5] In 2004, for example, there were 267 labor protests; the following year an unprecedented wave of pro-democracy demonstrations engulfed the country.[6] Another, even larger wave of workers' protests swept the country in 2006 and 2007.[7] After a poor showing in the 2000 parliamentary elections, the party tried to restructure itself to attract new members and voters. In particular, the NDP has sought to incorporate the new business elite that emerged as a consequence of economic reforms. The NDP faction associated with the new elite and led by President Mubarak's son Gamal has become more visible since 2002, when the Eighth General Congress of the NDP took place, and since then has gained an important voice in setting the party's agenda.[8]

Despite the incorporation of the new business elite, the NDP has continued to be torn by internal feuding, and its ineffectiveness in mobilizing support and establishing two-way communication between the elite and the public was underscored by the regime's increasing reliance on the security forces and military courts to silence its critics. These confrontations between the regime and pro-democracy activists intensified in the year prior to the 2005 presidential and parliamentary elections. In the parliamentary elections, the outlawed Muslim Brotherhood stunned the NDP by winning 87 seats in the 454 member assembly, more than six times the number they had had in the previous parliament. Since then, the pro-democracy movement has been retreating as government repression has grown.

At the same time, the regime has attempted to breathe new life into the stalled privatization program. The government of Prime Minister Ahmed Mohamed Nazif made accelerating privatization one of its central concerns and brought more businessmen into his cabinet. The push to accelerate public sector restructuring along with government's unfulfilled promises to increase bonus pay to workers in state firms have resulted in one of the most intense

---

5. *Business Monthly,* February 2002.

6. Land Center for Human Rights Annual Report 2004 cited in *Business Monthly,* May 2005.

7. Joel Beinin and Hossam el-Hamalawy, "Egyptian Textile Workers Confront the New Economic Order," *Middle East Report Online,* March 25, 2007.

8. Jason Brownlee, "Ruling Parties and Durable Authoritarianism" (CDDRL working paper 23, Center on Democracy, Development and the Rule of Law, Stanford University's Institute on International Studies, Stanford, October 28, 2004); Michele Dunne, "Evaluating Egyptian Reform," Carnegie Papers, Democracy and the Rule of Law Project, no. 66, Carnegie Endowment for International Peace, Washington, D.C., January 2006.

confrontations between the regime and labor in decades. By one estimate, there were about 222 strikes and demonstrations during 2006. The dissatisfaction among the rank and file with the ETUC leadership has also been on display, although calls to establish an independent union organization have still not found much support among workers.[9]

The relationship between organized labor and the state in Mexico became increasingly contentious during the Zedillo and Fox administrations. Here, as the reform program entered its second decade, divisions increasingly began to appear within the ruling party, including the defection of the left-wing under the leadership of Cuauthémoc Cárdenas. At the same time, the neoliberal reforms resulted in the closure of many industrial and manufacturing plants and the growth of the maquiladora sector in the northern part of the country. As union density declined, the informal sector became an increasingly important segment of the economy. With the main labor confederation (the CTM) less able to effectively represent the rank and file and to control them, independent union organizations were formed to better defend workers in the new economic environment. In November 1997 unions whose size approached a million and a half members broke away from the CTM and founded a new independent confederation, the National Union of Workers (UNT).

The increasingly independent and militant labor organizations, furthermore, could now count on finding allies within the increasingly divided PRI and not just among opposition parties. The first sign of the changing balance of power between state and labor came when, faced with labor opposition, the Zedillo administration (1994–2000) withdrew its plans to privatize the electricity sector. Furthermore, having ignored labor union demands since the reform program began, the PRI could no longer count on labor votes during elections. This was amply demonstrated in the 2000 presidential contest when the PRI, after seven decades in power, lost to Vicente Fox, candidate of the right-leaning PAN. In many ways, the state's success in ushering in a more market-dominated economy contributed to the PRI's fall from power by creating conditions that facilitated the emergence of a better organized and politically stronger private business sector that undermined organized labor's loyalty to the party. The continuation of economic reforms during Fox's tenure galvanized popular opposition and proved that the new independent labor movement had staying

9. Joel Beinin and Hossam el-Hamalawy, "Strikes in Egypt Spread from Center of Gravity," *Middle East Report Online,* May 9, 2007, http://www.merip.org/mero/mero050907.html (accessed May 12, 2007).

power. In 2002, the UNT was one of the founding members of the Union, Peasant, Social, Indigenous, and Popular Front (FSCISP), a broad coalition of organizations opposed to neoliberal reforms.[10] In the 2006 presidential elections large segments of the labor movement backed Party of the Democratic Revolution candidate Andrés Manuel López Obrador, who promised to champion the poor. After the victory of Felipe Calderón from the conservative National Action Party, the confrontations between organized labor and the state continued.

In Poland, the continuation of reforms has changed state-labor relations as well. The number of strikes has declined since the late 1990s. Faced with high unemployment and increasing economic insecurity, workers in many industrial and manufacturing sectors and regions of the country are less willing to go on strike. In some sectors workers and union leaders realized that strikes may well be self-defeating, since in many state firms even a short strike was likely to spell bankruptcy. Union density has been declining, although at different rates in different sectors of the economy. Unions continue to have a strong presence in industry, transportation, and communications sectors. However, they are not well represented in the increasingly important construction and services sectors. Consequently, unions have sought to devise new mechanisms for pressing their demands, in the process changing the dynamics of the state-labor relationship.

Perhaps even more important, unions' initial support for the economic reform program contributed to the growing disenchantment of the rank and file with labor organizations, with the vast majority of workers believing that the unions no longer represented their interests.[11] The tensions within the labor movement increased after the Solidarity-dominated party AWS formed a government in 1997. Once in power, the Solidarity leadership began pursing policies that were contradictory to the party's electoral platform and were not supported by the union's rank and file. The experience of running a government proved to be a disastrous one for the organization. In parliamentary elections held in the fall of 2001 not only was Solidarity voted out of office, but it was no longer represented in the parliament, having failed to garner 8 percent of the vote, a threshold required of political coalitions. The electoral rout, however, strengthened the position of those within Solidarity who had long

10. Dan La Botz, "Mexico's Labor Movement in Transition," *Monthly Review* 57, no. 2 (2005): 62–72.

11. For an exhaustive discussion of the views of the rank and file of their union leaders, see Juliusz Gardawski, "Członkowie i zakładowi liderzy związków zawodowych," in Juliusz Gardawski et al., *Rozpad bastionu? Związki zawodowe w gospodarce prywatyzowanej* (Warsaw: Instytut Spraw Publicznych, 1999), 115–62.

pushed for the organization to concentrate on more traditional trade union activities. They pointed out that unions had been largely unsuccessful in expanding from their old public sector base into the private sector. As a consequence of this difficulty in moving into the private sector, not only are current members growing frustrated with their leadership but the membership rolls themselves are dwindling as the center of production moves away from state firms. This faction wanted Solidarity to concentrate on devising a new strategy that would allow it to better adapt to the new market environment. Although the 2005 parliamentary elections briefly returned center-right parties to power, Solidarity was no longer actively involved in governing.

In the Czech Republic as well, the relationship between state and labor has been undergoing a slow evolution. Unions have managed to become better organized and more effective at ensuring that their views are taken into account during policy debates. Two developments have contributed to this transformation. First, the lack of government response to union demands made the latter less interested in a cooperative relationship. Second, as the Czech economic miracle began running into trouble, organized labor became more critical of the government's policies. Nonetheless, the unions faced an uphill battle. Although about 25 percent of the workforce is still unionized, this represents a sharp decline since the political transition, and in many enterprises they have no presence. The unions have not been fully rehabilitated in the eyes of the public and many continue to view them as too rigid and not sufficiently responsive to workers' needs. These public perceptions have hindered the ability of unions to attract new members. As one public opinion survey noted, "Decline in trade union membership is generally connected with certain 'public opinion legacies' from the past. To a certain extent, behavior and expectation patterns that are inherited from the past and support the formal or passive union membership that applied under the previous regime continue to be reproduced in society.[12] The same survey revealed that many workers were concerned about possible retaliation from employers for joining a union. The association of čmkos leadership with the Social Democratic party, which has proposed many of the policies that the unions opposed, has often made it difficult for the čmkos to build broader support for its positions. However, unlike during the first decade of reforms, the čmkos has been able to stage large demonstrations to demand policy changes. In September 2003 for example, twenty thousand union members

12. "Public Views of Trade Unions Analysed," http://www.eiro.eurofound.eu.int/2004/11/feature/cz0411105f.html.

demonstrated in Prague against an austerity package proposed by the government. Similarly, more than twenty-five thousand workers demonstrated in the capital in November 2005 against the proposed changes in the labor law. The new labor law passed by the parliament in April 2006 did include a number of provisions demanded by unions, reflecting the importance of this growing labor activism.

Historical legacies shape the resources available to the state and to interest groups and hence influence how conflicts between them play out and how they are resolved. Over time, these contentious encounters can significantly shift the balance of power between the state and interest groups. As we have seen in this study, economic reforms affect social groups that had a stake in the previously established institutions. Whether these groups were able to successfully resist or influence the processes of economic restructuring depended to a great extent on the resources they could bring to the negotiations over the form of new institutional arrangements. Those resources varied depending on how conflicts between the state and particular social groups were resolved in the past. In cases in which institutional evolution had redistributed resources away from a group threatened by change, it had difficulty in challenging economic restructuring. Where historical developments allowed the group to amass resources it was better able to influence policy design and implementation. The process of economic reform deepening and the contentious encounters between the state and interest groups it generates, however, initiates incremental changes in the balance of relative power between these actors. The shifting of resources available to the state and to interest groups will in turn shape how their future contentious encounters will be mediated and resolved.

........................................................

*The Uprising of 2011*

In December 2010, a wave of protests swept through Tunisia, fueled by anger at the self-immolation of a young street vendor, Mohamed Bouazizi. Soon the protests spread to other countries in the region. In Tunisia and Egypt the uprisings succeeded in deposing the countries' presidents, Ben Ali and Mubarak, respectively. There the military was unwilling to back the countries' rulers and regime change happened with relatively little violence. In Libya, Qaddafi's fall and death were preceded by a months-long civil war and NATO-led intervention; in Yemen, President Saleh was ousted but only after months of violent confrontations between the regime and its opponents; in Syria, the violence escalated and after a year and a half the conflict between the Assad regime and the rebel forces seemed ever more intractable; and in Bahrain the opposition movement was brutally suppressed by the regime.

In mid-2012 it is still too early to tell what these political changes will ultimately bring and what the structure of the emerging political systems will be. Tunisia, Egypt, and Libya have all held elections that were generally seen as free and fair by observers. Even in those countries, however, it is still unclear whether democratic reforms will be consolidated. The history of past revolutions and transitions away from authoritarianism, whether in Latin America or in East Central Europe, suggests that these processes are challenging and contentious and often suffer from reversals. Nonetheless, regardless of the ultimate outcomes, the political landscape of the region has shifted in fundamental ways.

## Roots of Discontent in Egypt

The government of Prime Minister Ahmed Mohamed Nazif, which came to office in July 2004, set out to accelerate the implementation of neoliberal reforms and in particular the privatization of the public sector. At the same time, the government sought to attract foreign direct investors both to purchase state-owned firms and to establish new enterprises. It was quite successful in meeting its objectives. The pace of sales of state firms accelerated noticeably, and flow of foreign investment picked up. GDP grew 7 percent a year, earning praise from the IMF, which noted in 2007 that "Egypt's economy delivered another impressive performance in 2006/2007, with high growth generated by reforms and solid macroeconomic management,"[1] and from the World Bank, which ranked Egypt as the most effective country in putting in place reforms that made it easy to conduct business.[2]

But while the economy was growing at impressive rates, socioeconomic inequalities deepened significantly. Increasing numbers of people fell below the poverty line as jobs became scarce and subsidies on basic consumer goods were slashed. The 2008 global rise in food prices put further pressure on household budgets. Unemployment among young people was especially high, hovering around 25 percent.[3] The economic misery of the majority, furthermore, was juxtaposed with the ever more conspicuous consumption of a narrow elite. Pervasive corruption, cronyism, and repression added to the growing public anger.

The military, too, was increasingly concerned by the situation. In particular, it was worried about the rise in influence of the NDP faction, led by the president's son, Gamal Mubarak, and aligned with the new business elites.[4] The military had benefited from the economic reforms implemented over the previous fifteen years, building up its economic empire, which included enterprises in such diverse industries as cement, construction, energy, and hotels. However, the military was anxious that the push to accelerate privatization

1. International Monetary Fund, *IMF Country Report,* no. 07/380 (Washington, D.C.: International Monetary Fund, December 2007), 3.
2. World Bank, *Public Financial Management Reform in the Middle East and North Africa: An Overview of Regional Experience, Part I: Overview and Summary,* Report no. 55061-MNA, June 2010, 39.
3. *Economist,* February 3, 2011.
4. Michele Dunne, *Evaluating Egyptian Reform,* Carnegie Papers, Middle East Working Paper Series, no. 66, Democracy and the Rule of Law Project (Washington, D.C.: Carnegie Endowment for International Peace, 2006).

might hamper its economic and political position as new generation of businessmen moved to cash in on neoliberal reforms.[5]

## Protests in Egypt Prior to 2011

During the five years preceding the January 25, 2011, uprising, workers' mobilization and protests intensified in response to quickened pace of privatizations and other neoliberal reforms as well as the deteriorating standards of living. The number of protests grew from over six hundred in 2007 to about nine hundred in 2010.[6] Workers organized primarily around economic grievances, many of which involved wage levels at individual enterprises. Few linkages existed between workers and other social groups within Egyptian society, and as a consequence these protests and strikes remained largely divorced from other opposition groups' activities.[7] However, the huge strikes that erupted in December 2006 at the textile plants in Mahalla al-Kubra, in which twenty-four thousand workers participated, began to create these linkages. Other segments of the labor force, including doctors and teachers, joined these protests. The linkages tightened further during another large strike at public sector textile enterprises in Mahalla in April 2008, when a group of young activists set up a Facebook page that called for a national solidarity strike with the workers.[8] This wave of protests also witnessed the unprecedented sight of demonstrators pulling down posters of Mubarak and calling for his resignation.[9] The workers in Mahalla won their major demands regarding their share of company profits, and this success encouraged workers in other factories to stage protests and strikes of their own.[10] The following year, after a national strike by fifty-five thousand tax collectors, the first new independent trade union since 1957 was established, the Real Estate Tax Authority Union (RETA).

5. *New York Times,* September 11, 2010.

6. Nadine Abdalla, "Egypt's January Revolution and the Eastern European Experience," *Visegrad Revue,* March 23, 2012.

7. For instance, there was no coordination between the workers' movement and the Kifaya (Enough) movement, which first emerged in 2004.

8. This movement came to be known as the April 6 Movement.

9. Anand Gopal, "Egypt's Cauldron of Revolt," *Foreign Policy,* February 16, 2011.

10. For an exhaustive discussion of workers' movement activities during this period, see Joel Beinin, *Justice for All: The Struggle for Workers' Rights in Egypt: A Report by the Solidarity Center* (Washington, D.C.: Solidarity Center, 2010).

In other words, in the years preceding the January 25 uprising, social tensions intensified and the number of protests, demonstrations, and labor strikes grew significant. As importantly, this dissatisfaction spread across ever-wider segments of the society, and the number of people willing to express their anger at the economic and political situation increased. Linkages were also formed between workers and opposition activists, and new connections between labor groups in public sector enterprises across the country were forged. Following the parliamentary election in November 2010, which were widely seen as rigged, public frustration with the political environment grew deeper.

## Labor and the Ouster of President Mubarak

On January 14, after weeks of popular protests sparked by the self-immolation of Mohamed Bouazizi, Tunisian president Zine El Abidine Ben Ali fled the country. The following day, the *Washington Post,* commenting on the events, noted that "the Jasmine Revolution [as the Tunisian uprising came to be known] should serve as a stark warning to Arab leaders—beginning with Egypt's 83-year-old Hosni Mubarak—that their refusal to allow more economic and political opportunity is dangerous and untenable."[11] In fact, ten days later, on January 25, protests were planned in front of the Ministry of Interior in Cairo to protest policy brutality and the all-pervasive corruption, and to demand an end to the country's emergency laws, which had been in place since President Sadat's assassination, and a limit on presidential terms. On the "Day of Revolt" thousands of protesters turned out in Cairo and other cities across Egypt. Organizers set up Facebook pages and used Twitter to spread the word about the demonstrations. Despite the government's shutting down of the Internet to hinder organizing, the protests continued and the numbers of demonstrators gathering in Tahrir Square in Cairo and other cities grew. While the protests were generally peaceful, clashes between demonstrators and government forces and supporters did erupt. In all, over eight hundred people would be killed in the Egyptian uprising and over six thousand would be wounded.[12] Protests continued unabated until February 11, 2011, when Vice President Omar Suleiman announced Mubarak's resignation. The Supreme Council of the Armed Forces (SCAF) took over power.

11. *Washington Post,* January 15, 2011.
12. BBC, July 8, 2011.

As in Poland, Egyptian labor had a long history of confronting the state and could therefore draw on that experience in 2011. Unlike in Poland, the labor movement in Egypt did not lead the protests and demonstrations that resulted in the ouster of Hosni Mubarak. However, workers played a central role in these events, and their participation proved crucial to the success of the effort to usher in political change.[13] Furthermore, although historically most labor demands and activism centered on economic rather than political issues, and only a small number of labor activists explicitly included democratic reforms as part of their objectives, workers mobilized in unprecedented numbers once the demonstrations in Tahrir Square began on January 25, 2011.[14] They joined demonstrations in Cairo, Alexandria, and other key cities, and beginning on February 8, workers also staged numerous strikes, demonstrations, and sit-ins across different sectors of the economy, including public transportation and railways, industry, and government administrative agencies in the majority of Egypt's twenty-nine governorates.[15] Many of workers' demands continued to focus on economic grievances, such as improving working conditions and wages and ending corruption within enterprises. However, in the days prior to Mubarak's departure, labor was also voicing explicitly political demands.

Among the most significant events prior to Mubarak's departure was the announcement on January 30, 2011, of the creation of the Egyptian Federation of Independent Trade Unions (EFITU). Because its establishment directly challenged the ETUC's monopoly on trade union organization, "it was a revolutionary act—one in which a crime becomes the basis of a new legality."[16] On February 8 the new labor organization called for a national strike in support of the revolution and demanded Mubarak's resignation. Tens of thousands of workers responded. One estimate suggested that on February 9 alone, between two hundred fifty and three hundred thousand workers participated in these various types of protests.[17] In other words, while workers did not initiate the revolution, their participation played a crucial role its success. Furthermore, as one commentator put it, "one of the important steps of this revolution was

---

13. Labor activist Hossam El-Hamalawy has argued that labor strikes in February were the key development that forced Mubarak's resignation. Cited in Hesham Sallam, "Striking Back at Egyptian Workers," *Jadaliyya*, June 16, 2011.

14. Joel Beinin, *The Rise of Egypt's Workers*, Carnegie Papers (Washington, D.C.: Carnegie Endowment for International Peace, June 2012).

15. The government closed all places of work in early February.

16. Beinin, *Rise of Egypt's Workers*, 7.

17. Dina Bishara, "Working Class Power in Egypt's 2011 Uprising?," paper presented at the Middle East Studies Association Conference, Washington, D.C., December 2011.

taken when they began to protest, giving the revolution an economic and social slant besides the political demands."[18]

## Post-Mubarak Egypt

The events that have unfolded since Mubarak's ouster in February 2011 suggest that the transition to democracy in Egypt will not be a smooth one. For one, the relationship between the SCAF and political parties and activists has been tense. Between November 2011 and January 2012, parliamentary elections were held, with the Muslim Brotherhood winning the most seats. In May the first round of presidential elections took place and the emergency laws were finally lifted. However, in June, just prior to the second round of voting in presidential elections, the Supreme Constitutional Court ruled that the process of electing one-third of parliamentarians was illegal, thereby effectively dissolving the parliament. At the same time, the SCAF in effect restored the emergency laws by "restoring vast powers to the security services to arrest civilians," and a constitutional annex was adopted that has sharply limited presidential powers.[19]

The newly elected president, Mohamed Morsy, leader of the Freedom and Justice Party, founded by the Muslim Brotherhood, therefore faced multiple challenges as he took office. Not only was the military still firmly at the center of political decision making, but there was no working parliament and the constitution had not yet been written. At the same time, economic conditions have continued to deteriorate, and labor unrest has not ceased. During summer 2012, workers in the textile industry struck, bringing sector's production to a virtual halt. Other industries have also experienced sporadic labor protests and strikes.[20] And while a new Labor Party has been established, tensions between emerging, independent labor organizations and the ETUC have not ceased.[21] Despite these challenges, the changes that have unfolded in Egypt since January 2011 have fundamentally shifted the country's political landscape and, as in Poland, underscored the crucial role that labor has played in the political transition. The Polish and Czech experience, furthermore, suggests that even in

18. Khalid 'Ali, cited in Beinin, *Rise of Egypt's Workers,* 7.
19. Marc Lynch, "That's It for Egypt's So-Called Transition," *Foreign Policy,* June 14, 2012.
20. *Egypt Independent,* July 18, 2012.
21. In addition to the EFITU, other independent labor organizations have been established.

cases of dramatic breaks with the past, the historical legacies of state-labor interaction continue to shape post-transition dynamics between them. This suggests, especially in light of persisting economic problems, that the relation-ship between labor and the new government is likely to remain contentious.

# Bibliography

'Abbas, Mahmoud, ed. *Niqabat wa al-'amaliya al-Misriya*. Kirasat Ishtirakiya, no. 3.

Abd El-Ehah, Wafaa. "An Overall Analysis of Economic Liberalization and Privatization in the People's Assembly." In *Privatization in Egypt: The Debate in the People's Assembly*, ed. Wadouda Badran and Azza Wahby. Giza, Egypt: Center for Political Research and Studies, Faculty of Economics and Political Science, Cairo University, 1996.

Adam, Jan. *Planning and Market in Soviet and East European Economic Thought*. London: Macmillan, 1993.

———. "Transforming to a Market Economy in the Former Czechoslovakia." *Europe-Asia Studies* 45, no. 4 (1993).

Adamczuk, Lucjan, et al. *Grudzień przed styczniem: W XXV rocznicę wydarzeń grudniowych*. Gdańsk, Poland: Instytut Konserwatywny im E. Burke'a, 1996.

'Adli, Huwaida. *Al-haraka al-niqabiya bayn al-madi wa al-mustqbal*. Cairo: Institute of Cooperative Housing for Printing and Publishing, 1975.

———. *Al-haraka al-'ummaliya wa aliyat muqawamat al-ifqar, 1987–1993*. Cairo: Center for Trade Union and Workers' Services, 1997.

———. *Al-'ummal wa al-siyasa: Al-dawar al-siyasiy li-l-haraka al-'ummaliya fi misr min 1952–1981*. Cairo: Ahali Books, 1993.

Akhavi, Shahrough. "Egypt: Diffused Elite in a Bureaucratic Society." In *Political Elites in Arab North Africa*, ed. I. William Zartman, Mark A. Tessler, John Entelis, Russell A. Stone, Raymond A. Hinnebusch, and Shahrough Akhavi. New York: Longman, 1982.

Al-Din Hilal, 'Ali. *Intikhabat Majlis al-Sha'b, 1990: Dirasah wa tahlil*. Cairo: Political and Economic Studies Center, 1991.

Alexander, Christopher. "The Architecture of Militancy: Workers and the State in Algeria, 1970–1990." *Comparative Politics* 34, no. 3 (2002).

Al-Hanani, Muhammad Salih, and Ahmed Maher. *Al-Khaskhasa: Bain al-nathariya wa al-tatbiq al-misriy*. Cairo: Al-Dar al-Jamma'iya, 1995.

Al-Hilali, Ahmed Nabil. *Hatha al-mashrua lan yamir*. Helwan, Egypt: Dar al-Khadamat al-Niqabiya bil-Helwan, 1994.

Al-Sayyid, Mustafa Kamel. *Al-mujtama' wa al-siyasa fi misr: Dur jama'at al-masalih fi al-nizam al-siyasiy al-misri, 1952–1981*. Cairo: House of the Arab Future, 1983.

———. *Privatization: The Egyptian Debate*. Cairo Papers in Social Science 13, no. 2. Cairo: American University in Cairo Press, 1990.

Alvarez, R. Michael, Geoffrey Garrett, and Peter Lange. "Government Partisanship, Labor Organization, and Macroeconomic Performance." *American Political Science Review* 85, no. 2 (1991).

The American Chamber of Commerce in Egypt. *The Egyptian Labor Force*. Cairo: American Chamber of Commerce in Egypt, 1996.

———. *Privatization in Egypt: An Update*. Cairo: American Chamber of Commerce in Egypt, 1997.

Amin, Galal A. *Egypt's Economic Predicament: A Study in the Interaction of External Pressure, Political Folly, and Social Tension in Egypt, 1960–1990.* Leiden, The Netherlands: E. J. Brill, 1995.

Anderson, Bo, and James D. Cockcroft. "Control and Cooperation in Mexican Politics." In *Latin American Radicalism: A Documentary Report on Left and Nationalist Movements,* ed. Irving Louis Horowitz, Josue de Castro, and John Gerassi. New York: Random House, 1969.

Anderson, Terry L., and Peter J. Hill, eds. *The Privatization Process: A Worldwide Perspective.* Lanham, Md.: Rowman and Littlefield, 1996.

Angresano, James. "Poland After the Shock." *Comparative Economic Studies* 38, no. 2/3 (1996).

Appel, Hilary. "The Ideological Determinants of Liberal Economic Reform: The Case of Privatization." *World Politics* 52, no. 4 (2000).

———. *A New Capitalist Order: Privatization and Ideology in Russia and Eastern Europe.* Pittsburgh: University of Pittsburgh Press, 2004.

Ascherson, Neal. *The Polish August.* New York: Viking Press, 1981.

Ashby, Joe C. *Organized Labor and the Mexican Revolution Under Lazaro Cardenas.* Chapel Hill: University of North Carolina Press, 1967.

Aspe, Pedro. *Economic Transformation the Mexican Way.* Cambridge: MIT Press, 1993.

Ayubi, Nazih N. *Over-stating the Arab State: Politics and Society in the Middle East.* London: I. B. Tauris, 1995.

———. *The State and Public Policies Since Sadat.* Ithaca: Reading, 1991.

Baczkowski, Andrzej. "Pakt o przedsiębiorstwie i partycypacja i akcjonariat pracowniczy." In *Partycypacja i akcjonariat pracowniczy w Polsce,* ed. Leszek Gilejko. Warsaw: Zakład Badań Przekształceń Własnościowych Instytut Studiów Politycznych PAN/Instytut Gospodarstwa Społecznego i Katedra Socjologii, SGH, 1995.

Badawi, Hassan. "Al-taharukat al-jam'iya li-l-'ummal, 1988–1991." In *Al-haraka al-'ummaliya fi ma'arakat al-tuhawwul,* ed. Mahmoud Abbas et al. Cairo: Arab Research Center, 1994.

Bailey, John, and Leopoldo Gomez. "The PRI and Political Liberalization." *Journal of International Affairs* 43, no. 2 (1990).

Baka, Władysław. *U źródeł wielkiej transformacji.* Warsaw: Oficyna Naukowa, 1999.

Baker, Raymond William. *Egypt's Uncertain Revolution Under Nasser and Sadat.* Cambridge: Harvard University Press, 1978.

Balassa, Bela, et al. *Development Strategies in Semi-industrial Economies.* Baltimore: Johns Hopkins University Press, 1992.

Balcerowicz, Leszek. *800 dni: Szok kontrolowany.* Warsaw: Polska Oficyna Wydawnicza, "BGW," 1992.

———. "Understanding Post-Communist Transitions." In *Political Economy of Policy Reform,* ed. John Williamson. Washington, D.C.: Institute for International Economics, 1994.

Bałtkowski, Maciej. *Prywatyzajca przedsiębiorstw państowych: Przebieg i ocena.* Warsaw: PWN, SA, 1998.

Barany, Zoltan, and Ivan Volgyes, eds. *The Legacies of Communism in Eastern Europe.* Baltimore: Johns Hopkins University Press, 1995.

Bartlett, David L. *The Political Economy of Dual Transitions: Market Reform and Economic Interaction in Economic Policy Reform; Evidence from Eight Countries.* Cambridge, U.K.: Blackwell, 1993.

Bayat, Assef. "Populism, Liberalization, and Popular Participation: Industrial Democracy in Egypt." *Economic and Industrial Democracy* 14, no. 2 (1993).

Beattie, Kirk J. *Egypt During the Nasser Years: Ideology, Politics, and Civil Society.* Boulder, Colo.: Westview Press, 1994.

———. *Egypt During the Sadat Years.* New York: Palgrave, 2000.

———. "Prospects for Democratization in Egypt." *American-Arab Affairs* 34 (1991).

Beck, Carl. "Control and Bureaucratization in Czechoslovakia." *Journal of Politics* 23, no. 2 (1961).

Be'eri, Eliezer. *Army Officers in Arab Politics and Society.* London: Praeger-Pall, 1979.

Beinin, Joel. "Labor, Capital, and the State in Nasserist Egypt, 1952–1961." *International Journal of Middle Eastern Studies* 21 (Fall 1989).

Beinin, Joel, and Hossam el-Hamalawy. "Egyptian Textile Workers Confront the New Economic Order." *Middle East Report Online*, March 25, 2007.

Beinin, Joel, and Zachary Lockman. *Workers on the Nile: Nationalism, Communism, Islam, and the Egyptian Working Class, 1882–1954.* Princeton: Princeton University Press, 1987.

Bejar, Alejandro Alvarez. "Economic Crisis and the Labor Movement in Mexico." In *Unions, Workers, and the State in Mexico,* ed. Kevin J. Middlebrook. San Diego: Center for U.S.-Mexican Studies, University of California, San Diego, 1991.

Belanger, Gerard. *Czech Republic: IMF Economic Review.* Washington, D.C.: International Monetary Fund, 1995.

Bellin, Eva. *Stalled Democracy: Capital, Labor, and the Paradox of State-Sponsored Development.* Ithaca: Cornell University Press, 2002.

Bhagwait, Jagdish N. "Directly Unproductive, Profit-Seeking (DUP) Activities." *Journal of Political Economy* 90 (October 1982).

Bianchi, Robert. "The Corporatization of the Egyptian Labor Movement." *Middle East Journal* 40, no. 3 (1986).

———. "Interest Groups and Politics in Mubarak's Egypt." In *The Political Economy of Contemporary Egypt,* ed. Ibrahim M. Oweiss. Washington, D.C.: Center for Contemporary Arab Studies, Georgetown University, 1990.

———. *Unruly Corporatism: Associational Life in Twentieth-Century Egypt.* New York: Oxford University Press, 1989.

Bielasiak, Jack. "The Party: Permanent Crisis." In *Poland: Genesis of a Revolution,* ed. Abraham Brumberg. New York: Random House, 1983.

Bienen, Henry. *Tanzania: Party Transformation and Economic Development.* Princeton: Princeton University Press, 1967.

Bienen, Henry, and Jeffrey Herbst. "The Relationship Between Political and Economic Reform in Africa." *Comparative Politics* 29, no. 1 (1996).

Bienkowski, Wojciech. "The Bermuda Triangle: Why Self-Governed Firms Work for Their Own Destruction." *Journal of Comparative Economics* 26, no. 4 (1992).

Biglaiser, Glen, and Michelle A. Danis. "Privatization and Democracy: The Effects of Regime Type in the Developing World." *Comparative Political Studies* 35, no. 1 (2002).

Binder, Leonard. *In a Moment of Enthusiasm: Political Power and Second Stratum in Egypt.* Chicago: University of Chicago Press, 1966.

Błaszczyk, Barbara. *Pierwsze lata prywatyzacji w Polsce (1989–1991): Dylematy, koncepcje i rywalizacja.* Studia Ekonomiczne, no. 30. Warsaw: Polska Academia Nauk, Instytut Nauk Ekonomicznych, 1993.

————. *Własność pracownicza i pracownicze udziały kapitałowe w krajach gospodarki rynkowej.* Warsaw: Fundacja im. Friedricha Eberta, 1992.

Błaszczyk, Barbara, and Richard Woodward, eds. *Privatization in Post-Communist Countries.* Vol. 1. Warsaw: Center for Social and Economic Research, 1996.

Blejer, Mario I., and Fabrizio Coricelli. *The Making of Economic Reform in Eastern Europe: Conversations with Leading Reformers in Poland, Hungary, and the Czech Republic.* Aldershot, U.K.: Edward Elgar, 1995.

Brandenburg, Frank. *The Making of Modern Mexico.* Englewood Cliffs, N.J.: Prentice Hall, 1964.

Bresser Pereira, Luiz Carlos, Jose Maria Maravall, and Adam Przeworski. *Economic Reforms in New Democracies: A Social-Democratic Approach.* New York: Cambridge University Press, 1993.

Bromke, Adam. *Poland: The Protracted Crisis.* Oakville: Mosaic Press, 1983.

Brownlee, Jason. "Ruling Parties and Durable Authoritarianism." CDDRL Working Paper 23. Center on Democracy, Development and the Rule of Law, Stanford University's Institute on International Affairs, October 28, 2004.

Buccianti, Alexandre. "Les élections législatives en Égypte." *Maghreb-Mashrek* 106 (October/November/December 1984).

Buchtikova, Alena. "Privatization in the Czech Republic." In *Privatization in Post-Communist Countries.* Vol. 1, ed. Barbara Błaszczyk and Richard Woodward. Warsaw: Center for Social and Economic Research, 1996.

Burgess, Katrina. "Loyalty Dilemmas and Market Reform: Party-Union Alliances Under Stress in Mexico, Spain, and Venezuela." *World Politics* 52 (October 1999).

————. *Parties and Unions in the New Global Economy.* Pittsburgh: University of Pittsburgh Press, 2004.

Callaghy, Thomas. "Lost Between State and Market: The Politics of Economic Adjustment in Ghana, Zambia, and Nigeria." In *Economic Crisis and Policy Choice: The Politics of Adjustment in the Third World,* ed. Joan M. Nelson. Princeton: Princeton University Press, 1995.

————. *The State-Society Struggle: Zaire in Comparative Perspective.* New York: Columbia University Press, 1984.

Camp, Roderic Ai. "Mexican Presidential Candidates: Changes and Prospects for the Future." *Polity* 16, no. 4 (1984).

————. *Mexico's Leaders: Their Educational Background and Recruitment.* Tucson: University of Arizona Press, 1980.

————. *Politics in Mexico.* New York: Oxford University Press, 1996.

Candland, Christopher, and Rudra Sil, eds. *The Politics of Labor in a Global Age: Continuity and Change in Late-Industrializing and Post-Socialist Economies.* New York: Oxford University Press, 2001.

Castaneda, Jorge G. *Perpetuating Power: How Mexican Presidents Are Chosen.* New York: New Press, 2000.

Castells, Manuel. *The Information Age.* Vol. 2, *The Power of Identity.* Oxford, U.K.: Blackwell, 1997.

Centeno, Miguel Angel. *Democracy Within Reason: Technocratic Revolution in Mexico.* University Park: Pennsylvania State University Press, 1994.

Centeno, Miguel Angel, and Sylvia Maxfield. "The Marriage of Finance and Order: Changes in the Mexican Political Elite." *Journal of Latin American Studies* 24, no. 1 (1992).

Chełmiński, D., and A. Czynczyk. *Społeczne bariery prywatyzacji: Prawomocność ładu instytucjonalnego w przedsiębiorstwach skomercjalizowanych.* Warsaw: Fundacja Centrum Prywatyzacji, 1991.

Chodorowski, Marcin. *"Sieć"—81: Powstanie, struktura, działanie.* Warsaw: Instytut Studiów Politycznych Polskiej Akademii Nauk, 1992.

Chossudovsky, Michel. *Globalization of Poverty: Impacts of IMF and World Bank Reforms.* Penang: Third World Network, 1997.

Clark, Marjorie Ruth. *Organized Labor in Mexico.* Chapel Hill: University of North Carolina Press, 1973.

Cohen, Youssef. "The Benevolent Leviathan: Political Consciousness Among Urban Workers Under State Corporatism." *American Political Science Review* 76, no. 1 (1982).

———. "The Impact of Bureaucratic Authoritarian Rule on Economic Growth." *Comparative Political Studies* 18, no. 1 (1985).

Collier, David. "Trajectory of a Concept: 'Corporatism' in the Study of Latin American Politics." In *Latin America in Comparative Perspective: New Approaches to Methods and Analysis,* ed. Peter H. Smith. Boulder, Colo.: Westview Press, 1995.

Collier, David, and Ruth Berins Collier. *Shaping the Political Arena: Critical Junctures, the Labor Movement, and Regime Dynamics in Latin America.* Princeton: Princeton University Press, 1991.

Collier, Ruth Berins. *The Contradictory Alliance: State-Labor Relations and Regime Change in Mexico.* Berkeley: University of California, International and Area Studies, 1992.

———. *Paths Towards Democracy: The Working Class and Elites in Western Europe and South America.* New York: Cambridge University Press, 1996.

Collier, Ruth Berins, and James Mahoney. "Adding Collective Actors to Collective Outcomes: Labor and Recent Democratization in South America and Southern Europe." *Comparative Politics* 30, no. 3 (1997).

Cook, Maria Lorena. *The Politics of Labor Reform in Latin America: Between Flexibility and Rights.* University Park: Pennsylvania State University Press, 2007.

Cooper, Mark N. *The Transformation of Egypt.* London: Croom Helm, 1982.

Crawford, Beverly. "Post-Communist Political Economy: A Framework for the Analysis of Reform." In *Markets, States, and Democracy: The Political Economy of Post-Communist Transformation,* ed. Beverly Crawford. Boulder, Colo.: Westview Press, 1995.

Crowley, Stephen. "Explaining Labor Weakness in Post-Communist Europe: Historical Legacies and Comparative Perspective." *East European Politics and Society* 18, no. 3 (2004).

Crowley, Stephen, and David Ost. *Workers After Workers' States: Labor and Politics in Postcommunist Eastern Europe.* New York: Rowman and Littlefield, 2001.

Curry, Jane Leftwich. "The Solidarity Crisis, 1980–81." In *Poland's Permanent Revolution: People vs. Elites, 1956 to the Present,* ed. Jane Leftwich Curry and Luba Fajfer. Washington, D.C.: American University Press, 1996.

Czajka, Zdzisław. *Związki zawodowe wobec polityki płac w okresie transformacji.* Warsaw: Instytut Pracy i Spraw Socjalnych, 1998.

Dąbrowski, Janusz. *Przedsiębiorstwa państwowe w roku 1990—wyniki badań.* Warsaw: Instytut Badań nad Gospodarka Rynkową i Prawami Własności, 1991.

Dąbrowski, Janusz, Michał Federowicz, and Anthony Levitas. "Polish State Enterprises and the Properties of Performance: Stabilization, Marketization, Privatization." *Politics and Society* 19, no. 4 (1991).

Davis, Charles L., and Kenneth M. Coleman. "Labor and the State: Union Incorporation and Working-Class Politicization in Latin America." *Comparative Political Studies* 18, no. 4 (1986).

Dawisha, Karen. *The Kremlin and the Prague Spring.* Berkeley and Los Angeles: University of California Press, 1984.

Dekmejian, R. Hrair. *Egypt Under Nasir: A Study of Political Dynamics.* Albany: State University of New York Press, 1971.

De Sola Pool, Ithiel. "Public Opinion in Czechoslovakia." *Public Opinion Quarterly* 34, no. 1 (1970).

Dessouki, Ali E. Hillal. "Dynamics of Change and Continuity in Egypt Today." In *Cairo Papers: The 20th Anniversary Symposium, Twenty Years of Development in Egypt, 1977–1997.* Part 1, *Economy, Politics, Regional Relations,* ed. Mark C. Kennedy. Cairo Papers in Social Science 21, no. 3. Cairo: American University in Cairo Press, 1999.

Deutsch, Karl. "Social Mobilization and Political Development." In *Political Development and Social Change,* ed. Jason Finkle and Richard Gable. New York: Wiley, 1971.

De Veydenthal, Jan B. "Poland: Workers and Politics." In *Blue-Collar Workers in Eastern Europe,* ed. Jan F. Triska and Charles Gati. London: George Allen and Unwin, 1981.

Diamond, Larry, and Marc Platter, eds. *Economic Reforms and Democracy.* Baltimore: Johns Hopkins University Press, 1995.

Djankov, Simon, and Peter Murreil. *Enterprise Restructuring in Transition: A Quantitative Survey.* Working Paper 244, University of Maryland, Center for Institutional Reform and Informal Sector, November 2000.

Drake, Paul W. *Labor Movements and Dictatorships: The Southern Cone in Comparative Perspective.* Baltimore: Johns Hopkins University Press, 1996.

Duchacek, Ivo. "The February Coup in Czechoslovakia." *World Politics* 2, no. 4 (1950).

Dudek, Antoni, and Tomasz Marszałkowski. *Walki uliczne w PRL, 1956–1989.* Kraków: Wydawnictwo Geo, 1999.

Dunne, Michele. "Evaluating Egyptian Reform." Carnegie Papers, Democracy and the Rule of Law Project 66, Carnegie Endowment for International Peace, Washington, D.C., January 2006.

Duverger, Maurice. *Political Parties: Their Organization and Activity in the Modern State.* London: Methuen, 1969.

Dyba, Karel, and Jan Svejnar. *An Overview of Recent Economic Developments in the Czech Republic.* Working Paper 61, Center for Economic Research and Graduate Education, Charles University, and Economic Institute of the Academy of Science of the Czech Republic, Prague, April 1994.

Eddin Ibrahim, Saad. "Qui va capter l'ame de Hosni Mubarak?" *Maghreb-Mashrek* 97 (July/August/September 1982).

Ekiert, Grzegorz. *The State Against Society: Political Crises and Their Aftermath in East Central Europe.* Princeton: Princeton University Press, 1996.

Ekiert, Grzegorz, and Stephen E. Hanson, eds. *Capitalism and Democracy in Central and Eastern Europe.* New York: Cambridge University Press, 2003.

El-Mikway, Noha. *The Building of Consensus in Egypt's Transition Process.* Cairo: American University in Cairo Press, 1999.

El-Naggar, Said. "Problems and Prospects of Privatization." In *The Political Economy of Contemporary Egypt*, ed. Ibrahim M. Oweiss. Washington, D.C.: Center for Contemporary Arab Studies, Georgetown University, 1990.

El-Sayed, Salah. *Workers' Participation in Management*. Cairo: American University in Cairo Press, 1978.

El-Shafai, Omar. *Workers, Trade Unions, and the State in Egypt: 1984–1989*. Cairo Papers in Social Science 18, no. 2. Cairo: American University in Cairo Press, 1995.

Elster, Jan, Claus Offe, and Ulrich K. Preuss. *Institutional Design in Post-Communist Societies: Rebuilding the Ship at Sea*. New York: Cambridge University Press, 1998.

Evans, Peter. *Embedded Autonomy: States and Industrial Transformation*. Princeton: Princeton University Press, 1995.

———. "The State as Problem and Solution: Predation, Embedded Autonomy, and Structural Change." In *The Politics of Economic Adjustment: International Constraints, Distributive Conflicts, and the State*, ed. Stephan Haggard and Robert R. Kaufman. Princeton: Princeton University Press, 1992.

———. "State Structures, Government-Business Relations, and Economic Transformation." In *Business and the State in Developing Countries*, ed. Sylvia Maxfield and Ben Ross Schneider. Ithaca: Cornell University Press, 1997.

Evanson, Robert K. "Regime and Working Class in Czechoslovakia, 1948–1968." *Soviet Studies* 37, no. 2 (1985).

Fan, Qimiao, and Mark E. Schaffer. "Government Financial Transfer and Enterprise Adjustment in Russia with Comparison to Central and East Europe." *Economics of Transition* 2, no. 2 (1994).

Farag, Imam. "Le politique a l'égyptienne: Lectures des élections législative." *Maghreb-Mashrek* 133 (July/September 1991).

Federowicz, Michał, Wiesława Kozek, and Witold Morawski. *Stosunki przemysłowe w Polsce: Studium czterech przypadków*. Warsaw: Instytut Socjologii Uniwersytetu Warszawskiego, 1995.

Fernandez, Raquel, and Dani Rodrik. "Resistence to Reform: Status Quo Bias in the Presence of Individual-Specific Uncertainty." *American Economic Review* 81, no. 5 (1991).

Fisera, Vladimir. *Workers' Councils in Czechoslovakia, 1968–69: Documents and Essays*. London: Allison and Busby, 1978.

Frieden, Jeffry. *Debt, Development, and Democracy*. Princeton: Princeton University Press, 1992.

———. "Invested Interests: The Politics of National Economic Policies in a World of Global Finance." *International Organization* 45, no. 4 (1991).

Frydman, Roman, and Andrzej Rapaczynski. *Privatization in Eastern Europe: Is the State Withering Away?* New York: Central European University Press, 1994.

Gadomski, Witold. *Instytucjonalne bariery rozwoju gospodarczego*. Warsaw: Centrum im. Adama Smitha, 1996.

Galal, Amin. *Country Economic Memorandum for Egypt*. Washington, D.C.: World Bank, December 1996.

Gardawski, Juliusz. *Poland's Industrial Workers and Return to Democracy and Market Economy*. Warsaw: Fridrich Ebert Stiftung, 1996.

Gardawski, Juliusz, and Leszek Gilejko. *Poles and Polish Industrial Elites on Privatization*. Warsaw: Warsaw School of Economics, 1997.

Gardawski, Juliusz, and Tomasz Żukowski. *Robotnicy 1993—wybory ekonomiczne i polityczne*. Warsaw: Fundacja im. Friedricha Eberta, 1994.

Gardawski, Juliusz, Barbara Gąciarz, Andrzej Mokrzyszewski, and Włodzimierz Pańkow. *Rozpad bastionu? Związki zawodowe w gospodarce prywatyzowanej.* Warsaw: Instytut Spraw Publicznych, 1999.

Garrett, Geoffrey, and Peter Lange. "Internationalization, Institutions, and Political Change." *International Organization* 49, no. 5 (1995).

Garrett, Geoffrey, and Christopher Way. "The Rise of Public Sector Unions, Corporatism, and Macroeconomic Performance, 1970–1990." In *The Political Economy of European Integration,* ed. Barry Eichengreen and Jeffry Frieden. New York: Springer-Verlag.

Geddes, Barbara. "Challenging the Conventional Wisdom." *Journal of Democracy* 5, no. 4 (1994).

———. "Economic Reform in New Democracies: A Social-Democratic Approach." *Latin American Research Review* (Spring 1995).

———. *Politician's Dilemma: Building State Capacity in Latin America.* Berkeley and Los Angeles: University of California Press, 1994.

Gereffi, Gary, and Donald L. Wyman, eds. *Manufacturing Miracles: Paths of Industrialization in Latin America and East Asia.* Princeton: Princeton University Press, 1990.

Gieorgica, J. Paweł, ed. *Problemy restrukturyzacji górnictwa.* Warsaw: Centrum Partnerstwa Społecznego "Dialog" im. Andrzeja Bączkowskiego, 1998.

Gilejko, Leszek, ed. *Partycypacja i akcjonariat pracowniczy w Polsce.* Warsaw: Zakład Badań Przekształceń Własnosciowych, Instytut Studiów Politycznych Polskiej Akademii Nauk, 1995.

———. *Robotnicy i społeczeństwo, 1980–81, 1989–90.* Warsaw: Szkoła Główna Handlowa, 1995.

———, ed. *Własność pracownicza w Polsce.* Monografie i Opracowania 436. Warsaw: Szkoła Główna Handlowa, 1997.

Gilejko, Leszek, and Przemysław Wójcik, eds. *Położenie klasy robotniczej w Polsce— potrzeby i aspiracje robotników, tom 7.* Warsaw: Akademia Nauk Spoecznych i Instytut Badań Klasy Robotniczej, 1987.

Giugale, Marcelo M., and Hamed Mobarak, eds. *Private Sector Development in Egypt.* Cairo: American University in Cairo Press, 1996.

Goldberg, Ellis Jay. "Reading from Left to Right: The Social History of Egyptian Labor." In *The Social History of Labor in the Middle East,* ed. Ellis Jay Goldberg. Boulder, Colo.: Westview Press, 1996.

Goldschmidt, Arthur, Jr. *Modern Egypt: The Formation of a Nation-State.* Boulder, Colo.: Westview Press, 1988.

Gomulka, Stanislawa, and Piotr Jasinski. *Privatization in Poland: 1989–1993: Policies, Methods, and Results.* Warsaw: Polska Akademia Nauk, Instytut Nauk Ekonomicznych, 1994.

Gomulka, Stanislawa, and Antony Polonsky, eds. *Polish Paradoxes.* London: Routledge, 1990.

Gordon, Joel. *Nasser's Blessed Movement: Egypt's Free Officers and the July Revolution.* New York: Oxford University Press, 1992.

Grindle, Merilee S. *Challenging the State: Crisis and Innovation in Latin America and Africa.* New York: Cambridge University Press, 1996.

———. "Policy Change in an Authoritarian Regime: Mexico Under Echeverria." *Journal of InterAmerican Studies and World Politics* 19, no. 4 (1977).

Grindle, Merilee S., and John W. Thomas. *Public Choice and Policy Change: The Political Economy of Reform in Developing Countries*. Baltimore: Johns Hopkins University Press, 1991.

Haggard, Stephan, and Robert R. Kaufman. "The Challenge of Consolidation." *Journal of Democracy* 5, no. 4 (1994).

———. *The Political Economy of Democratic Transitions*. Princeton: Princeton University Press, 1995.

———, eds. *The Politics of Economic Adjustment*. Princeton: Princeton University Press, 1992.

Haggard, Stephan, and Steven B. Webb, eds. *Voting for Reform: Democracy, Political Liberalization, and Economic Adjustment*. New York: Oxford University Press, 1994.

Hahn, Werner G. *Democracy in a Communist Party: Poland's Experience Since 1980*. New York: Columbia University Press, 1987.

Hall, Peter. *Governing the Economy: The Politics of State Inervention in Britain and France*. New York: Oxford University Press, 1986.

Hamilton, Nora L. *The Limits of State Autonomy: Post-revolutionary Mexico*. Princeton: Princeton University Press, 1982.

Handelman, Howard. "The Politics of Labor Protest in Mexico." *Journal of InterAmerican Studies and World Affairs* 18, no. 3 (1976).

Hanson, Stephen E. "The Leninist Legacy and Institutional Change." *Comparative Political Studies* 28, no. 2 (1995).

Harik, Ilya. "The Single Party as a Subordinate Movement: The Case of Egypt." *World Politics* 26, no. 1 (1973).

Hausner, Jerzy. "Formowanie się systemu stosunków pracy i reprezentacji interesów w Polsce w warunkach transformacji ustrojowej." In *Negocjacje: Droga do paktu społecznego: doświadczenia, treść, partnerzy, formy*. Warsaw: Polskie Towarzystwo Polityki Społecznej i Instytut Pracy i Spraw Socjalnych, 1995.

———. "Miedzy starymi i nowymi czasy—struktury reprezentacji interesów w Polsce." *Przegląd Społeczny*, no. 7 (1992).

Havlovic, Stephen J., and William M. Moore. "Workers' Councils, Trade Unions, and Industrial Democracy in Poland." *Economic and Industrial Democracy* 18, no. 2 (1997).

Haworth, Nigel, and Stephen Hughes. "Internationalisation, Industrial Relations Theory, and International Relations." *Journal of Industrial Relations* 42, no. 2 (2000).

Heeger, Gerald A. "Bureaucracy, Political Parties, and Political Development." *World Politics* 25, no. 4 (1973).

Hellman, Joel S. "Winner Takes All: The Politics of Partial Reform in Post-Communist Transitions." *World Politics* 50, no. 2 (1998).

Hellman, Judith Adler. *Mexico in Crisis*. New York: Holmes and Meier, 1983.

Hendriks, Bertus. "Egypt's Elections, Mubarak's Bind." *MERIP*, January 1985.

Henly, John S., and Mohamed M. Ereisha. "State Control and Labor Productivity Crisis: The Egyptian Textile Industry at Work." *Economic Development and Social Change* 35, no. 3 (1987).

Henry, Clement M., and Robert Springborg. *Globalization and the Politics of Development in the Middle East*. New York: Cambridge University Press, 2001.

Hinnebusch, Raymond A. "The National Progressive Unionist Party: The Nationalist-Left Opposition in Post-populist Egypt." *Arab Studies Quarterly* 3, no. 4 (1981).

Hirst, David, and Irene Beeson. *Sadat.* London: Faber and Faber, 1981.

Hirszowicz, Maria, and Andre Mailer. "Trade Unions as an Active Factor in Economic Transformation." *Polish Sociological Review* 13, no. 115 (1996).

Hollister, Robinson, Jr., and Markus Goldstein. *Reforming Labor Markets in the Middle East: Implications for Structural Adjustment and Market Economies.* Sector Study 8. San Francisco: International Center for Economic Growth, 1994.

Huntington, Samuel P. *Political Order in Changing Societies.* New Haven: Yale University Press, 1968.

———. *The Third Wave: Democratization in the Late Twentieth Century.* Norman: University of Oklahoma Press, 1993.

Huntington, Samuel P., and Clement H. Moore, eds. *Authoritarian Politics in Modern Societies: The Dynamics of Established One-Party Systems.* New York: Basic Books, 1970.

Huntington, Samuel P., and Joan M. Nelson. *No Easy Choice: Political Participation in Developing Countries.* Cambridge: Harvard University Press, 1976.

Huntington, Samuel P., and Myron Weiner, eds. *Understanding Political Development.* Boston: Little, Brown, 1987.

Hussein, Mahmoud. *Class Conflict in Egypt, 1945–1970.* New York: Monthly Review Press, 1973.

Inglot, Tomasz. "Between High Politics and Civil Society." *Perspectives on Political Science* 27, no. 3 (1998).

Institute for World Economics. *Transformation in Progress: Proceedings of the First Roundtable Conference, Budapest, March 2–3, 1994.* Budapest: Institute for World Economics, 1994.

Jacoby, Stanford, ed. *The Workers of Nations: Industrial Relations in a Global Economy.* New York: Oxford University Press, 1995.

Janowski, Karol B. *Polska 1981–1989: Między konfrontacją a porozumieniem, studium historyczno-politologiczne.* Warsaw: Wydawnictwo Naukowe SCHOLAR, 1996.

Jarosz, Maria, ed. *Blaski i cienie spółek pracowniczych, 1991–1994.* Warsaw: Instytut Studiów Politycznych Polskiej Akademii Nauk, 1995.

———. *Spółki pracownicze '95.* Warsaw: Instytut Studiów Politycznych Polskiej Akademii Nauk, 1996.

Johnson, Juliet. "Path Contingency in Postcommunist Transformations." *Comparative Politics* 33, no. 3 (2001).

Kaliński, Janusz. *Gospodarka polski w latach 1944–1989: Przemiany strukturalne.* Warsaw: Państwowe Wydawnictwo Ekonomiczne, 1995.

Kamiński, Tytus. "Zaniechanie prywatyzacji: Bariery i konsekwencje." *Transformacja Gospodarki* 86 (1997).

Katzenstein, Peter J. *Small States in World Markets.* Ithaca: Cornell University Press, 1983.

Kaufman Purcell, Susan. "Decision-Making in an Authoritarian Regime: Theoretical Implications from the Mexican Case Study." *World Politics* 26, no. 1 (1973).

Kavan, Zdenek, and Bernard Wheaton. *The Velvet Revolution: Czechoslovakia, 1988–1991.* Boulder, Colo.: Westview Press, 1992.

Keinle, Eberhard. *A Grand Delusion: Democracy and Economic Reform in Egypt.* London: I. B. Tauris, 2001.

Kemp-Walsh, A. *The Birth of Solidarity: The Gdansk Negotiations, 1980.* New York: St. Martin's Press, 1983.

Kenway, Peter, and Eva Klvacova. "The Web of Cross-Ownership Among Czech Financial Intermediaries: An Assessment." *Europe-Asia Studies* 48, no. 5 (1996).

Kersten, Krystyna. *Narodziny systemu władzy: Polska 1942–1948.* Paris: Libella, 1986.

Khalid, Muhammad. *Al-haraka al-niqabiya bayna al-madi wa al-mustaqbal.* Cairo: Cooperative Institute for Printing and Publishing, 1975.

Kingstone, Peter. *Crafting Coalitions for Reform: Business Preferences, Political Institutions, and Neoliberal Reform in Brazil.* University Park: Pennsylvania State University Press, 1999.

Kirscheimer, Otto. "The Transformation of the West European Party System." In *Political Parties and Political Development,* ed. Joseph LaPalombara and Myron Weiner. Princeton: Princeton University Press, 1966.

Klaus, Vaclav. "Policy Dilemmas of Eastern European Reform: Notes of an Insider." Paper presented at the symposium "Central Banking in Emerging Market-Oriented Economies," organized by the Federal Reserve Bank of Kansas City, Jackson Hole, Wyoming, August 1990.

Kloc, Kazimierz. "Trade Unions and Economic Transformation in Poland." *Journal of Communist Studies* 9, no. 4 (1993).

Kloc, Kazimierz, and Władysław Rychlowski. "Spory zbiorowe i strajki w przemyśle." *Przegląd Społeczny* 18–19 (1993).

Kohli, Atul. "Democracy and Development." In *Development Strategies Reconsidered,* ed. John P. Lewis and Valeriana Kallab. Washington, D.C.: Overseas Development Council, 1986.

Kolankiewicz, George. "Employee Self-Management and Socialist Trade Unionism." In *Policy and Politics in Contemporary Poland,* ed. Jean Woodall. New York: St. Martin's Press, 1982.

———. "Poland 1980: The Working Class Under 'Anomie Socialism.'" In *Blue-Collar Workers in Eastern Europe,* ed. Jan F. Triska and Charles Gati. London: George Allen and Unwin, 1981.

Kolankiewicz, George, and Paul G. Lewis. *Poland: Politics, Economic, and Society.* New York: Pinter, 1988.

Kolarska-Bobinska, Lena. "The Myth of the Market and the Reality of Reform." In *Polish Paradoxes,* ed. Stanislaw Gomulka and Antony Polonsky. London: Routledge, 1990.

Kotrba, Josef. *Czech Privatization: Players and Winners.* Working Paper series 58, CERGE-EI, Prague, April 1994.

Kozek, Wiesława, and Jolanta Kulpińska, eds. *Zbiorowe stosunki pracy w Polsce: Obraz zmian.* Warsaw: Wydawnictwo Naukowe SCHOLAR, 1998.

Kozłowski, Paweł. *Szukanie sposobu: Społeczne uwarunkowania procesu transformacji w Polsce w latach 1989–1993.* Warsaw: Polska Akademia Nauk, Instytut Nauk Ekonomicznych, 1997.

Kramer, Mark. "Polish Workers and the Post-Communist Transition, 1989–1993." *Europe-Asia Studies* 47, no. 4 (1984).

Krasner, Stephen. "Approaches to the State—Alternative Conceptions and Historical Dynamics." *Comparative Politics* 16, no. 2 (1984).

Krueger, Anne O. *Economic Policy Reform in Developing Countries: The Kuznets Memorial Lectures at the Economic Growth Center, Yale University.* Cambridge, U.K.: Blackwell, 1992.

———. "The Political Economy of Rent-Seeking Society." *American Economic Review* 64 (1974).

Krystufek, Zdenek. *The Soviet Regime in Czechoslovakia.* Boulder, Colo.: East European Monographs, 1981.

Kubicek, Paul. *Organized Labor in Postcommunist States: From Solidarity to Infirmity.* Pittsburgh: University of Pittsburgh Press, 2004.

———. "Organized Labor in Post-Communist States: Will the Western Sun Set on It Too?" *Comparative Politics* 32, no. 1 (1999).

Kupka, Martin. "Transformation of Ownership in Czechoslovakia." *Soviet Studies* 44, no. 2 (1992).

Kuroń, Jacek, and Jacek Żakowski. *Siedmiolatka czyli kto ukradł Polskę?* Wrocław, Poland: Wydawnictwo Dolnośląskie, 1997.

Kusin, Vladimir V. *From Dubcek to Charter 77: A Study of "Normalization" in Czechoslovakia, 1968–1978.* New York: St. Martin's Press, 1978.

La Botz, Dan. *The Mask of Democracy: Labor Suppression in Mexico Today.* Boston: South End Books, 1992.

———. "Mexico's Labor Movement in Transition." *Monthly Review* 57, no. 2 (2005).

Lakhadar, Lafif. "The Development of Class Struggle in Egypt." *Khamsin: Journal of Revolutionary Socialists of the Middle East* 5 (1978).

Lal, Deepak. *The Poverty of Development Economics.* London: Institute of Economic Affairs, 1983.

Land Center for Human Rights. *Ahwal al-'ummal fi bir Misr 'am 1998.* Cairo: Land Center for Human Rights, 1998.

———. *Conditions in Egypt, First Half of 1999.* Cairo: Land Center for Human Rights, 1999.

Lange, Peter. "Unions, Workers, and Wage Regulation: The Rational Bases of Consent." In *Order and Conflict in Contemporary Capitalism,* ed. John H. Goldthorpe. Oxford: Clarendon Press, 1984.

LaPalombara, Joseph, and Myron Weiner, eds. *Political Parties and Political Development.* Princeton: Princeton University Press, 1966.

Levitsky, Stephen, and Lucan Way. "Between a Shock and a Hard Place: The Dynamics of Labor-Backed Adjustment in Poland and Argentina." *Comparative Politics* 30, no. 2 (1998).

Lewandowski, Janusz, and Jan Szomburg. "Model transformacji gospodarski polskiej." *Transformacja Gospodarki* 1 (1990).

———. "Strategia prywatyzacji." *Transformacja Gospodarki* 7 (1990).

Lewis, John P., and Valeriana Kallab, eds. *Development Strategies Reconsidered.* Washington, D.C.: Overseas Development Council, 1986.

Lewis, Paul G. *Political Authority and Party Secretaries in Poland, 1975–1986.* New York: Cambridge University Press, 1989.

Linz, Juan J., and Alfred Stepan. *Problems of Democratic Transition and Consolidation: Southern Europe, South America, and Post-Communist Europe.* Baltimore: Johns Hopkins University Press, 1996.

Lipowski, Adam. "O przywilejach w polskiej gospodarce w okresie transformacji." In *Transformacja gospodarki: Spojrzenie retrospęktywne,* ed. Witold Jakobik. Warsaw: Instytut Studiów Politycznych Akademii Nauk i Fundacji im. Friedricha Eberta, 1997.

Lipowski, Adam, and Jan Macieja. "Wnioski z analizy rządowych programów restrukturyzacji gazownictwa, górnictwa węgla kamiennego, hutnictwa żelaza i stali oraz przemysłu stoczniowego." Working Paper 10, Polish Academy of Sciences, Institute of Economics, Warsaw, 1998.

Lippman, Thomas, W. *Egypt After Nasser: Sadat, Peace, and the Mirage of Prosperity.* New York: Paragon House, 1989.

Lipset, Seymour Martin. "Some Social Requisites of Democracy: Economic Development and Political Legitimacy." *American Political Science Review* 53, no. 1 (1959).

Lipset, Seymour Martin, and Stein Rokkam, eds. *Party Systems and Voter Alignments: Cross-National Perspectives.* New York: Free Press, 1967.

Lipton, David, and Jeffrey Sachs. "Privatization in Eastern Europe: The Case of Poland." *Brookings Papers on Economic Affairs* 21, no. 3 (1990).

Lustig, Nora. *Mexico: The Remaking of an Economy.* Washington, D.C.: Brookings Institution, 1992.

Mabro, Robert, and Samir Radwan. *The Industrialization of Egypt, 1939–1976.* Oxford: Clarendon Press, 1976.

MacLeod, Dag. "Privatization and the Limits of State Autonomy in Mexico: Rethinking the Orthodox Paradox." *Latin American Perspectives* 32, no. 4 (2005).

Makram Ebeid, Mona. "Political Opposition in Egypt: Democratic Myth or Reality." *Middle East Journal* 43, no. 3 (1989).

Makrar, Ahmed Muhammad. *Al-Khaskhasa: Nitham qanuniy lil-tanwil al-qita' al-'am ila qita' al-khas.* Cairo: Economic al-Ahram Books, 1996.

Mansfeldova, Zdenka. "Professional and Political Strategies in Economic Discourse." Paper prepared for the conference "Symbolic Politics and the Processes of Democratization in Eastern Europe," Berlin, August 21–28, 1994.

Maravall, Jose Maria. "The Myth of Authoritarian Advantage." *Journal of Democracy* 5, no. 4 (1994).

Matejko, Alexander. *Social Change and Stratification in Eastern Europe: An Interpretive Analysis of Poland and Her Neighbors.* New York: Praeger, 1974.

Maxfield, Sylvia. *Governing Capital: International Finance and Mexican Politics.* Ithaca: Cornell University Press, 1990.

Maxfield, Sylvia, and Ben Ross Schneider, eds. *Business and State in Developing Countries.* Ithaca: Cornell University Press, 1997.

Mazur, Jay. "Labor's New Internationalism." *Foreign Affairs,* January/February 2000.

McAdam, Doug. "Conceptual Origins, Current Problems, Future Directions." In *Comparative Perspectives on Social Movements: Political Opportunities, Mobilizing Structures, and Cultural Framings,* ed. Doug McAdam, John D. McCarthy, and Mayer N. Zald. New York: Cambridge University Press, 1996.

Meier, Gerald, ed. *Politics and Policy Making in Developing Countries: Perspectives on the New Political Economy.* San Francisco: International Center for Economic Growth Publications, ICS Press, 1991.

Mejstrik, Michael, and James Burger. "Vouchers, Buy-Outs, Auctions: The Battle for Privatization in the Czech and Slovak Republics." In *Privatization in the Transition Process: Recent Experience in Eastern Europe.* Budapest: Kopint-Datorg, 1989.

Mericle, Kenneth S. "Corporatist Control of the Working Class: Authoritarian Brazil Since 1964." In *Authoritarianism and Corporatism in Latin America,* ed. James M. Malloy. Pittsburgh: University of Pittsburgh Press, 1977.

Mertlik, Pavel. "Czech Privatization: From Public Ownership to Private Ownership in Five Years?" In *Privatization in Post-Communist Countries.* Vol. 1, ed. Barbara Błaszczyk and Richard Woodward. Warsaw: Center for Social and Economic Research, 1996.

Michalski, Janusz. *Restrukturyzacja i prywatyzacja: Pozycja i zadania związków zawodowych.* Poznań, Poland: Oficyna Wydawnicza Sami Sobie, 1997.

Michels, Robert. *Political Parties: A Sociological Study of the Oligarchic Tendencies of Modern Democracy.* New York: Dover, 1959.

Middlebrook, Kevin J. "Dilemmas of Change in Mexican Politics." *World Politics* 41, no. 1 (1988).

————. "Organized Labor and Democratization in Postrevolutionary Regimes: Transition Politics in Russia, Nicaragua, and Mexico." Paper presented at the American Political Science Association conference, Washington, D.C., 1997.

————. *The Paradox of Revolution: Labor, the State, and Authoritarianism in Mexico.* Baltimore: Johns Hopkins University Press, 1995.

————. "Sounds of Silence: Organized Labour's Response to Economic Crisis in Mexico." *Journal of Latin American Studies* 21, no. 2 (1989).

Migdal, Joel S., Atul Kohli, and Vivienne Shue, eds. *State Power and Social Forces: Domination and Transformation in the Third World.* New York: Cambridge University Press, 1994.

Mitchell, Timothy. "No Factories, No Problem: The Logic of Neo-liberalism in Egypt." *African Political Economy Review* 82 (1999).

Mladek, Jan. "Privatizing the Czech Republic." *World Policy Journal* 12, no. 3 (1995).

Moerel, Hans, ed. *Labour Relations in Transition.* Nijmegen, Netherlands: Institute for Applied Social Sciences, 1994.

Moore, Clement Henry. "Authoritarian Politics in Unincorporated Society: The Case of Egypt." *Comparative Politics* 6, no. 2 (1974).

Morawski, Witold, ed. *Zmierzch socjalizmu państwowego.* Warsaw: Wydawnictwo Naukowe, PWN, 1994.

Mujzel, Jan. *The Problems of Post-Communism Transformation, Recession, and Privatization.* Warsaw: Polish Academy of Sciences, Institute of Economics, 1991.

Muller, Alexander. *U źródeł polskiego kryzysu: Społeczno-ekonomiczne uwarunkowania rozwoju gospodarczego Polski w latach osiemdziesiątych.* Warsaw: Państwowe Wydawnictwo Naukowe, 1985.

Murillo, Maria Victoria. "From Populism to Neoliberalism: Labor Unions and Market Reforms in Latin America." *World Politics* 52, no. 1 (2000).

————. *Labor Unions, Partisan Coalitions, and Market Reforms.* New York: Cambridge University Press, 2001.

Myant, Martin. "Czech and Slovak Trade Unions." In *Parties, Trade Unions, and Society in East-Central Europe,* ed. Michael Waller and Martin Myant. Portland, Ore.: Frank Cass, 1994.

Nafi', Ibrahim, ed. *Khaskhasa . . . Limatha? Wa Kaifa?* Cairo: Economic al-Ahram Books, 1993.

Nash, John. "Mexico: Adjustment and Stabilization." In *Restructuring Economies in Distress: Policy Reform and the World Bank,* ed. Vinod Thomas, Ajay Chhibber, Mansoor Dailami, and Jaime de Melo. New York: Oxford University Press for the World Bank, 1991.

Needleman, Carolyn, and Martin Needleman. "Who Rules Mexico? A Critique of Some Current Views on the Mexican Political Process." *Journal of Politics* 31, no. 4 (1969).

Neelder, Martin C. "Political Developments in Mexico," *American Political Science Review* 55 (June 1961).

Nelson, Joan M., ed. *Economic Crisis and Policy Choice: The Politics of Adjustment in the Third World.* Princeton: Princeton University Press, 1990.

————. *Intricate Links: Democratic and Market Reforms in Latin America and Eastern Europe.* New Brunswick, N.J.: Transaction Books, 1994.

Nelson, Joan M., and contributors. *Fragile Coalitions: The Politics of Economic Adjustment.* New Brunswick, N.J: Transaction Books, 1989.

North, Douglass C. "Institutional Change: A Framework for Analysis." In *Institutional Change: Theory and Empirical Findings,* ed. Sven-Erik Sjostrand. New York: M. E. Sharpe, 1993.

————. *Institutions, Institutional Change, and Economic Performance.* New York: Cambridge University Press, 1990.

Olson, Mancur. *The Rise and Decline of Nations: Economic Growth, Stagnation, and Social Rigidities.* New Haven: Yale University Press, 1982.

Orenstein, Mitchell. "The Czech Tripartite Council and Its Contribution to Social Peace." In *Evolution of Interest Representation and Development of the Labour Market in Post-Socialist Countries,* ed. Jerzy Hausner, Ove K. Pedersen, and Karsten Ronit. Kraków, Poland: Cracow Academy of Economics, 1995.

————. "The Failure of Neo-liberal Social Policy in Central Europe." *Transition* 2, no. 14 (1996).

Osa, Maryjane. *Solidarity and Contention: Networks of Polish Opposition.* Minneapolis: University of Minnesota Press, 2003.

Ost, David. *The Defeat of Solidarity: Anger and Politics in Postcommunist Europe.* Ithaca: Cornell University Press, 2005.

————. "Labor, Class, and Democracy: Shaping Political Antagonisms in Post-Communist Society." In *Markets, States, and Democracy: The Political Economy of Post-Communist Transformation,* ed. Beverly Crawford. Boulder, Colo.: Westview Press, 1995.

————. *Solidarity and the Politics of Anti-politics: Opposition and Reform in Poland Since 1968.* Philadelphia: Temple University Press, 1990.

Ostrowski, K. *Rola związków zawodowych w polskim systemie politycznym.* Wrocław, Poland: PAN, 1970.

Oweiss, Ibrahim M., ed. *The Political Economy of Contemporary Egypt.* Washington, D.C.: Center for Contemporary Arab Studies, Georgetown University, 1990.

Ożyński, Antoni. *My i oni w procesie restrukturyzacji: Studium przypadku pracy zespołowej w polskich warunkach.* Warsaw: Wydawnictwo Wyższej Szkoły Przedsiębiorczości i Zarządzania im. Leona Koźmińskiego, 1998.

Packenham, Robert. *Liberal America and the Third World: Political Development Ideas in Foreign Aid and Social Sciences.* Princeton: Princeton University Press, 1973.

Paczkowski, Andrzej. *Pół wieku dziejów Polski, 1939–1989.* Warsaw: Wydawnictwo Naukowe PWN, 1998.

Padgett, L. Vincent. *The Mexican Political System.* Boston: Houghton Mifflin, 1976.

Palmer, Monte, Ali Leila, and El Sayed Yassin. *The Egyptian Bureaucracy.* Syracuse: Syracuse University Press, 1988.

Panebianco, Angelo. *Political Parties: Organization and Power.* New York: Cambridge University Press, 1988.

Pastor, Manuel, and Carol Wise. "State Policy, Distribution, and Neoliberal Reform in Mexico." *Journal of Latin American Studies* 29, no. 2 (1997).

Paszkiewicz, Krystyna A., ed. *Polskie partie polityczne: Charakterystyki, dokumenty.* Wrocław, Poland: Drukarnia i Oficyna Wydawnicza Hektor, 1996.

Paul, David W. *Czechoslovakia: Profile of a Socialist Republic at the Crossroads of Europe.* Boulder, Colo.: Westview Press, 1981.

Payne, Douglas W. "Mexican Labor: Cracks in the Monolith." *Dissent* 45, no. 1 (1998).

Pei, Minixin. "The Puzzle of East Asian Exceptionalism." *Journal of Democracy* 5, no. 4 (1994).

Piazza, James A. "Globalizing Quiescence: Globalization, Union Density, and Strikes in 15 Industrial Countries." *Economic and Industrial Democracy* 26, no. 2 (2005).

Porket, Joseph L. "Czechoslovak Trade Unions Under Soviet-Type Socialism." In *Trade Unions in Communist States,* ed. Alex Pravda and Blair A. Ruble. Boston: Allen and Unwin, 1986.

Poznanski, Kazimierz Z. *Poland's Protracted Transition: Institutional Change and Economic Growth.* New York: Cambridge University Press, 1996.

———. "Political Economy of Privatization in Eastern Europe." In *Markets, States, and Democracy: The Political Economy of Post-Communist Transformation,* ed. Beverly Crawford. Boulder, Colo.: Westview Press, 1995.

Pravda, Alex, and Blair A. Ruble, eds. *Trade Unions in Communist States.* Boston: Allen and Unwin, 1986.

Pripstein, Marsha Posusney. *Labor and the State in Egypt: Workers, Unions, and Economic Restructuring.* New York: Columbia University Press, 1997.

———. "Labor as an Obstacle to Privatization: The Case of Egypt." In *Privatization and Liberalization in the Middle East,* ed. Ilya Harik and Denis J. Sullivan. Bloomington: Indiana University Press, 1992.

Przeworski, Adam. *Democracy and the Market: Political and Economic Reforms in Eastern Europe and Latin America.* New York: Cambridge University Press, 1991.

———. "The Neoliberal Fallacy." *Journal of Democracy* 3, no. 3 (1992).

Przeworski, Adam, and Fernando Limongi. "Political Regimes and Economic Growth." *Journal of Economic Perspectives* 7 (Summer 1993).

Przeworski, Adam, and James Raymond Vreeland. "The Effects of IMF Programs on Economic Growth." *Journal of Development Economics* 62 (2000).

Qasim, Mona. *Islah al-iqtisadiy fi Misr: Dur al-bunuk fi khaskhasa wa aham al-taqarib al-dawla.* Cairo: Maktabat al-Usra, 1998.

Raina, Peter. *Droga do 'Okrągłego Stołu,' zakulisowe rozmowy przygotowawcze.* Warsaw: Wydawnictwo von Borowiecky, 1999.

Rainnie, Al, and Jane Hardy. "Desperately Seeking Capitalism: Solidarity and Polish Industrial Relations in the 1990s." *Industrial Relations Journal* 21, no. 4 (1995).

Ramadan, 'Abd al-'Zim. *Al-sira' ijtima'iya wa siyasiya fi Misr munthu qiyam thawra 23 yuliu ila nihaya azmat maris 1954.* Cairo: Maktabat Matbuli, 1994.

Ranis, Peter. *Class, Democracy, and Labor in Contemporary Argentina.* New Brunswick, N.J: Transaction Books, 1995.

Rapacki, Ryszard, and Susan J. Linz. "Insytucjonalne uwarunkowania i bariery prywatyzacji w Polsce." *Ekonomista* 1 (1993).

*Raport: Polska 5 lat po sierpniu.* Międzyzakładowa Struktura "Solidarność." 1985.

Reed, Stanley. "The Battle of Egypt." *Foreign Affairs,* September/October 1993.

Remmer, Karen. "Democracy and Economic Crisis: The Latin American Experience." *World Politics* 42 (1998).

———. "The Politics of Economic Stabilization: IMF Standby Programs in Latin America, 1954–1984." *Comparative Politics* 19, no. 1 (1986).

Renner, Hans. *The History of Czechoslovakia Since 1945.* London: Routledge, 1989.

Richards, Alan. "The Political Economy of Dilatory Reform: Egypt in the 1980s." *World Development* 19, no. 12 (1991).

Rivlin, Paul. *The Dynamics of Economic Policy Making in Egypt.* New York: Praeger, 1985.

Rodriguez, Rogelio Hernandez. "The Partido Revolucionario Institucional." In *Governing Mexico: Political Parties and Elections,* ed. Monica Serrano. London: Institute of Latin American Studies, 1998.

Rodrik, Dani. "Understanding Economic Policy Reform." *Journal of Economic Literature* 34 (March 1996).

Roett, Riordan, ed. *The Challenge of Institutional Reform in Mexico.* Boulder, Colo.: Lynne Rienner, 1995.

Rolicki, Janusz. *Edward Gierek: Przerwana dekada.* Warsaw: Wydawnictwo FAKT, 1990.

Ronfeldt, David. "Prospects for Elite Cohesion." In *Mexico's Alternative Political Futures,* ed. Wayne A. Cornelius, Judith Gentleman, and Peter H. Smith. San Diego: Center for U.S.-Mexican Studies, University of California, San Diego, 1989.

Roszkowski, Wojciech. *Historia Polski, 1914–1993.* Warsaw: Wydawnictwo Naukowe PWN, 1994.

Rothschild, Joseph. *Return to Diversity.* New York: Oxford University Press, 1989.

Ruiz, Ramon Eduardo. *The Great Rebellion: Mexico, 1905–1924.* New York: W. W. Norton, 1980.

———. *Labor and the Ambivalent Revolutionaries: Mexico, 1911–1923.* Baltimore: Johns Hopkins University Press, 1976.

Ruszkowski, Paweł, ed. *Społeczne aspekty zmiany systemowej w gospodarce.* Warsaw: Fundacja Wspierania Własności Pracowniczej Zmiany, 1999.

Sachs, Jeffrey. "Life in the Economic Emergency Room." In *The Political Economy of Policy Reform,* ed. John Williamson. Washington, D.C.: Institute for International Economics, 1994.

Sadowski, Yahya. *Political Vegetables? Businessman and Bureaucrat in the Development of Egyptian Agriculture.* Washington, D.C.: Brookings Institution, 1991.

———. "The Sphinx's New Riddle: Why Does Egypt Delay Economic Reform?" *Arab-American Affairs* 22 (Fall 1987).

Salinas-Leon, Roberto. "Between Mercantalism and Market: An Analysis of Privatization in Mexico." In *The Privatization Process: A Worldwide Perspectives,* ed. Terry L. Anderson and Peter J. Hill. Lanham, Md.: Rowman and Littlefield, 1996.

Salwa, Zbigniew. *Uprawnienia związków zawodowych.* Bydgoszcz, Poland: Oficyna Wydawnicza "BRANTA," 1998.

Samstead, James G., and Ruth Berins Collier. "Mexican Labor and Structural Reform Under Salinas: New Unionism or Old Stalemate?" In *The Challenge of Institutional Reform in Mexico,* ed. Riordan Roett. Boulder, Colo.: Lynne Rienner, 1995.

Sanderson, Steven E. "Presidential Succession and Political Rationality in Mexico." *World Politics* 35, no. 3 (1983).

Sartori, Giovanni. "European Political Parties: The Case of Polarized Pluralism." In *Political Parties and Political Development,* ed. Joseph LaPalombara and Myron Weiner. Princeton: Princeton University Press, 1966.

———. *Parties and Party Systems: A Framework for Analysis.* New York: Cambridge University Press, 1976.

Schapiro, Leonard B. *The Communist Party of the Soviet Union.* New York: Random House, 1960.

Scarrow, Howard A. "The Functions of Political Parties: A Critique of the Literature and the Approach." *Journal of Politics* 29, no. 4 (1967).

Schmitter, Phillipe. *Interest Conflict and Political Change in Brazil.* Stanford: Stanford University Press, 1971.

———. "Still a Century of Corporatism?" *Review of Politics* 36, no. 1 (1974).

Serrano, Monica, ed. *Governing Mexico: Political Parties and Elections.* London: Institute for Latin American Studies, 1998.

Shafter, Michael. "Political Economy of Sectors and Sectoral Change: Korea Then and Now." In *Business and the State in Developing Countries,* ed. Sylvia Maxfield and Ben Ross Schneider. Ithaca: Cornell University Press, 1997.

Shalev, Michael. "The Resurgence of Labor Quiescence." In *The Future of Labour Movements,* ed. Marino Regini. London: Sage, 1992.

Silver, Beverly J. *Workers' Movements and Globalization Since 1870.* New York: Cambridge University Press, 2002.

Skalnik, Carol Leff. *The Czech and Slovak Republics: Nation Versus State.* Boulder, Colo.: Westview Press, 1997.

Sloan, John. "The Mexican Variant of Corporatism." *Inter-American Economic Affairs* 38, no. 4 (1985).

Sloan, John, and Kent Tedin. "The Consequences of Regime Type for Public Policy Outputs." *Comparative Political Studies* 20, no. 1 (1987).

Sniecikowski, Andrzej K., ed. *Interesy i wartości pracownicze w dekadzie przekształceń systemowych polskiej gospodarki.* Warsaw: Zmiany, 1999.

Snyder, Jack. *Myths of Empire.* Ithaca: Cornell University Press, 1991.

Sobell, Vlad. "Czechoslovakia: The Legacy of Normalization." *East European Politics and Society* 2, no. 1 (1988).

Springborg, Robert. *Mubarak's Egypt: Fragmentation of the Political Order.* Boulder, Colo.: Westview Press, 1989.

———. "Patrimonialism and Policy-Making in Egypt: Nasser and Sadat and the Tenure Policy for Reclaimed Lands." *Middle East Studies* 15, no. 1 (1979).

———. "Patterns of Association in the Egyptian Political Elite." In *Political Elites in the Middle East,* ed. George Lenczowski. Washington, D.C.: American Enterprise Institute for Public Policy Research, 1975.

———. "Professional Syndicates in Egyptian Politics, 1952–1970." *International Journal of Middle Eastern Studies* 9, no. 3 (1978).

Squires Meaney, Constance. "Foreign Experts, Capitalists, and Competing Agendas: Privatization in Poland, the Czech Republic, and Hungary." *Comparative Political Studies* 28, no. 2 (1995).

Stallings, H. Gordon. "Czechoslovakia: Government in Communist Hands." *Journal of Politics* 17, no. 3 (1955).

Staniszkis, Jadwiga. *Poland's Self-Limiting Revolution.* Princeton: Princeton University Press, 1984.

Stankiewicz, Tomasz. *Akcjonariat pracowniczy w polskiej prywatyzacji kapitałowej.* Warsaw: Centrum Prywatyzacji Biznes i Finanse, 1997.

Stark, David, and Laszlo Bruszt. *Postsocialist Pathways: Transforming Politics and Property in East Central Europe.* New York: Cambridge University Press, 1998.

Steinmo, Sven, Kathleen Thelen, and Frank Longstreth, eds. *Structuring Politics: Historical Institutionalism in Comparative Perspective.* New York: Cambridge University Press, 1992.

Stelmachowski, Andrzej. *Kształtowanie się ustroju III Rzeczypospolitej.* Warsaw: Wydawnictwo Ośrodek Doradztwa i Szkolenia "Tur," 1998.

Stepan, Alfred. *The State and Society: Peru in Comparative Perspective.* Princeton: Princeton University Press, 1978.

Stevens, Evelyn P. "Mexico's PRI: The Institutionalization of Corporatism?" In *Authoritarianism and Corporatism in Latin America,* ed. James M. Malloy. Pittsburgh: University of Pittsburgh Press, 1977.

Stevens, John N. *Czechoslovakia at the Crossroads: The Economic Dilemmas of Communism in Postwar Czechoslovakia.* Boulder, Colo.: East European Monographs, 1985.

Subramanian, Arvind. "The Egyptian Stabilization Experience: An Analytical Retrospective." IMF Working Paper, International Monetary Fund, Washington, D.C., September 1997.

Suleiman, Ezra N., and John Waterbury, eds. *The Political Economy of Public Sector Reform and Privatization.* Boulder, Colo.: Westview Press, 1990.

Sullivan, Denis J. "The Political Economy of Reform in Egypt." *International Journal of Middle Eastern Studies* 22, no. 3 (1990).

Surdykowska, Stanisława Teresa. *Prywatyzacja.* Warsaw: Wydawnictwo Naukowe PWN, 1997.

Svejnar, J. "Workers' Participation in Management in Czechoslovakia." *Annals of Public and Cooperative Economy,* April–June 1978.

Swenson, Peter. "Labor and the Limits of the Welfare State." *Comparative Politics* 23, no. 4 (1991).

Szurdowicz, Alojzy. *Solidarność: NSZZ Solidarność 1980–1981; Zarys działalności w świetle prasy i innych źródeł.* Bydgoszcz, Poland: Margrafsen, 1998.

Taborsky, Edward. *Communism in Czechoslovakia, 1948–1960.* Princeton: Princeton University Press, 1961.

———. "Czechoslovakia: Return to 'Normalcy,'" *Problems of Communism* 19, no. 6 (1970).

Tannebaum, Frank. *The Mexican Agricultural Revolution.* New York: Macmillan, 1929.

Tarrow, Sindey. *Power in Movement: Social Movements and Contentious Politics.* New York: Cambridge University Press, 1998.

Teichman, Judith A. *Privatization and Political Change in Mexico.* Pittsburgh: University of Pittsburgh Press, 1995.

Thelen, Kathleen. "Historical Institutionalism in Comparative Perspective." *Annual Review of Political Science* 2 (1999).

———. *How Institutions Evolve: The Political Economy of Skills in Germany, Britain, the United States, and Japan.* New York: Cambridge University Press, 2004.

Thomas, Vinod, Ajay Chhibber, Mansoor Dailami, and Jaime de Melo, eds. *Restructuring Economies in Distress: Policy Reform and the World Bank.* New York: Oxford University Press for the World Bank, 1991.

Tomiche, F. J. *Syndicalisme et certains aspects du travail en République Arab Unie (Égypte), 1900–1967.* Paris: G.-P. Maisonneuve and Larose, 1974.

Torańska, Teresa. *Oni.* Warsaw: Agencja Omipress, 1989.

Triska, Dusan. *Political, Legislative, and Technical Aspects of Privatization in the Czech Republic.* Prague: Meridian, 1994.

Turkowski, Romuald, ed. *Opozycja parlamentarna w Krajowej Radzie Narodowej i Sejmie Ustawodawczym, 1945–1947.* Warsaw: Wydawnictwo Sejmowe, 1997.

Turnovec, Frantisek. *Political Background of the Economic Transition in the Czech Republic.* Working Paper series 44, Center for Economic Research and Graduate

Education, Charles University, and Economic Institute of the Academy of Social Sciences of the Czech Republic, Prague, April 1994.

Tonelson, Alan. *Race to the Bottom.* Boulder, Colo.: Westview Press, 2000.

Ulc, Otto. "Pilsen: The Unknown Revolt." *Problems of Communism* 14, no. 3 (1972).

———. "Political Participation in Czechoslovakia." *Journal of Politics* 33, no. 2 (1971).

Valenta, Jiri. "Czechoslovakia: A Proletariat Embourgeoisie?" In *Blue-Collar Workers in Eastern Europe,* ed. Jan F. Triska and Charles Gati. London: George Allen and Unwin, 1981.

Valenzuela, J. Samuel. "Labor Movements in Transition to Democracy: A Framework for Analysis." *Comparative Political Studies,* July 1989.

Van der Hoeven, Rolph, and Gyorgy Sziraczki, eds. *Lessons from Privatization: Labour Issues in Developing and Tranisitional Countries.* Geneva: International Labour Organization, 1997.

Waterbury, John. *Egypt: Burdens of the Past, Options for the Future.* Hanover, N.H.: American Universities Field Staff Reports, 1977.

———. *Egypt of Nasser and Sadat: The Political Economy of Two Regimes.* Princeton: Princeton University Press, 1983.

———. *Exposed to Innumerable Delusions: Public Enterprise and State Power in Egypt, India, Mexico, and Turkey.* New York: Cambridge University Press, 1993.

Ważniewski, Władysław. *Walka polityczna w kierownictwie PPR i PZPR, 1944–1964.* Toruń, Poland: Wydawnictwo Adam Marszałek, 1991.

Weiner, Myron. "Traditional Role Performance and the Development of Modern Political Parties: The Indian Case." *Journal of Politics* 26, no. 4 (1964).

Weinstein, Marc. "Solidarity's Abandonment of Workers' Councils: Redefining Postsocialist Poland." *British Journal of Industrial Relations* 38, no. 1 (2000).

Western, Bruce. "A Comparative Study of Working-Class Disorganization: Union Decline in Eighteen Advanced Capitalist Countries." *American Sociological Review* 60, no. 2 (1995).

Weyland, Kurt. *The Politics of Market Reform in Fragile Democracies: Argentina, Brazil, Peru, and Venezuela.* Princeton: Princeton University Press, 2002.

Wheelock, Keith. *Nasser's New Egypt: A Critical Analysis.* Westport, Conn.: Greenwood Press, 1960.

Wiadera, Wojciech. *Robotnicy i liderzy związkowi.* Warsaw: Szkoła Główna Handlowa, 1992.

Williamson, John, ed. *Latin American Adjustment: How Much Has Happened?* Washington, D.C.: Institute for International Economics, 1990.

———. *The Political Economy of Policy Reform.* Washington, D.C.: Institute for International Economics, 1994.

Winiecki, Jan, ed. *Polska niezakończona transformacja: Instytucjonalne bariery rozwoju gospodarczego.* Warsaw: Centrum im. Adama Smitha, 1996.

Włodka, Zbigniew. *Tajne dokumenty Biura Politycznego PZPR a "Solidarność," 1980–1981.* London: Aneks, 1992.

Wolchik, Sharon L. "The Czech Republic and Slovakia." In *The Legacies of Communism in Eastern Europe,* ed. Zoltan Barany and Ivan Volgyes. Baltimore: Johns Hopkins University Press, 1995.

World Bank. *Bureaucrats in Business: The Economics and Politics of Government Ownership: A World Bank Policy Research Report.* New York: Oxford University Press for the World Bank, 1995.

Wratny, Jerzy. *Ewolucja zbiorowego prawa pracy w Polsce w latach 1989–1991*. Zeszyt 16. Warsaw: Instytut Pracy i Spraw Socjalnych, 1991.

———. *Prawne i ekonomiczne aspekty reprezentacji interesów pracowniczych w przedsiębiorstwach państwowych: Raport z badań*. Warsaw: Instytut Pracy i Spraw Socjalnych/Fundacja Friedricha Eberta, 1995.

Yashar, Deborah J. *Demanding Democracy: Reform and Reaction in Costa Rica and Guatemala, 1870s–1950s*. Stanford: Stanford University Press, 1997.

Zalewski, Dariusz. *Partnterstwo polityczne—NSZZ "Solidarność" i OPZZ jako reprezentacje zbiorowych interesów,* Warsaw: Instytut Pracy i Spraw Socjalnych, 1998.

Zolberg, Aristide. "Response: Working-Class Dissolution." *International Labour and Working Class History* 47 (1995).

# Index

........................................................

Page numbers in *italics* refer to tables.

www.ingramcontent.com/pod-product-compliance
Lightning Source LLC
Chambersburg PA
CBHW032119020426
42334CB00016B/1009